SERIES ON
Economic Development
AND GROWTH VOL. 4

INCLUSIVE
VALUE CHAINS

A Pathway Out of Poverty

Series on Economic Development and Growth   (ISSN: 1793-3668)

Published

Vol. 1   Globalisation and Economic Growth in China
edited by Yang Yao & Linda Yueh

Vol. 2   Elderly Entrepreneurship in an Aging U.S. Economy
It's Never Too Late
by Ting Zhang

Vol. 3   Industrial Development in East Asia
A Comparative Look at Japan, Korea, Taiwan, and Singapore
(With CD-ROM)
by K. Ali Akkemik

Vol. 4   Inclusive Value Chains: A Pathway Out of Poverty
by Malcolm Harper

SERIES ON
ECONOMIC DEVELOPMENT
AND GROWTH   VOL. 4

INCLUSIVE VALUE CHAINS

A PATHWAY OUT OF POVERTY

Malcolm Harper

Emeritus Professor, Cranfield School of Management, UK

World Scientific

NEW JERSEY · LONDON · SINGAPORE · BEIJING · SHANGHAI · HONG KONG · TAIPEI · CHENNAI

Published by

World Scientific Publishing Co. Pte. Ltd.

5 Toh Tuck Link, Singapore 596224

USA office: 27 Warren Street, Suite 401-402, Hackensack, NJ 07601

UK office: 57 Shelton Street, Covent Garden, London WC2H 9HE

British Library Cataloguing-in-Publication Data
A catalogue record for this book is available from the British Library.

Series on Economic Development and Growth — Vol. 4
INCLUSIVE VALUE CHAINS
A Pathway Out of Poverty

Copyright © 2010 by Malcolm Harper

ISBN-13 978-981-4293-89-1
ISBN-10 981-4293-89-X

Typeset by Stallion Press
Email: enquiries@stallionpress.com

Printed in Singapore.

About the Author

Malcolm Harper was educated at Oxford University, the Harvard Business School and the University of Nairobi. He worked for nine years in a household hardware manufacturing business in England, mainly in marketing. He then taught at the University of Nairobi from 1970 to 1974, before coming to Cranfield School of Management, where he was Professor of Enterprise Development. Since 1995 he has worked independently, mainly in India. He has published over twenty-five books and numerous articles on various aspects of self-employment, enterprise development, livelihoods and micro-finance. His most recent publications include *'What's Wrong with Microfinance?'* (co-edited with T Dichter) and *'Development, Divinity and Dharma: The Role of Religion in Development and Microfinance Institutions'* (co-authored with DSK Rao and A K Sahu).

From 1996 until 2006, he was Chairman of Basix Finance of Hyderabad, and he is Chairman of M-CRIL of New Delhi, the leading micro-finance credit and social rating institution in Asia. He was also the founding Editor-in-chief of the *Journal of Enterprise Development and Microfinance*, and is a director and trustee of a number of other institutions, including Homeless International, EDA (UK) Limited and APT Enterprise Development.

Contents

About the Author   v

Acknowledgments   ix

CHAPTER 1: **Poverty in India and Value Chains**   **1**

CHAPTER 2: **Retail Winners and Losers — The Impact**   **16**
            of Organised Retailing

CHAPTER 3: **Inclusive Value Chains in Fresh Fruit and**   **28**
            Vegetables

Introduction   29

Case Study 1: Namdhari Fresh Limited   31
            BN Dhananjaya and A Umesh Rao

Case Study 2: ITC Choupal Fresh   47
            Rewa Shankar Misra

Case Study 3: INFAM in Wayanad, Kerala   67
            Jacob D Vakkayil

Case Study 4: Spencer's Retail   81
            Sukhpal Singh

CHAPTER 4: Inclusive Value Chains in Commodity Crops   **94**

Introduction   95

Case Study 5: Contract Farming of Potatoes: An Attempt to   97
Include Poor Farmers in the Value Chain
Braja S Mishra

Case Study 6: Basmati Rice and Kohinoor Foods Limited   115
Anup Kumar Singh

Case Study 7: Agrocel Industries   133
Anamika Purohit

Case Study 8: bioRe Organic Cotton   149
Rajeev Baruah

CHAPTER 5: Inclusive Value Chains in Fisheries, Honey,   **160**
Coffee and Poultry

Introduction   161

Case Study 9: Falcon Marine Exports   163
Rajeev Roy

Case Study 10: Honey in Muzaffarpur   181
Ashok Kumar

Case Study 11: Fairtrade and Organic Coffee   200
Priti Rao

Case Study 12: Small-Holder Broiler Farming in Kesla   222
Anish Kumar

CHAPTER 6: Inclusive Value Chains in Non-Food Artisan   **241**
Products

Introduction   242

Case Study 13: ITC Limited and the Agarbatti Industry   245
Nagendra Nath Sharma

Case Study 14: Operation Mojari   258
Vipin Sharma and Mallika Ahluwalia

CHAPTER 7: What Do the Case Studies Tell Us?   **278**
Lessons for the Future

Glossary   295

Acknowledgments

The preparation of a book of this kind involves many different people, and it is only possible to acknowledge a few of them by name. The most important contributors are of course the small-scale farmers and artisans who are participating in the value chains which are described. Most of them are benefiting substantially from their participation, but all of them took a significant risk when they made the decision to join the value chain.

For most of us, if a decision of this kind turns out to have been a mistake, the results are unfortunate but are not life-threatening. For marginal producers, however, it can lead to the loss of their entire livelihood. They deserve our admiration for this, and I would also like to express my gratitude to those of them who talked to the writers of the cases about their experiences; without this information, the case studies would mean very little.

But, some names can be named. The Ford Foundation has supported my work in various ways and places for around 25 years, and Ajit Kanitkar is a worthy successor to the many representatives and programme officers who have preceded him in the New Delhi office. He and his colleagues Mona Challu and Renuka Agarwal, and Vinita Tripathi of the Institute of International Education, ingeniously engineered support for the book from the foundation, and they also introduced me to a number of useful sources of information.

Ranjana Rajan and Bhupathiraju Shalini of World Scientific Publishing Co. have encouraged and assisted in the evolution of the book since its original inception, and laboured mightily to ensure that it appeared on schedule. Natasha Kirwan and Liz Riley helped with some critical editing at a critical time, and Adrian Macer rescued my computer when disaster threatened; I am grateful to all of them.

The Indian edition of the book was launched at the first "Livelihoods India" conference in New Delhi in November 2008. I must thank Vipin Sharma and his colleagues at ACCESS Development Services for making this possible.

The contributors of the case studies are of course responsible for the main content of the book, and the only reason why their names do not appear on the cover is that there are too many of them. They have produced some remarkable material, and I hope that they will not be dissatisfied with the way in which it has been used. The following list is a very inadequate expression of my gratitude to them.

- Anamika Purohit works for International Resources for Fairer Trade in Mumbai. She is an economic development professional, engaged in counselling community businesses and building the capacities of producer groups for sustainable livelihoods. She also works for the domestic fair trade initiative in India.
- Anish Kumar works with PRADAN on rural livelihood issues. He has worked with rural enterprises since 1994. He facilitated the formation of Kesla Poultry Society in 2001 and was its first CEO. His related areas of interest include business organisations of poor people and small-holders in modern value chains.
- Anup Kumar Singh is a Delhi based development professional working on promotion and development of small and micro-enterprises in India, Nepal and Bhutan.
- Ashok Kumar has over 15 years experience in value chain and subsector development, micro and small enterprise promotion, and value chain finance. He has worked in several farm and non-farm sub-sectors, with a focus on the integration of small and micro-enterprises into markets.
- Rajeev Baruah has a Masters degree in sociology from the Delhi School of Economics. He worked for ten years in the tea plantations in Assam and then pioneered the organic cotton movement in India and its integration into the "bioRe" textile chain. He is the Managing Director of bioRe India Limited.

- B N Dhananjaya is a post-graduate in agricultural economics. He has over ten years experience in rural water supply, sanitation and water-shed development. He has worked in research, project implementation and training. Currently he is associated with The Livelihood School as a Senior Faculty Associate.
- Braja S. Mishra has a PhD in Development Studies. He worked with the government of India for 14 years as an Education Officer, three years with The Livelihood School, Hyderabad as a faculty member and is now working as an Associate Professor with KIIT University, Bhubaneswar.
- Rewa Shankar Misra works at the Mastercard foundation in Canada, specialising in micro-finance and livelihoods. She has eight years of experience with agencies such as the ILO, Action Aid and CARE. Her main interests are in impact research, policy evaluation and organisational development.
- Nagendra Nath Sharma has worked in development for 25 years, with development banks and support institutions for SMEs promoted by banks, financial institutions and the government. He has been a consultant to projects assisted by the World Bank, UNDP, UNIDO, DFID and others.
- Priti Rao was a consultant to the Naandi Foundation for the Araku Coffee Programme. She has worked for a decade on small farmer livelihoods chiefly in the Himalayas. She did her Masters at IDS, Sussex and is currently pursuing a doctorate in service design.
- Rajeev Roy teaches entrepreneurship and marketing at Xavier Institute of Management, Bhubaneswar. Before joining academia, he was an entrepreneur. He now wants to encourage and facilitate sensible entrepreneurship.
- Vipin Sharma has worked for 26 years in development banking and enterprise development, with the Reserve Bank of India, National Bank for Agriculture and Rural Development, and the Rural Non-Farm Development Agency (RUDA). He joined CARE in 2000 and in 2007 he set up ACCESS, a national technical services institution that supports microfinance and sustainable livelihoods.
- Mallika Ahluwalia graduated from the Woodrow Wilson School at Princeton University and is now completing her MPA-MBA at Harvard. She works for ACCESS on micro-finance and livelihoods,

and has also worked on food security with the UN World Food Programme in Namibia and on education reform for inner-city public schools in Chicago.

- Sukhpal Singh, Indian Institute of Management, Ahmedabad, has published widely, including three books. He was a visiting fellow at the Institute of Development Studies, Sussex, and Chulalongkorn University, Bangkok and a member of committees of the Planning Commission. His research interests include value chain governance and small producers.

- A. Umesh Rao is a graduate in agriculture and a post-graduate in business. He has worked in rural development since 1970, for the Karnataka Government and most recently for the Livelihood School in Bangalore. He specialises in soil conservation and watershed management.

- Jacob D Vakkayil comes from a family of small-scale farmers in Kerala, India. He teaches organisational behaviour at the Indian Institute of Management, Calcutta. Driven by his personal and academic experiences, he constantly explores how the fruits of economic development can be more appropriately shared.

Chapter **1**

Poverty in India and Value Chains

INDIA IS POOR

This book is about inclusive value chains, which can be one way of alleviating poverty. They are not the only way, and nor can value chains on their own eliminate poverty. Value chains, the links between producers and consumers, have always been with us, but they have only recently been seen to be a tool for reducing poverty.

Poverty is everywhere, but the examples in the book are all from India; there are good reasons for this.

India is in absolute terms the poorest nation on earth. This statement may appear inconsistent with the popular view of India as one of the world's fastest growing economies, whose software industry is a major global player and whose rapid development is regarded more as a competitive threat than a human tragedy.

The facts, however, speak for themselves. China is the largest country in the world by population, but India achieves far higher numbers of people than any other country by the two main poverty indicators, number of people living under the $1.25 per day income line, corrected for purchasing power, and number of malnourished children (see Table 1).

Table 1: Comparative poverty and malnutrition data.

Country	Numbers living under $1.25 a day	Numbers of malnourished children under five years old
India	456 million	52 million
China	208 million	6 million
Nigeria	88 million	7 million

Source: On-line atlas of millennium development goals, World Bank 2009.

This chapter draws extensively on the author's paper "Emerging Marketing Channels for Small Producers", in *Finding Pathways, Social Inclusion in Rural Development,* Premchander, Dudin, Reid (eds.). Books for Change, Bangalore (2009).
Note: Units of measurement in the Indian numbering system: lakh = 100,000; crore = 10,000,000. Indian Rupees (Rs.) where appropriate are converted into USD at a rate of approximately Rs. 50 = $1.00; Rs. 1 lakh = $2,000; Rs. 1 crore = $200,000.

Table 2: South Asia — Comparative child nutrition data.

Country	% of low birth-weight babies	% of under-five children under-weight
India	28%	43%
Pakistan	19%	31%
Bangladesh	22%	41%
Nepal	21%	39%

Source: State of the World's Children, UNICEF 2009.

The figures given in Table 1 are of course in part a function of India's large population, although the comparison with China is sadly remarkable.

Relative figures, irrespective of absolute numbers, are almost as shocking. The data (Table 2) from UNICEF shows how India compares with its South Asian neighbours on two critical measures relating to the health of children.

A country which has enjoyed rapid economic growth, and aspires to be a world power, but which fails so dramatically to take care of so many of its children, must be suffering from some serious deficiencies.

India is of course made up of many different states. The largest state, Uttar Pradesh, which is one of the poorest, has a population of about 170 million people, the state of Maharashtra has about 100 million, and another seven all have populations of between 50–100 million. Reliable information on their poverty levels is notoriously difficult to find, even more so if it is required to be comparable with international data, but the Indian national averages conceal very wide variations, between North and South, and, even more, between rural and urban areas. If internationally comparable data was available at the state level, a fair number of these nine states would be among the very poorest countries in the world.

WHY IS INDIA POOR?

India's poverty is well-known, although it has in recent years been concealed by the more exciting news of growth, billionaires, Bollywood movies and acquisitive India-based multinationals. Many explanations have been put forward for the persistence of poverty, in spite of so much economic success, and there can of course be no single explanation for such a complex phenomenon, which affects almost a fifth of the world's population.

Some, albeit a declining number as time passes, blame the British, who destroyed or throttled Indian industry and encouraged and exacerbated existing communalist tendencies in order to more effectively divide and rule. Others blame the governments of India since independence in 1947. As far back as 1997, at the 50th anniversary of independence, the Hindu newspaper wrote that "the persistence of poverty in India is the world's greatest public policy failure". It is certainly true that many well-intentioned poverty alleviation programmes have tended to strengthen rather than to break down the social and economic structures which perpetuate poverty.

The shock and dislocation of partition, and the resulting and continuing diversion of resources for military rather than more productive purposes, have also played some part, as have corruption, inefficiency and simple bad management. It can also be claimed that India is too big; although its territory is much smaller than that of many countries, its population is enormous, and, more importantly, desperately fissured by language, caste, race and culture. Many Indians agree that the country is effectively ungovernable, because of its size and variety, but nevertheless few are willing to countenance any reduction in its size, in spite of the fact that there are several groups who are struggling to secede and make the country smaller.

India is certainly a vibrant democracy, and the proportion of its people who play an active part in its government by using their votes, particularly the poor, is much higher than in some better-off societies. This may paradoxically contribute to bad government, since India has persistently failed to invest in effective education for its citizens; an uneducated electorate may be less functional than a benign autocracy.

Religion also plays a part. It is of course divisive, but Hinduism, the dominant religion of India, is generally a tolerant creed. There are some exceptions, particularly in recent years when the religion, like others, has been distorted for political purposes, but people who adhere to an almost infinitely polytheist faith necessarily find it easier to accept other Gods than those such as Christians or Muslims who believe in one God.

Tolerance extends not only to other people's religions but also to one's own and others' economic and social condition. One verse of a well-known 19th century Church of England hymn reads "The rich man in his castle, the poor man at his gate, God made them high and lowly, and ordered their estate". This verse is nowadays regarded with amusement, or horror, and is not included in recent hymn books, but the sentiment may be still be relevant in India today, among both rich and poor.

One major feature of Indian society, which is partly a cause and partly an effect of poverty, is the rural-urban divide. This has been in part perpetuated by the heritage of Mahatma Gandhi's passion to preserve village self-sufficiency. It may, or may not, have been possible in the 1940s for villages to feed and clothe themselves from their own resources, when India's total population was less than a third of what it is today, and expectations were so much lower, but it is abundantly clear that this is not possible in the 21st century. In the year 2000 average annual income per capita was just over Rs. 30,000 in urban areas, and about Rs. 11,500 in rural areas (National Accounts Statistics, CSO, Delhi, 2009). This book is about one way in which this yawning gulf can be bridged.

WHAT CAN BE DONE?

There are probably as many possible solutions for India's poverty as there are causes of it. Some political parties on the left propose a return to the earlier policy of economic isolation; this policy can at least in part be blamed for the so-called "Hindu rate of growth" which allowed China and other countries in South-East Asia to leap ahead of India in the years before liberalisation in 1991. It may also, however, have protected India from some of the glaring inequities which have become evident since 1991. "Globalisation", the process of which India has slowly and hesitantly become a part since that year, has certainly not promoted equity, anywhere, and shared poverty may be less painful than dramatic contrast.

The problem is not usually a matter of adopting the right policies or programmes, so much as that of implementing them effectively. There are comprehensive programmes and laws in place to deal with just about every issue, including abortion of female foetuses, bride burning, the need for old age pensions and the low standards of primary education and health care. But they are incompletely enforced and delivered. Even the well-designed National Rural Employment Guarantee Act (NREGA) is in many places failing to deliver the basic right to 100 days work for every rural household which it provides, because of apathy, mismanagement, state level disinterest and corruption. It might be possible to impose higher taxes on the country's growing middle class and thus to spend more on basic services, but there is little evidence that the taxes would be paid or the programmes would be delivered.

Others promote more drastic solutions. The present situation is surely an emergency, but there seems to be little enthusiasm for repeating Mrs. Gandhi's 1975 attempt to put democracy on a temporary hold. The so-called "Naxalites", quasi-Maoist guerrillas who have for many years been waging a desultory struggle against the establishment, largely in rural areas and among the "tribal" people, the descendants of the original aboriginal inhabitants of what is now India, believe that only a violent revolution can redeem India. They are quite small in number, but they have recently become more visible and active, and the Prime Minister has stated that they constitute "India's most serious internal security problem". The apparent success of their colleagues in neighbouring Nepal has of course added some credibility to their claims.

BRIDGING THE RURAL-URBAN DIVIDE

The rural-urban divide is one of the most abiding features of India's poverty, and many of the possible solutions which have been mentioned above, such as the NREGA, or the Naxalite movement, are intended to address it, albeit in very different way. This book describes some isolated attempts to bridge it which have little or nothing to do with government, and which do not depend on non-government organisations, or on corporate subsidy, for their continuation or success. These attempts are as yet modest in scale, but they do show that Marx need not always be right, that globalisation, growth and the power of capital need not always lead to further inequity and marginalisation of the poor.

About two thirds of India's 1.1 billion people live in rural areas and farming is the mainstay of their livelihoods. There are almost 92 million small farms in India, and the average farm size in 1996 was 1.4 hectares (Nagayets, 2005). This figure is steadily decreasing as the population grows and family land is shared between succeeding generations.

The divide between rural and urban people is not only a division of location, or lifestyle, or wealth. They are also becoming increasingly divided by new types of retailing, such as "modern" supermarkets of the type which have been familiar in wealthier countries for over half a century. These supply goods to urban people through channels, or value chains, in ways which urban consumers are coming to prefer over traditional markets and vendors. They can exclude not only the small traders from whom urban consumers have traditionally bought their supplies; but also the small producers, notably small farmers as well as individual artisans.

"Modern" retailing, self-service supermarkets and superstores, have come late to India. This is mainly because governments have tried to preserve employment and have resisted change in retailing for longer than in any other country. These barriers have now been lowered, and it is estimated that modern retailing is growing at 40% annually in India. (Reardon and Gulati, 2008).

Similar changes have long since happened in China, Thailand, Latin America, and in Eastern Europe (Dries *et al.*, 2004) but at a somewhat slower pace. The rate of change in India is unprecedented.

How does modern retailing affect India's small producers? Modern retail chains, and importers, require large quantities of standardised products, delivered at precise times and to closely specified standards. There is a widening mismatch between traditional small producers and the new large multi-branch retailers. As Gulati and Reardon stated in the IFPRI report (ibid.), India's farmers are in for a "painful shock". Modern retailers demand standardised specifications, high-quality, and large quantities, delivered at stated times. They also tend to pay slowly.

Shepherd (2005) writes of the impact of modern retailing in Thailand and Malaysia, where the changes have taken place earlier than in India. One supermarket chain in Malaysia cut the number of its fresh produce suppliers from 200 to 30 in two years. In Thailand, individual supermarkets initially procured produce on a local basis, from 250 suppliers. Within a few years the company switched to centralised buying for all its outlets, using fewer suppliers in total than each branch had used before.

In India such changes have already caused serious tensions; rioters have attacked and burned modern supermarkets, and in the state of Uttar Pradesh, which is home to about 170 million people, including many of India's poorest small farmers, supermarkets have been forbidden by the state governments to carry fresh produce. The protesters often march under the hammer and sickle, which is still a powerful political symbol in

India. Marx seems to have been right: progress seems inevitably to be associated with increasing inequity.

India cannot retreat, however, to the economic isolation which characterised its first 54 years of independence. There is an urgent need to establish "value chains", which can include rather than exclude the smallest producers. The term is used to describe the set of institutions through which a product passes from the initial producer (or producers) to the final consumer. For edible agricultural products, the phrase "farm to fork" is used to encapsulate what the chain does.

Traditional value chains were, and in India still are, made up of large numbers of small-scale actors. Small farmers and artisans sell through networks of local traders and other middlemen who in turn supply to local grocery shops, market traders and mobile vendors. Now this equilibrium of scale is being upset, as large multi-outlet retailers begin to take over from small traders whose buying power more nearly matches the production capacity of the small producers who supply them.

The "natural" tendency, as has happened in Europe and elsewhere, is for small producers to be consolidated into larger units which can more nearly match the requirements of the traders to whom they sell. In India, this is not socially or politically possible, because of the predominance of small farmers and their lack of alternative opportunities. Ways have to be found to include small producers without preventing the development of new forms of retailing which customers prefer. In fact, inclusive value chains.

International trade has also become far more important in the Indian economy. The following table (Table 3) shows the dramatic rate of this change:

Table 3: India's international trade data, 1987–1997–2007.

	1987	1997	2007
% of GDP from exports of goods and services	5.7%	10.8%	21.3%
% of GDP from imports of goods and services	7.1%	12.1%	24.4%

Source: World Bank Development Indicators, 2009.

Farmers and other small-scale producers in India thus have to cope not just with a totally new and unfamiliar type of domestic buyer. They face increasing competition from foreign producers, which usually operate at a far larger scale, and they must also adjust to the demands of export markets, which require the same kind of consolidation as domestic modern retailers.

The majority of India's poor, particularly those in rural areas, are generally not employed, or un-employed. They are self-employed, as small and marginal farmers or independent artisans. It might or might not be possible to create jobs for them, but this is not the solution. If they are not to be left even further behind, millions of very small independent producers must be included in value chains which will enable them to increase or at least to maintain their incomes. The examples in this book show that this can be done.

There are many obvious reasons why small and marginal producers, like marginal communities, districts, states and even nations, are often excluded from the benefits of economic and social development. These barriers are more difficult to overcome in rural India, than perhaps anywhere else in the world.

The physical distances are not great, except in a very few mountain or desert regions, and the word "remote" is often used in India to describe communities which may only be a few miles or even a few minutes drive or walk from more "mainstream" areas. The boundaries of caste and tribe are more powerful than miles or mountains, and small producers are often still defined by caste. A weaver whose hut is a few yards from a Brahmin's house is far further away from his neighbour than a nomadic shepherd or farmer who measures the distance from his neighbours in days of walking.

Such people also lack the means to find out about new opportunities; they cannot access effective means of communication. They may speak minority languages, many if not most of their adult population, particularly women, are illiterate in any language, and they lack the skills and the equipment which might enable them to communicate at a distance through technology, such as radio or television, telephones or computers.

They also have low-quality physical communication; they are often only linked to mainstream markets by low-quality roads, which may be totally impassable during floods, and even the better roads are poorly maintained and are often blocked.

Even if these people can establish physical contact, or if they can use equipment for communication at a distance, and if they can find a common language, such groups are often socially excluded. They dare not even go into a bank or clinic or government office, still less the office of a large formal business which might be a buyer for what they produce, or to telephone them; if they do summon up the courage to make the initial contact, the staff may be uncomprehending, unwelcoming, or downright rude.

Such exclusion also reinforces itself. If someone believes that he or she is unlikely to be welcomed or given a fair hearing, this will be transferred through body language, voice or even written words, to whoever is the intended recipient of the communication, and will be reinforced by their reaction.

The Indian Government's policies since independence have unwittingly but strongly reinforced such people's lack of self-esteem. All manner of preferences and reservations are in force to ensure positive discrimination in favour of lower caste people and the so-called tribals, and these have become powerful tools of political patronage. These have nurtured the belief that lower caste and tribal people must have preferential treatment to succeed. There is no better way of creating and perpetuating a sense of personal and community inadequacy than the use of the very common Indian official label "the weaker sections".

These barriers lead to low expectations by those who are the "gatekeepers" to the formal and informal institutions through which mainstream resources can be accessed, and low aspirations on the part of the excluded. The problems are compounded by ill-health, by people's lack of "modern" marketable skills, and by wide-ranging family and community responsibilities which make long-term planning very difficult.

In India, the rural poor, most of whom are very small-scale farmers or artisans, have been excluded for thousands of years. They have always been isolated from mainstream activities, within their own villages and local areas — except for paying taxes, whether to local rulers, the British Raj or post-independence authorities — but the impact of this isolation has been partly mitigated by the narrow compass of the activities within which rural communities have traditionally moved.

When individual households and villages are nearly self-sufficient, for goods and for services, exclusion is less damaging than when information, services, markets and physical supplies have to be accessed from much further away, and even globally. Progress and change were always difficult, but the *status quo* could be more or less maintained. In a globalised world, those who are excluded and cannot be linked to wider networks rapidly become worse off, both relatively and absolutely.

Small and marginal producers in India do have some advantages, even or perhaps particularly in the contemporary globalised world to which they are forced to belong. These may be very modest, and may even seem insignificant by comparison with their weaknesses, but if they are not recognised there are only two alternatives: to ignore the excluded people and their poverty, or to increase and perpetuate their dependence on ineffective and pauperising policies such as reservations and subsidy.

The first and most obvious strength is that they are cheap. Women and men who are used to working for long hours, for Rs. 50 a day or less, clearly have an enormous price advantage when compared with their better-paid competitors, even in India. The long-term aim should of course be to enable small producers to increase their earnings, not merely to maintain them. Poverty is as much a matter of uncertainty and vulnerability as it is of low income, however, and regular income, even at a very low level, is better than the same amount or more, which is unreliable.

Poor producers are cheap; they are also flexible. They are willing to work whenever and wherever work is available. They will travel large distances, even at short notice, to work, and they will work at unsocial hours, in difficult conditions, as the task demands. They are also able to fit several activities into the same day, in ways which help them to be competitive with more formal producers. This is of course the result of their poverty, but it also confers advantages over more fortunate workers, which can be exploited for their benefit as well as their employers.

Small farmers and artisans can also mobilize even lower cost workers to assist and supplement their own work. It is easy to dismiss all underage labour as illegal and immoral, but small-scale producers can work effectively as family units, for very low wages per person, which when aggregated may be well over what an individual worker would earn if he traveled to a job and left his family behind.

The increasing importance of the English language, more demanding phyto-sanitary and other regulations, the increasing scale of demand and the need for larger quantities of standardised varieties, shapes, qualities and sizes, are all factors that threaten to exclude small producers from local, national and international markets.

Self-service retail chains, as well as exporters, find it easier to deal with similarly large formal producers than with small informal ones. The scale of an individual Indian farmer's crop, or of an individual weaver's output, is well-matched to the scale of demand of traders and customers in a local village market or of vendors and "mom and pop stores" in a small town marketplace, and to the capacity of the intervening intermediaries in the value chain which connects them, if there are any.

Just one self-service outlet, even a small-scale "mini-market", which is becoming common in urban India, needs much larger quantities than what an individual producer can provide. They must be delivered to a strict schedule and of a standard quality. Chains of many such outlets, widely spread in cities throughout a whole region or even the whole of India, clearly place greater demands on their producers, particularly for fresh produce. There are increasing number of such chains in India, operating at the level of individual cities, states or nationally. In Bhubaneswar, for instance, the relatively small capital of the State of Orissa that has under one million inhabitants, there were no such retailers in the year 2003. By 2008, there were 21 of them.

Value chains, like any other relationships, are more likely to be efficient and beneficial to all parties if each institution in the link is reasonably similar to the others in scale, and power. If one stage in the chain is undertaken by a large number of small independent entities, which together have to deal with one large individual institution, either as a supplier, a customer, or both, the mismatch may be dysfunctional for the whole chain.

There are nevertheless some trends in global markets, some of which are local, others which are India-wide and others which may be outside India and way beyond the normal knowledge of traditional producers. These can allow some small producers to improve their livelihoods and even to attain some relative prosperity.

The threats are powerful, immediate and visible, and are a part of the "normal" marginalising impact of economic progress which has been gradually excluding India's small producers for many generations. The opportunities are mainly new, and sometimes counter-intuitive, and it is not easy to grasp them. They do however hold out hope for some of India's excluded millions.

Many of these new developments are at the forefront of progress, and have arisen because of the greater incomes and more sophisticated taste of better-off communities, which have moved beyond basic needs. The modern communication technologies that bring those who are "connected" closer together, and exclude those who are not, can also make it easier for small producers to learn about what sophisticated urban and foreign consumers want, and what is required to satisfy them. Organic crops are perhaps the best example of this.

Small producers may lack formal education and "modern" skills, but they do have traditional knowledge and skills in crafts, and farming, which can confer special advantages. They are in a good position to exploit the growing demand for organic foodstuff, mainly from higher income consumers, initially abroad and now also within India. Organic farming usually substitutes labour for purchased inputs. Hand weeding replaces herbicides, integrated pest management replaces pesticides, composting replaces purchased chemical fertilizers, and "micro-drip" irrigation replaces more capital- and water-intensive techniques. All these practices require more sustained labour inputs than the "modern" inputs they replace, and small producers' labour is cheap.

Organic farming also requires local knowledge of soil conditions, pests and weather. Marginal farmers know their small plots intimately, and they are better able to grow organic crops than large-scale farmers who in effect standardise their land by the application of chemicals.

Over a quarter of a million farmers have committed suicide in India in the last 10 years, in large part because of unsustainable levels of debt, from banks and from moneylenders. This massive tragedy graphically demonstrates the dangers of heavy farm inputs, and the credit which is needed to finance them. Organic farming reduces the need for credit, and it is particularly suitable for small-scale producers who are often excluded from formal bank loans.

"Fair-trade" products can further improve the position of small producers, as wealthier consumers are willing to pay higher prices for products which are certified as having been bought at "fair" prices, often through producer-owned co-operatives or other forms of community institutions. These institutions have always been prone to failure, often because of government or political interference, but there are now the beginnings of some customer preference for their products.

In some wealthy and sophisticated markets, there is a reaction against over-standardised products and designs. This often applies to non-food items, such as garments, home furnishings, furniture and decorative items, but it is also used in some markets for custom-packaged foodstuffs. Modern communication can even make it possible for customers to send their individual requirements direct to producers, and more flexible and secure small-unit transport services which enable small producers to send custom-made products direct to the final customers. There has thus far been very little use of this form of direct marketing by Indian producers, perhaps because of inadequate infrastructure and unreliable transport, but the potential is there.

Small-scale producers are already excluded from some mainstream markets, and globalisation, integrated value chains and new technologies can make this worse. There are also many opportunities which such producers can exploit. The following table (Table 4) briefly summarises the position, following the traditional SWOT approach of strengths, weaknesses, opportunities and threats.

Table 4: Small producers in emerging markets: A simplified SWOT analysis.

Strengths	Weaknesses
Low cost	Socially and physically "remote"
Family labour	Illiteracy
Traditional knowledge and skills	Lack of language skills
Flexibility	Ill-health
	Low aspirations and self-esteem
	Digitally divided from mainstream
	"Weaker sections"
Opportunities	**Threats**
Low input organic farming	Standardisation
Custom-designed individual products	Bulk requirements
Fair trade preferences	Inexorable growing world-wide inequity
Resurgence of co-operatives	Government subsidies and preferences

These strengths and opportunities are not merely optimistic visions of what might be. There are many examples of totally modern inclusive value chains which have been developed in recent years. Fourteen examples are described in the pages that follow. They demonstrate that even the smallest producers can be linked to modern markets in ways which are profitable for all parties.

REFERENCES

Nagayets, O (2005). Small Farms: Current Status and Key Trends, Information Brief, Prepared for the Future of Small Farms Research Workshop, Wye College, Ashford.

Reardon, T and A Gulati (2008). The Rise of Supermarkets and their Development Implications — International Experience and Relevance for India, IFPRI, Washington DC.

Dries, L, T Reardon and JFM Swinnen (2004). The Rapid Rise of Supermarkets in Central and Eastern Europe: Implications for the Agrifood Sector and Rural Development. Development Policy Review.

Shepherd, A (2005). The Implications of Supermarket Development for Horticultural Farmers and Traditional Marketing Systems in Asia, FAO, Rome.

Chapter 2

Retail Winners and Losers — The Impact of Organised Retailing

THE MIDDLEMEN AND WOMEN

There are three main categories of people who are engaged in any value chain; the actual producers, who grow, manufacture or process the products which pass through the chain, the consumers who buy and consume the products, and the much maligned "middlemen" (and middle-women) who buy and sell and distribute and store and transport and otherwise add the intangible values of time, place, quantity and information which are required by the final consumer.

There is some evidence, which is generally supported by the case studies in this book, that it is possible for both producers and consumers to benefit from the "modernisation" of value chains, particularly for fresh produce. Table 1 shows the extent of price reductions for consumers, and price increases for farmers, which were achieved for a sample of fresh produce items in one area.

Less is known, however, about the impact on the second group, the middlemen (and middle-women). Middlemen have traditionally been despised and even derided. Growing and making things is somehow an acceptable way of making a living, but trading in them, buying and selling them without physically making them any different, has never been considered as a decent occupation. Napoleon's worst insult was to call England "a nation of shopkeepers", and none of the fathers of Jane Austen's heroines had ever been "in trade". This opprobrium continues in India to this day; one of the major goals of the 2008 budget was to release farmers from the "clutches of the middlemen".

This traditional view of what is after all no different from "marketing" may in part explain why Indian retailing is so under-developed in comparison with other countries at a similar stage of development. The AT Kearney Global Retail Development Index (AT Kearney, 2007) has for the last three years ranked India first in its list of potential markets for international retailers. India scores well in part because of its low country risk and growing wealth, but the main reason for its high ranking is the

The author wishes to acknowledge valuable assistance from Braja Mishra and Sukhpal Singh.

Note: Units of measurement in the Indian numbering system: lakh = 100,000; crore = 10,000,000. Indian Rupees (Rs.) where appropriate are converted into USD at a rate of approximately Rs. 50 = $1.00; Rs. 1 lakh = $2,000; Rs. 1 crore = $200,000.

Table 1: Comparative benefits to farmers and consumers from modernisation of fruit and vegetable supply chains.

	Tomato (%)	Potato (%)	Cabbage (%)	Cauliflower (%)	Banana (%)
Consumer's reduction in prices	21	8	9	11	13
Farmers' increase in prices	25	4	1	22	3

Source: Raghunath and Ashok (with Mathur and Joseph).

under-developed condition of Indian retailing, and hence its potential for growth. "Modern" retailers are said to occupy less than 3% of the total Indian retail market; this is the lowest rate of penetration of any major country in the world except Egypt.

MODERN RETAILING IN INDIA

The Kearney report estimates that modern retailing is growing at a compound rate of 40% a year in India, but because the whole market is growing at around 10% annually this means that modern retailers will still only have about 5% of the market by the year 2010. Markets such as Thailand, Brazil, China, Malaysia and even Indonesia are said to be relatively saturated, so that new entrants are being compelled to look for smaller niche markets, secondary towns or new formats; the report says that India is "hot".

The case studies in this book are about the producers, about ways in which even the smallest and most marginalised of them can profitably be included in modern integrated value chains. We have identified a number of examples where this is being done successfully, but even if India's millions of small farmers and artisans could somehow participate in inclusive value chains of this kind, which is itself very unlikely, this would still leave out the millions of small-scale and usually informal middlemen and middle-women who at present constitute the marketing channels for most Indian products, and particularly for foodstuffs.

A number of organisations and individuals have opposed the entry of modern organised retailers into India. Much of their wrath has been directed at foreign multinationals, and in particular at Wal-Mart, the world's largest retailer. Foreign investors are always an attractive target for the political left, and if they can also be branded as "middlemen" so much the better. It is already clear, however, that modern retailing is coming to India irrespective of foreign entrants. Reliance Fresh has been the main indigenous target, perhaps because it is an arm of one of India's largest and best-known companies, but there are large number of other companies already active in the field.

The Ministry for Commerce and Industry of the Government of India commissioned a study of the likely impact of "supermarketisation" on Indian producers and consumers, and on the traditional retailers who it is feared may be displaced by modern retailing. This was carried out for the Indian Council for Research on International Economic Relations (ICRIER) by the International Food Policy Research Institute (IFPRI) and Michigan State University (Reardon and Gulati, 2008).

This study drew on international experience in order to predict how the rapid changes in Indian retailing might be expected to affect the three major interest groups in India. It did not examine the Indian experience as such, but because modern retail has come later to India than to other so-called developing countries such as Indonesia, China and much of Latin America it was argued that it is possible to draw some conclusions as to the probable outcomes in India.

THE IMPACT ON TRADITIONAL RETAILING

There is no escape from the fact that modern retailing, which includes not only large supermarkets and so-called "hypermarkets" but also quite small self-service chain stores such as are already familiar in most Indian cities, displaces large number of traditional "mom and pop" retailers, the equivalent of India's *kirana* shops. The IFPRI study states that the number of such small shops fell by 30% in Hong Kong between 1974 and 1985, and that they fell by the same percentage in Argentina between 1984 and 1993. Modern retailing in India in 2008 expanded at a similar or slightly faster rate than it did in Hong Kong and Argentina during those periods, so that it is likely that 30% of the present numbers employed, or some 12 million people, will be displaced from Indian traditional retailing by 2018. To place this in context, this is perhaps ten times the total number now employed in business process outsourcing and call centres.

Altenburg (2007) summarised some aspects of the socio-economic impact of "modern" value chains on producers and intermediaries. Among other effects, he suggests that there will be a reduction of direct employment in retailing because "mom and pop" stores will be crowded out, and that wage levels in retailing will increase for those who are employed. He also argues that the changes will reduce opportunities for women's livelihoods more than men's, because small producers and informal traders will suffer and they tend to be owned by and to employ women.

There has been much well-publicised opposition to retail modernisation in India, but this seems to be based on local political agitation rather than on objective data as to the extent of the job losses that may be expected. There seems to be general agreement that some 40 million people are employed in the approximately 12 million existing retail outlets in India, but although there have been a number of modern retail grocery outlets in some metro cities for several years, there appear to have been very few attempts to assess what impact they have had on neighbouring traditional retailers.

A study by Anuradha Kalhan of Jai Hind University in Mumbai, (see India FDI watch, website accessed 24 March 2008, and Economic Times, 3 March 2007) surveyed 82 *kirana* shops and 29 vendors in Mumbai, of which 96 were selling general grocery or food items. They were all within a range of one kilometer of a modern retail mall. Seventy eight of them, or over 70%, reported that that their sales had decreased since the malls had been opened. No data was reported, however, as to the amount by which their sales had dropped, nor was there any comparative data from a "control group" of similar traditional retailers which were not near neighbours of a "modern retail" shopping centre.

One might also expect a certain degree of contextual bias in such a response. Just about every small-scale retailer and vendor in Mumbai, as in most Indian cities, must be aware of the debate on the issue of the entry of "modern" retailing, and small-scale business people are in any case always alive to the possibility of some form of official recompense for their problems, whether real or imagined.

A paper by SA and M Scalem is one of the few reports which focuses on the interaction between traditional and modern retailing. This is based on a survey which was carried out in and around Delhi and in Indore, Jaipur, Jamshedpur and Kanpur. The survey covered some 700 customers, 200 vendors, 340 workers and 180 managers or owners of traditional and modern retail outlets. These latter included Reliance, Big Bazaar, Pantaloons, Shoppers Stop and other supermarket and department store chains, as well as some branches of exclusive retailers such as Adidas and Levis.

The authors start their paper with a number of quotations which demonstrate the wide range of opinions of the dramatic changes which are taking place in Indian retailing.

"...These so called organised retail players, I tell you, are going to eat us small fishes. Mark my words as this is going to happen! Who can come in the way of such big corporates with unlimited money behind them? What can we, small kirana storekeepers, do to retain customers given our average spend and/or income? How can we compete in such an unbalanced fight? ..."

— A local *kirana* shop owner-cum-keeper

"...We are essentially enabling the consumers. Be it the wholesome retail environment, AC atmosphere, strategies to capture sales, retaining customers by various loyalty schemes, a haggling-less shopping experience as is mostly the case at local kirana shops, providing the benefit of organised retail supply chain to the end user thereby providing at a lesser cost, and so on. The conflict of business doesn't arise at all as the clientele that the local kirana shop is targeting is not our primary customer as such. However who are we to stop a customer if he/she so wishes to come and experience our environment?"

— Organised sector player's representative

"...The organised retail in India has the potential to add over $45 billion business by the year 2010, generating employment for some 2.5 million people in various retail operations and over 10 million additional workforce in retail support activities – contract

production & processing, supply chain & logistics, retail real estate development & management, etc..."

— Union Minister for Commerce & Industry, GoI

"...With around 12 million outlets, India has the largest density of small shops in the world ... Corporate retailers plan to grow the share of organised retail from the current 3% to approximately 15–20% in four years by investing more than $25 billion, of this 60–65% of all investments will go towards food and grocery retail in setting up the supply chain, which means direct corporate investment in agricultural (sector). Analysts are saying that India is attempting to do in 10 years what took 25–30 years in other global major markets ... The entry of the giant corporate retail in India's food market will have direct impact on India's 650 million farmers and 40 million people employed in retail. If we take examples of other countries, we can see that nowhere has these (organised) corporations ever thought about the people, society and the ecology"

— India Foreign Direct Investment Watch Campaign

The most important finding of the Scalem study is that monthly sales per employee are about Rs. 60,000 in modern retailers, as opposed to Rs. 8,000 for traditional outlets. Some tasks that small shopkeepers perform for themselves, or do not do at all, such as housekeeping, maintenance, technology support or security, are outsourced to other businesses by organised retailers, but this is not likely to make a material difference to the comparison.

This seven and a half times multiple is similar to data from between 1965 and 1975 from Recife in Brazil, from Nairobi in Kenya and from Santiago in Chile; in all three places, sales per employee in "modern" supermarkets were between six and seven times those of traditional retail shops (Slater C *et al.*, 1969; Bennett PD, 1966; Harper M, 1975).

Chile is now well into middle-income status. The Nordestina region is much poorer than the rest of Brazil, but is still well ahead of India, and Kenya is marginally less well-off than India. In all three countries, however, retailing has long since undergone the same kind of revolution that is now taking place in India. It is of course impossible to state even approximately how many jobs have been lost in the process, but the conclusion from the sales per employee figures is irrefutable. For a given volume of retail sales, only about one-sixth as many people will be employed in organised retailing as in traditional small shops.

A small survey of recent developments in retailing was carried out in Bhubaneswar, the capital of Orissa, India's poorest state. It is a rapidly growing city with a population of around 1 million. No city is typical, but Bhubaneswar's situation is probably not very different from that of many similar-sized places in India. Until 2003, there were no modern-format food and grocery retailers in Bhubaneswar. By 2008, there were 21 such outlets, including department stores with self-service grocery departments and single-purpose grocery shops. Only one was locally owned.

The daily sales of one of the eight Reliance Fresh outlets which had been open for less than 12 months were informally estimated to be around Rs. 60,000. This store had some 16 employees, working in two shifts, leading to an average figure of Rs. 3,750 sales per day, per employee. The sales levels of the *kirana* shops vary very widely, and many of them employ part-time family labour so that it is difficult to calculate an equivalent figure. Rs. 1,000 sales per day is typical for such shops, however, with the equivalent of one and a half full time employees. This gives an average of Rs. 670 sales per day, per employee. Table 2 shows the ratio of sales per employee in traditional and modern retail from Brazil, Kenya, Chile and two studies in India, from a period of some 30 years; the similarity is remarkable.

An attempt was also made in the Bhubaneswar study to compare the gender, the wages, and the education of the staff in the two types of retail outlet. The findings are given in Table 3.

One or two of the modern retail staff in Bhubaneswar had previously worked in *kirana* shops, and they remarked that they had been given

Table 2: Ratio of sales per employee in "modern" to "traditional" retailing.

Chile 1966, Santiago	Brazil 1969, Recife	Kenya 1973, Nairobi	India 2007, Delhi + 4 intermediate cities	India 2008, Bhubaneswar
7 times	7 times	6 times	7.3 times	5.6 times

Table 3: Comparison of gender, wages, and education of staff in two types of retail outlets.

	Gender	Earnings per month (in Rs.)	Education
Kirana shops	50:50 male:female	1,000–1,500	Graduates
"Modern" retailers	Two-thirds male	2,000–4,000	7th–10th grade

preference because of their prior experience. The majority, however, had no previous retail experience. 30% of the staff of modern retailers in the Scalem study said that they had previously worked in *kirana* shops; this suggests that some of the people who are displaced from traditional retailing may find employment in the new format outlets.

The *kirana* shop owners in Bhubaneswar and in the five cities covered in the Scalem study were asked whether the new format retailers had affected their business. It is of course by definition impossible to survey shops which have gone out of business, and there does not appear to have been any longitudinal study to observe changes in the numbers of *kirana* shops or vendors before and after the arrival of modern retailers.

The majority of the respondents said that their sales had gone down, and some mentioned that other neighbouring shops had gone out of business. A number of the Bhubaneswar shopkeepers mentioned that many of their older customers had deserted them for two or three months but had then returned because they preferred the personal services, proximity and price flexibility of their familiar neighbourhood store.

CONCLUSIONS

The broad conclusion seems inescapable. The numbers are inevitably imprecise, but it is likely that at least one million traditional retailing jobs will be lost every year for at least the next 10 years and probably for longer, as a result of the "modernisation" of retail. Around one fifth of that number or less new jobs will be created in new format retailing.

Most of the job losers will be women, and most of the new jobs will be for men. Those who are displaced will be less educated than those who displace them, and the salaries of the "winners" will be double or more those of the "losers".

There may be some mitigating factors, but it seems inevitable that this change will take place. Its pace may differ from one place to another because of local opposition, or the overall rate of change may be reduced as a result of major political changes or if India for any reason becomes a less attractive investment destination. In such a case, however, there would probably be even fewer new alternative employment opportunities for those who are displaced, so the overall level of socio-economic pain would be similar.

The IFPRI report which was referred to earlier described a number of programmes which have been used to mitigate the livelihood destruction effects of these changes in other countries where modern retailing has grown very rapidly and has inevitably displaced labour from traditional outlets. One aspect which can easily be overlooked is the impact on small shopkeepers of officially imposed standards. "Modern" regulations on issues such as sanitation, food standards, and preservation, weights and measures and waste disposal, which are introduced in the interests of consumers, can often inadvertently damage smaller traditional retailers which may have neither the scale, the skills nor the resources to conform to them. Similarly, zoning and other planning rules may make life even harder for small retailers, and may also deprive consumers of conveniently located sources of supply.

Such regulations are often not properly enforced, and this has always been a major source of opportunities for corruption. If they are enforced completely, they will inevitably make business harder for small shopkeepers, and if enforcement is incomplete, or partial, and subject to political manipulation or corrupt behaviour by the responsible authorities, as is more likely in the Indian context, the effect will be to increase costs and uncertainty. The continuing conflict over "locking" of unauthorised premises in Delhi is a classic example of this.

There are many examples from outside India of ways in which the authorities have attempted to mitigate the impact of modernisation and improved standards on small-scale retailers. Whole streets may be closed to traffic at certain periods to allow market vendors to operate, public cold storage facilities have been opened to enable retailers of perishable produce to store their stocks overnight, and special areas are set aside for small-scale retailers.

Such expedients are by no means unknown in India, although they are less developed because retailing itself has only recently started to be "modernised". They may also do little to help small shopkeepers because the areas which are set aside for them are often in marginal areas with low customer footfall; the premium locations are inevitably monopolised by large retail chains which can pay the highest rent. The old adage that the three rules of success in retail are "location, location, location" applies in Indian cities as much as anywhere else, or maybe more, because of poor local transport facilities and the physical difficulty of moving on foot.

Many attempts have been made to "rehabilitate" people who have been displaced from traditional activities such as informal retailing, by training them in new skills and helping them to secure new livelihoods. These programmes have achieved some limited successes, usually with people such as handloom weavers or other artisans, whose traditional skills could be "re-engineered" to fit new markets.

The skills of vendors and *kirana* shopkeepers, however, are not readily transferable to modern retailing, and there are few alternatives. As we have seen, some people who work in traditional retailing may be able to find jobs in the supermarkets which have replaced them, but there are insufficient opportunities to absorb more than a small number of those who are being displaced. New format retailers are unlikely to employ large numbers of illiterate women.

The case studies in this collection show that more efficient value chains need not necessarily displace or injure the smallest producers, and that at least some of them can indeed benefit from change. It does not at present seem possible to hold out any similar hope for most of the middlemen and middle-women who presently intermediate between the producers and the final customers. Indian policy makers and politicians have for many years inveighed against these intermediaries; "elimination of the middleman" has been seen as the solution to small producers' problems. Perhaps the politicians are right, as was Karl Marx. At least in retailing, progress under the capitalist mode of production may inevitably be associated with further marginalisation and impoverishment of the poor. We can only hope that future innovations in retailing will be more labour intensive and more inclusive than the present retail revolution.

REFERENCES

Altenburg, T (2007). Donor approaches to supporting pro-poor value chains. Report prepared for the Donor Committee for Enterprise Development, Working Group on Linkages and Value Chains, by German Development Institute. July 2006, revised January 2007.

AT Kearney (2007). Global Development Retail Index. Chicago.

Bennett, PD (1966). Retailing evolution or revolution in Chile? *Journal of Marketing*, 30(3), 38–41.

Harper, M (1975). The employment of finance in small business. *The Journal of Development Studies*, 11(4), 366–375.

Raghunath, S and D Ashok (with PP Mathur and T Joseph). Indian Agricultural Produce Distribution System — Towards an Integrated Agri Produce Flow, a PPT presentation, IIM, Bangalore (undated).

Reardon, T and A Gulati (2008). The Rise of Supermarkets and their development implications — International experience and relevance for India, Washington DC: IFPRI.

SA and M Scalem (2008). Organised Indian Retail Market. Unpublished draft report prepared for the Indian School of Livelihoods.

Slater, C *et al.* (1969). Market Processes in the Recife area of NE Brazil, East Lansing, Latin American Studies Centre.

Chapter 3

Inclusive Value Chains in Fresh Fruit and Vegetables

Introduction

It is appropriate that this collection should start with value chains in fresh fruit and vegetables, because this is probably the most challenging category of products to fit into modern integrated value chains, and is for that very reason the one which offers the most opportunities.

"Fresh" is the operative word. Apart from uncooked meat, fresh fruit, fish and vegetables are the most perishable products which consumers regularly want to purchase. The maximum permissible delay between "farm and fork" may for some items be measured in hours rather than days, and the prices which discerning consumers are prepared to pay drop steeply as time goes by. Refrigeration can extend the period for some items, as can less expensive and more labour-intensive expedients such as sprinkling the produce with clean or not so clean water, but the key to success is to minimise the time it takes to bring the produce into the consumer's hands.

This explains why the retailing of fresh fruit and vegetables is in India still overwhelmingly dominated by informal vendors operating from roadside stalls, fixed markets or mobile push-carts. *Kirana* shops, and the few department stores or quasi-supermarkets which had opened before the start of the 21st century, do not stock fresh produce. Some of the produce, such as apples or oranges, may have traveled long distances from where it was grown, but the last link in the supply chain is no different from what it has been for centuries. These outlets also provide employment for large numbers of poor people, and particularly for women, which is why most popular agitation against new format retailing has been focused on retailers of fresh produce.

The "under-developed" nature of fresh produce retailing may also explain why fresh fruit is often not available in institutions that require large quantities of high quality produce on a regular basis. Visitors to India are often astonished to find that fresh fruit is completely unavailable in most hotels, while the streets outside are crowded with vendors who sell it. There is no effective interface between the informal and the formal, so that producers cannot access customers who may be literally only a few yards away.

The case studies in this section show how four very different institutions are attempting to fill this gap. ITC, previously the "Imperial Tobacco Company", is working with a project funded by the government of the United States, to try to integrate small farmers in the Punjab and elsewhere into its own and other companies' "new format" retail operations. Spencer's, another large company with roots going back to pre-independence times, is doing similar work mainly in the South, without any subsidised assistance, and Namdharis, part of a large traditional family group of firms with a long tradition of philanthropy, is building on its original seed production business to link small farmers in Karnataka to new markets abroad, and, more recently, in India.

INFAM in Kerala has very different roots. It arose from a church-based initiative in Wayanad District, where indebted farmer suicides are a major problem. It has engaged with a number of different initiatives and institutions in an effort to alleviate the problems of small farmers, some of which have succeeded while others are struggling. One approach which has great potential for farmers in Wayanad, and elsewhere, is organic farming. INFAM is one of several institutions which are described in this book which has found that the requirements of organic cultivation closely match the strengths of small farmers. The growing demand for organic produce, in Europe and more recently in India, offers an enormous market for Indian farmers, particularly for the smallest and most vulnerable of them, and integrated value chains of the kind which are described are vital to make this market work.

Case Study **1**

Namdhari Fresh Limited

BN Dhananjaya and A Umesh Rao*

INTRODUCTION

The marketing of consumer goods in India has changed greatly over the past two decades. Until the end of the 20th century, producers tradition-ally reached consumers through large wholesalers or individuals with storage space and transport. These agencies appointed a network of dealers for the different regions. The dealers would supply products to retailers — usually the neighbourhood convenience or *"kirana"* store — who would sell it to consumers. All the stake holders in this chain got a fee in the form of discounts, thereby adding to the price paid by the con-sumer. This model was mainly for processed, manufactured fast-moving consumer goods and durables with a relatively long shelf-life.

In the case of farm produce, in particular food grains, the chain was the same with some extra players: small scale buyers who collected small

* The writers wish to thank Dr. VSS Rao, Director (Quality Control), Namdhari Seeds, and M/S Sunil Awari, and Anand Nanjappanavar, Managers, and Mr Shiva, Field Supervisor, all of Namdhari Fresh, for their assistance. They also acknowledge the contributions of the contract farmers who shared their experiences.
Note: Units of measurement in the Indian numbering system: lakh = 100,000; crore = 10,000,000. Indian Rupees (Rs.) where appropriate are converted into USD at a rate of approximately Rs. 50 = $1.00; Rs. 1 lakh = $2,000; Rs. 1 crore = $200,000.

quantities of farm produce from the small and marginal farmers who make up the majority of food grain producers in India, especially in Karnataka which is the focus of this case. Here, the small-scale procurers, who are themselves very poor, gather farm produce for a small fee on behalf of small-scale traders who then sell to wholesale traders either directly or through commission agents. There are usually between one and three of these small-scale gatherers in each village. The high numbers of intermediaries mean that there is a big difference between the price the farmer receives and the price paid by the consumer.

Fresh fruit and vegetables are different because they are perishable, so the time available for the produce to reach the market is shorter. Farmers usually transport these commodities to the market on their own or using a representative of a group of farmers. When they get to the market, these commodities are sold to wholesale traders or retailers through commission agents who often form a cartel and fix the price paid for a commodity on a given day. The agents and wholesale traders often exploit the farmers by manipulating prices in their favour. There is typically no quality control or grading of produce at this stage of the traditional value chain.

Department stores, convenience stores, hypermarkets and supermarkets arrived in India towards the end of the 20th century and led to new marketing models. There were fundamental social changes, particularly in cities, as less people lived in extended families and more couples went out to work. There was less time for shopping, and consumers wanted to buy everything from one place. Supermarkets and shopping malls only came to India in the 1990s. Most of the early arrivals sold manufactured, processed and packaged goods with relatively long shelf lives, but since around 2006 there has been a rush to start marketing and selling perishables such as meat, fish, vegetables and fruit through the new types of retail outlets.

The perishable nature of these products and the continuous demand for them means that the links between the retail outlet and the producer have to be closely integrated. Perishable goods also need sophisticated infrastructure such as refrigerated transport and cold storage, and controlled environment shelves and show cases at the retail level. These value chains are more efficient than their predecessors, and they have profoundly influenced the livelihoods of the various stakeholders who participate in them.

The big retail chains in the West, especially in the USA, have for many years used integrated value chains for many farm products, in order to bring the products to the consumer at a competitive price by controlling the entire chain from producer to consumer. The value chains also allow the flow of produce to be controlled in order to meet demand, especially of perishables and other products with a short shelf-life. These models are being adopted in India. The majority of the large companies who have gone into mass retailing have merely streamlined existing value chains in order to bring in economies of scale in marketing. Others such as Namdhari have gone further and have set up complete "farm to fork" systems for production, quality control, grading, cold storage, packaging, refrigerated transport to modern malls and even processing fresh produce into ready-to-use products.

The promoters of the Namdhari company come from a line of chieftains in Punjab. They belong to a deeply religious sect whose members are meant to adopt a strict vegetarian diet and to abstain from any drugs or alcohol. They tend to be philanthropic and are involved in various charities. The Namdharis are known as good horsemen and breeders of thoroughbred horses. They first came to Karnataka to set up a stud farm for breeding horses in the village of Urugahalli in Bidadi hobli of Ramanagar District, which was known for its regular horse racing events. They bought a 180 acre plot in 1982, from the family of one of the erstwhile court staff of the Maharaja of Mysore. Up to that time it had been farmed by share croppers.

Bidadi hobli, which is now the head quarters of the Namdhari business group, is about 30 kms away from Bangalore, and suffers from frequent drought. The local rural population is very poor because of the low productivity of agriculture in the area. Bangalore, however, is one of the biggest markets in the state for all commodities including food grains, fruit and vegetables. It is well connected to Bidadi by rail and by road.

Some of the larger and more enterprising farmers in Bidadi sell small quantities of perishable commodities such as fruit and vegetables direct to Bangalore. Neighbouring districts such as Devanahalli, Chikkaballapur and Kolar sell large quantities to Bangalore, but the climatic and socio-economic conditions of Bidadi are such that the farmers have no access to inputs such as water and improved agronomic practices, which could earn them higher returns. The products which they can grow from rain-fed agriculture are sold through commission agents either to wholesale traders or retailers, but the farmers get very low prices through these traditional channels.

While they were about to set up the stud, the Namdharis saw how poor the local village farmers were. They abandoned their plan to set up a horse stud. They were already involved in seed production for the international market, and they decided instead to set up a processing plant for treating and packaging seeds on the site, and to involve local farmers.

The Company leased more land from neighbouring small-holders in addition to their own 180 acres, and they bored tube wells to get ground water for irrigation. For five years the land was then used to produce seeds for the international market and later for the growing Indian market. Nothing was paid to the farmers who owned the land — the deal was that the company would develop the land and install the irrigation. During this period, most of the farmers who owned the land worked as wage labourers for the company.

After five years, the land reverted to the farmers, and they had the option to use it for growing quality seeds for Namdhari Seeds under the close supervision of the Company's technical staff. The Company distributed all the required inputs and ensured that the seed was cultivated according to the correct procedures for seed production.

Many workers were hired from nearby villages to work in seed production and processing. A large number of them were women who were employed to sort and pack the seeds. This gave the management an insight into the diet and general socio-economic conditions of the workers, in particular the women, and they decided to try to help to address their many problems.

At the same time, the Namdhari company identified a growing demand for Indian types of vegetables in the European market. They were being grown in Africa and exported to Britain. The management took advantage of this and started to grow vegetables to meet the British and the European market specifications. In 2000 they started the "Namdhari Fresh" brand, and in 2007 they incorporated "Namdhari Farm Fresh Limited" to handle the business. These initiatives have provided work for more than 10,000 workers in the fields and in various processing plants. More than 4,000 farmers are producing seeds and growing fruit and vegetables.

Namdhari Fresh aims to be the leader in the fresh produce market and to be recognised as a customer-focused grower, exporter and retailer of quality produce. To achieve this, Namdhari is committed to providing safe, hygienic and fresh vegetables and fruit using environmentally friendly inputs and integrated pest management practices. "Customer safety and satisfaction is our prime concern", says the management. It has instilled quality consciousness and the practice of on-farm grading amongst the farmers, so that their produce fetches a good price. This model has generated a deep sense of loyalty among the farmers.

THE OPERATIONAL MODEL OF NAMDHARI FRESH

Namdhari Fresh has a centralised production, procurement and distribution system. It has both captive production, on its own as well as on leased land, and contract farming with carefully vetted farmers. The ratio of captive to contract farming is approximately 20:80. Based on an assessment of the demand for export, institutional and domestic supplies, Namdhari Fresh plans production meticulously to avoid over-production and to ensure that the daily supply of fresh produce matches requirements. This planning helps to maintain the quality of the produce. Farmers are informed about the production plan, and they stagger their sowing and planting dates in order to ensure sequential dates for harvesting. The company supplies inputs such as seeds, fertilisers and pesticides. Harvest dates are given in advance, and the dates are fixed according to production trials conducted on Namdhari's own farms. The farmers also receive technical guidance. The cost of the inputs is initially borne by the company but is then deducted when the farmers are paid.

The company also provides interest free one to three-year loans to help farmers improve their irrigation facilities. This has helped to build long-term bonds between the company and the farmers. Even when the Company has leased the land, they pay for leveling and the cost of irrigation. The farmers are allowed these terms if they agree to lease the land to the company for three to five years with no return. During this period the company improves the land, and cultivates and harvests the crops, and it may employ the farmer during that time. Once the period is over, the developed land is returned to the farmer, and he then has the option to grow crops for the company if he wishes. This method of capital assistance and infrastructure development has been used for seed growers and also for a few vegetable farmers for Namdhari Fresh.

Namdhari manages the whole production process with hired labour on its own or leased land, but for contract farming, the farmer and his hired labour are responsible for planting and harvesting the produce. The produce is weighed in the presence of the farmer, and is then transported to the packing house by Namdhari. The company has it own refrigerated trucks to collect the produce from the farms and to transport it over long distances. The packing houses were built with an initial investment of $5 million and they have state-of-the-art cold storage and packing facilities. Namdhari has a workforce of about 500 people, along with supervisory staff, and the produce is sorted, graded and packed in the pack houses according to EUREP GAP standards.

Table 1 shows how farmers benefit from the system. They have to produce higher quality produce, and they grade it themselves on the farm to Namdhari's standards before it is weighed and taken away by Namdhari. They have to market their lower-grade produce themselves on the open market, since Namdhari will only accept the highest quality.

The produce is air-freighted to foreign markets. In the domestic market, some produce is sent to institutional buyers such as five star hotels and large-scale caterers such as those which supply airline meals. Namdhari Fresh has also established its own chain of retail outlets to sell fruit and vegetables direct to the consumer, and has introduced salad bars which serve ready-made fruit and vegetable salads. Stringent efforts are made to ensure that no pesticide residues remain in the produce. The Company uses Integrated Pest Management on its own fields, to reduce the amount of pesticides, and ensures that contract farmers do the same.

Namdhari Fresh is the only Indian company that has received the British Retail Consortium (BRC) and European Retailers Certified Vegetable Growing and Exporting Firm (EUEP GAP) certifications. Their operating system emphasises strict quality and centralised production control.

Namdhari Fresh manages 250 acres of captive farm land and over 1250 acres through contract farming. Over 1200 farmers are involved in contract farming, and in 2008 the average total volume of production was

Table 1: Value Chain Price Analysis — Namdhari compared with the Traditional System.

Product	System	Farmers level/ farm gate (in Rs./kg)	Value addition/ processing	Bulk price (in Rs./kg)	Retail price (in Rs./kg)	Remarks
Baby Corn	Traditional	4	No grading, packing or cold storage	12	18	'A' grade quality is usually not available at all in the traditional market.
	Namdhari	7	Grading, packing, cold storage	160	200	Namdhari takes only 'A' grade quality produce.
Bhendi (*Okra*)	Traditional	4	No grading, packing or cold storage	10–12	16–20	Price will vary depending upon tenderness. 20% wastage during transportation/selling.
	Namdhari	9	Grading, packing, cold storage	25	32	Tenderness of the produce is ensured. < 5 % wastage in transportation/ selling

Figure 1: Namdhari's operational areas in India.

approximately 160 tonnes per week, of which about 110 tonnes came from contract farming. The land is located in Bangalore Rural, Ramanagara, Koppal and Tumkur Districts, and in a few small pockets elsewhere in the state. Namdhari is also starting production in Ooty in Tamil Nadu and in some villages near Ludhiana in the Punjab. Figure 1 shows the areas where Namdhari is producing crops.

Namdhari Farm Fresh Limited exports fresh vegetables to Britain and other European countries, in particular to France and Germany, to Japan and to the Middle East. Namdhari Fresh Ltd, which caters to the domestic market, sells through 30 company-owned retail outlets, of which 20 are in Bangalore, and five each in Delhi and Ludhiana. The domestic market also includes a number of five star hotels all over India and in other SAARC countries, large industrial canteens and catering establishments and airline caterers. Seven of the Bangalore retail outlets have salad bars. Figure 2 shows the relationships between the different participants and their functions in the Namdhari value chain.

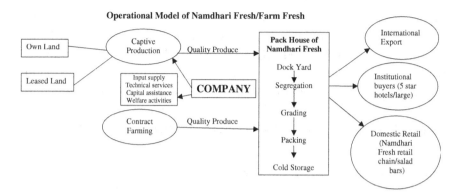

Figure 2: Relationships between the different participants and their functions in the Namdhari value chain.

FARMER CASES

Kumar, Son of Lakshmaiah — Contract Farmer for Namdhari Fresh

Kumar farms seven acres in Avaragere village in Bannikuppe near Bidadi in Ramnagar District. He has five family members and he used to farm ragi and, when conditions allowed, some paddy in his lower lying land. Because of recurrent droughts, he had debts of $2,000.

He saw how some of his neighbours were benefiting from farming with Namdhari, so he approached them to start vegetable cultivation. He had no irrigation, but Namdhari lent him Rs. 30,000 to buy a pump and pipes to lift water from a nearby pond. This completely changed his cultivation practices. Since 2006 he has grown baby corn in one and then two acres, green leaf vegetables such as dill and fenugreek in three quarters of an acre, broccoli in quarter of an acre and some other vegetables such as cabbage and brinjal in smaller patches. Kumar now grows four different crops a year, of which one is always a green vegetable, with about one month of rest. This provides him with year round employment and guaranteed good returns. He gets all the inputs for toxin-free produce in advance, and the cost of these is taken off the selling price at harvest. In the unlikely event of loss or crop failure due to natural calamities the cost of inputs is waived, which mitigates his loss. Thus far this has not happened.

Since starting contract farming for Namdhari, Kumar has paid off his debts and has also repaid the Rs. 30,000 he borrowed from Namdhari for irrigation equipment. He now has a bank balance of Rs. 200,000. Namdhari pays him by cheque, and this saves him the cost of transport to the wholesale market in Bangalore and helps him to avoid the risk of being exploited by unscrupulous traders. He gets additional income from the second crop which he sells on the open market in Bangalore. He sends his children to good fee-paying schools, and hopes that his children will have a good future. Thirty other farmers in the village do contract farming for Namdhari.

Munithimmaiah, A Marginal Farmer

Munithimmaiah farms three acres in M. Karenahalli village in Bidadi, and has five family members. He used to grow ragi every year and when there was good rainfall he would also grow Paddy in about half an acre. He was an early convert to contract farming for Namdhari, and started in the year 2000, with guidance from Namdhari's technical staff. He says that he used to be chronically debt ridden, but he now has some financial independence.

In the most recent season, he grew okra and brinjal, followed by baby corn. He used to have irrigation only for half an acre, and the following table gives details of the results of his previous cultivation of ragi and paddy. His own labour is valued at the prevailing daily average wage rate of Rs. 50 per day, with 20 labour days required per season.

The table below (Table 2) gives details of Munithimmaiah's land use and income with contract farming under Namdhari. The whole three acres is now irrigated.

In 2008, he grew okra, baby corn, sweet corn and brinjal with half to one acre of land for each crop. The company supplied all the seed and other inputs. He did not keep a record of the costs, but he estimated that about one fifth of his income was spent on inputs, and another fifth of his income covered his other costs including his own family's time and some hired labour.

In addition to their higher incomes, the farmers' working conditions have improved and their crop risks are reduced.

A Sharecroppers Experience

Chikkahombaiah and Hombaiah are landless sharecroppers from Avaragere village. They used to subsist by hiring themselves out as field

Table 2: Munithimmaiah — Expenditure and income details

Expenditure		Income	
Seed cost for ragi (Rs. 40/ acre cultivation)	Rs. 100	Sale of ragi (25 quintals @ Rs. 400/qt)	Rs. 10,000
Seed cost for paddy (Rs. 400/acre cultivation)	Rs. 200	Sale of by products, husk and straw	Rs. 2000
Cost of tillage, harvest/ labour for ragi cultivation	Rs. 1000	Sale of paddy (8 quintals @ Rs. 600/qt)	Rs. 4800
Cost of tillage/labour for paddy cultivation	Rs. 1000	Sale of paddy husk and straw	Rs. 1000
Cost of fertiliser for paddy	Rs. 800		
Cost of fertiliser for ragi	Rs. 500		
Other miscellaneous costs	Rs. 500		
Total Expenditure	**Rs. 4100**	**Total Income**	**Rs. 17,800**
		Net Income	**Rs. 13,700**

Crops grown	Area (in acres)	Yield (in tonnes)	Rate (in Rs./kg)	Total (in Rs.)
Baby Corn	1	4	7	28,000
Sweet Corn	1	3	6	18,000
Okra	1/2	1	8	8000
Brinjal	1/2	3	5	15,000
Total Income/season				**69,000**
Deduction for seed and input cost (20% of the income)				13,800
Electricity, labour and other miscellaneous costs (20%)				13,800
Net Income/Season				**41,400**
Net Income/Year (assuming three crops greens not grown in 2008)				**124,200**

labourers to other farmers, and by sharecropping some ragi and paddy. As they had a good reputation, some farmers who had more land than they could cultivate agreed to lease out their lands to them on a share-cropping basis. They approached Namdhari and started to grow vegetables under their technical supervision. Now they farm regularly for Namdharis although they do not possess any land of their own. They used to earn Rs. 4,000–5,000 a year from their share-cropping in addition to their wages for agricultural labor, but now their earnings have gone up four times. They are each growing one acre of baby corn.

CONCLUSIONS

Namdhari Fresh maintains strict quality controls on its own and its farmers' operations. The farmers must continue to maintain high standards and adhere to the timings and other rules, if they wish to become and remain as contract farmers for Namdhari Fresh. When selecting contract farmers, the company analyses their past history. Positive attitudes towards farming, willingness to work hard and a good reputation in the village are the main considerations. Many farmers, including some with large holdings, have been rejected. The company needs assured irrigation facilities at a farm to maintain productivity and quality, and the requirements would seem to prevent small and marginal farmers from becoming involved. In reality, however, most of the contract farmers are not rich and do not own much land. Most of the contract farmers with Namdhari Fresh own three to seven acres of land, and they all have some assured irrigation facilities, which they may have installed with help from Namdhari.

The farmers are generally satisfied with their relationship with Namdhari. They no longer have to transport their produce to market or be involved in any way in the marketing process, and this saves them time and money. They avoid distress sale of produce and exploitation by middlemen in the market and they receive better prices.

The staggered production and procurement plans of Namdhari Fresh help the farmers and the company. They avoid production gluts and the consequent price reductions, and the planning helps to meet consumers' demand for continuous supplies. Namdhari only wants young tender produce, so the farmers generally harvest after four to seven weeks. This means that they can grow three to four crops a year and they can also grow many varieties of vegetable in smaller areas which provides higher returns.

Namdhari's payments by cheque have made the whole system more transparent and has enhanced farmers' trust in the company. This has helped them to save and has increased their credit worthiness in the banks.

Because of the centralised system, the farmers get quality seeds and other inputs directly from Namdhari Fresh. This greatly reduces their day to day problems, since the lack of regular availability of quality seeds and inputs was previously one of the farmers' main problems.

Namdhari provides seeds and inputs on credit to the contract farmers, and the cost is recovered when paying the farmers for their produce. This helps the farmers' cash flow position, and Namdhari also provides a form of partial crop insurance against natural calamities such as floods, pest or disease infestation or total crop failure, since the Company undertakes to waive the farmers' liabilities in such cases. The pre-fixed prices give farmers confidence when planning their crops as they do not need to gamble on the markets as they had to before, and second quality produce and rejects still can be sold on the open market.

The price chain shown in Table 1 shows that the gap between the farm gate price and the price to the ultimate consumer has widened with this approach. This is to be expected, because Namdhari Fresh deals with superior quality produce and their customers are better off than most people. The farmer, who is the actual producer, receives only 10–20% of what the ultimate consumer pays. However, value additions such as keeping produce in cold storage, packing, transport, and reaching out to export markets are all done by the company which employs more than 500 labourers and many supervisors and management staff for this purpose. By targeting better off customers Namdhari has helped the producer to realise twice the price offered by the traditional market.

The highly centralised Namdhari Fresh model, with a mix of quality conscious export and domestic markets, has made it necessary for the Company to be involved in most of the operations from production up to consumer level and to create a standardised system. Namdhari initially invested about $8 million to set up the system, including about $5 million for the packing houses. The system leaves no scope for any of the traditional value chain participants.

Over the years production has increased from two tonnes to about 150 tonnes per week of which about a third goes for export. This volume of production is processed entirely in-house, employing about 500 labourers, mostly women from nearby villages. It is planned to increase production level to 180 tonnes per week in 2008.

The system has not, however, displaced any of the traditional value chain agents. It is a completely new system, from "farm to fork", and it does not compete with or hijack the existing system. The model needs a high initial investment and total commitment to quality, and there is so far little or no scope for competition from others. It supplements and complements the existing system, enhancing the farmers' incomes and the local economy. It creates employment for young people from the villages and especially for women. Namdhari's management believes that this model can be successful up to $200 million turnover but beyond this they believe it would be very difficult to exercise the necessary quality control.

Since the start of Namdhari Fresh, the company has taken the calculated risk of putting in place a complex system to ensure strict quality control. The company had some experience of seed production and of export business, but it faced many challenges in this fresh products venture.

Initially the company wanted to contract large-scale farmers who had assured irrigation facilities and lower costs. It was not possible to identify many such farmers, and the company was compelled to work with small and marginal farmers. This was at first considered a major challenge as it would mean high transaction costs. As the system developed, however, the company realised that it was better to work with smaller farmers. Contract farming with them was easier than with larger farmers, because they proved to be more disciplined and more willing to conform to the company's requirements. Over 50% of the contract farmers have land holdings in the range of three to five acres.

The marketing of high quality fruit and vegetable with no residual pesticides in the domestic market is also difficult. Namdhari has opened its own retail shops in many parts of Bangalore, but it generally only attracts high-income consumers who are health conscious. In areas where traditional pushcart or stall vendors have built up long-lasting relationship with their established customers, there have been some major problems such as boycotts and popular agitations when Namdhari outlets have been opened.

In some of the traditionally non-vegetarian areas of the city, the Namdhari retail outlets are struggling to sell their produce and are losing money. Some may have to be closed.

Occasions have also arisen when the open market prices for a given item were temporarily higher than Namdhari's prices. Some farmers were tempted to sell their produce on the open market rather than to Namdhari so that the company's retail outlets did not receive enough stock. This problem was overcome by dropping those farmers from Namdhari's supply chain for a period, and as such situations are quite rare there have been few recurrences. In few cases the company has faced problems when some farmers have not followed the production cycle strictly and have demanded that Namdhari should buy all their produce, irrespective of its quality or timing. The company has overcome such problems gradually through careful selection of the farmers and strengthening their understanding of what is required of them.

Unlike many other corporate value chain operators for farm produce in India, Namdhari Farm Fresh has focused on the international market. It has studied the quality preferences of consumers in Europe and other countries and has attempted to maintain the quality of its farm produce accordingly. The EUREP GAP and BRC Certificates permit export of quality farm produce to European countries and Britain, and these markets pay higher prices for the produce. This benefits the company and the farmers.

After starting with exports, Namdhari has tried to capture high-income and health conscious consumers in India. It relies on customers who can afford the high cost of their products, such as institutional buyers, five star hotels, large-scale caterers and airline companies, as well as consumers who live in areas with a high concentration of high-income households. The "Namdhari Farm Fresh" brand is not familiar to the common consumer. This policy of targeting a select consumer segment has created a unique brand image and has helped both the company and its farmers without affecting the existing traditional system. The company is also not yet in direct competition with any other modern corporate retail chain as their target consumer segment is different and more specific.

Namdhari combines social ethics and business principles to sustain its growth. It demands strict discipline from its farmers so that their relationship with the company can continue for a long period. It has helped many small and marginal farmers to irrigate their fields by providing capital assistance. It has hired many labourers from nearby villages to work in its packing houses, and most of these were very poor, with no land. Namdhari has also built ten or more new houses every year free of cost for deserving laborers, and such gestures have enhanced the company's reputation in the community as a whole.

The Namdhari Fresh model is still in its early years, but the top management are convinced that it is a viable long-term operation. They plan gradually to expand it, without compromising on quality. Produce turnover has grown from two tonnes to about 150 tonnes per week in six years, which shows that the model is fundamentally sound.

Over the years Namdhari has created a good brand image in Europe and other countries, and demand for their produce is increasing. However, the company is intentionally expanding slowly. Management believe that rapid expansion would make it difficult to maintain quality, which is the key to the success of the whole model.

REFERENCES

Namdhari Samachar (2006). Volume 12, October.
Reardon, T and A Gulati (2008). The Rise of Supermarkets and Their Development Implications: International Experience Relevant for India, IFPRI Discussion Paper.
www.namdharifresh.org

Case Study **2**

ITC Choupal Fresh

Rewa Shankar Misra

INTRODUCTION

The Growth Oriented Microenterprise Development (GMED) Program was initiated in September 2004 at a time when the transformation of India's retail sector had just started. The program is funded by the United States Agency for International Development and implemented by ACDI VOCA. The name ACDI/VOCA dates back to the 1997 merger of Agricultural Cooperative Development International and Volunteers in Overseas Cooperative Assistance. Both these institutions were American non-profit economic development organisations working largely in agriculture.

Between 2005 and 2007 India consistently topped AT Kearney's Global Retail Development Index ranking of markets which are ripe for investment in "modern" retailing. In 2006 single brand retailers were allowed to own a majority stake of 51% in a joint venture with a local company. Since only single brand retailers were given this opportunity, this provided a space for Indian companies like Reliance, Subhiksha, and Foodland to take advantage of the high growth groceries market.

Note: Units of measurement in the Indian numbering system: lakh = 100,000; crore = 10,000,000. Indian Rupees (Rs.) where appropriate are converted into USD at a rate of approximately Rs. 50 = \$1.00; Rs. 1 lakh = \$2,000; Rs. 1 crore = \$200,000.

But this was only the beginning. Organising fresh produce supply chains is the most challenging aspect of the retail groceries business. Ensuring that the customer has the same product, of the same quality, at the same place, fresh and at any time during the year presents a tremendous challenge. This is particularly true in a context where there are few large farmers, and organising small ones to reach scale and reliability of supply is notoriously expensive and risky.

This case describes how one large Indian company is supporting the development of a value chain that can potentially integrate over 125,000 small-holder farmers. For the purpose of this case study, a value chain is defined as all the firms that buy and sell from each other in order to supply a particular set of products or services to final consumers (Lusby and Panlibuton, 2007). The information in the case study is based on interviews with GMED project staff, and primary data available with the GMED. The case study highlights three particular aspects of the case: the types of activities, firms and strategies which yield higher value than others for small-holders, the types of relationships, contractual and otherwise, which work best in the value chain and, what models work best for service delivery. The case aims to show that it is possible to integrate small-holder farmers in fruit and vegetable value chains, provided that the lead firms fulfill certain key functions, that efficient extension services are delivered on a sustainable basis by firms embedded in the value chain, and that inter-firm relations are market-based and mutually beneficial.

Horticulture includes fruit, vegetables, spices, flowers and plantation farming. There are many opportunities and constraints for Indian small-holder farmers in fresh fruit and vegetables.

India is a country of small-holder farmers. The average size of operational farm holdings in India has declined from 2.28 hectares in 1971 to 1.57 hectares in 1991 and to 1.41 hectares in 1995–96. According to some estimates it has further declined to 1.22 hectares in recent years (ICRIER, 2006).

As can be seen from Table 1, India's marginal, small and semi-medium holdings of less than four hectares of farmland together comprise 95% of the country's total holdings. Future growth in agriculture can only be achieved by increases in yields or by transition to high-value crops. This coupled with changing consumer trends and rising consumer income,

Table 1: Distribution of farm holdings by size.

Classification by size of holding	Percentage of all operational holdings
Marginal holdings (of 1 hectare or less)	70%
Small holdings (1–2 hectares)	16%
Semi medium holdings (2–4 hectares)	9%
Medium holdings (4–10 hectares)	4%
Large holdings (over 10 hectares)	<1%

Source: National Sample Survey Organisation 59th Round (2006).

especially in the non-farm sector and in urban areas, is creating opportunities for high-value agricultural products such as fruit, vegetables, fish, eggs, milk and meat.

India is the second largest producer of both fruit and vegetables in the world, and the National Horticulture Mission (NHM) aims to double horticultural production by 2012 (Economic Survey, 2006–07). 15.3% of farm households grow vegetables and 4.6% grow fruits. Nearly 16% of households with less than two hectares grow vegetables. The corresponding figures for medium and large farm households are 14.8% and 10.4%, respectively. The growing markets for these products present an opportunity for farmers to diversify their production away from cereals and to raise their incomes. The major challenge is to include marginal, small and even medium farmers in this growth. The average size of land holdings in the GMED project ranges from 2.5–3 acres depending on the region. This includes some of the farms which are officially defined as small and semi-medium, but they are all called small-holders in this case. Changes in retailing are expected to create opportunities for small-holders, but they also threaten their continued access to remunerative markets.

Unless domestic supplies can be improved and the present constraints in fresh produce supply chains are resolved, the important urban retail markets may be dominated by imported fresh produce. This has happened in supermarkets in Manila, where many of the fresh vegetables are supplied from Australia, and in Jakarta, where domestically sourced vegetables still prevail, but a significant volume of tropical fruit is imported from Thailand and Malaysia. In both of these cases, local farmers are able to produce vegetables and fruit that is competitive in both quality and price; the problem lies in the inadequacy of the supply chains (Taylor and Jones, 2005).

Bringing small-holders into supply chains for organised retail is therefore not only an "additional option" but also a necessity. Otherwise their access to high-value markets will become increasingly distant and constrained, and there will be no real incentives for the private sector to integrate small-holders into knowledge or service networks.

Organised retailing and the success of brands such as Namdharis and Choupal Fresh and others are a trigger for value chain development in the fresh fruit and vegetables sub-sector in India. Private partnerships can play a key role in creating "farm to fork" linkages that can satisfy market demands for high-quality and safe food, while retaining small-holders in the value chain. While the private sector in India has been fast to enter organised retailing and most companies have definite plans for at least some kind of linkage to small farmers, relatively few companies are actually reaching the farm gate.

"When we first started there was no established model", says Donald Taylor, Chief of Party, GMED India. "And it was a hard sell to get anyone interested in working with small-holders". Most major organised retailers followed a cash and carry and wholesale approach to procurement. In the Indian context this might include direct procurement from local markets or *mandis*, or the use of private agents at collection points such as warehouses, but without any linkage back to the actual producers. This was partly because of the regulations but was also because it is costly and complex to develop a "farm to fork" value chain. As a result, the retailers have little control on volume or quality, and small-holders lack access to potential market opportunities.

There are many constraints along the chain. Existing policy measures adversely affect agricultural marketing, in particular the Agricultural Produce Marketing Act (APMA). This is enacted and administered at the state level. It requires all agricultural produce to be purchased only through state government-operated markets (*mandis*), although there are a number of exceptions in some states. As originally structured, the APMAs forbid farmers from selling produce directly to private buyers. The original purpose of this regulation was to protect farmers from being exploited by intermediaries and traders, and to ensure better prices and timely payment. "Over a period of time these markets have, however, acquired the status of restrictive and monopolistic markets, providing no help in direct and free marketing, organised retailing, smooth raw material supplies to agro — processing, competitive trading, information exchange and adoption of innovative marketing systems and technologies".[1] Under the APMC Act, only State Governments are permitted to set up markets. Farmers cannot sell their produce directly in bulk except by retailing direct to consumers. They also have to bring their own produce to the market yard.

The Ministry of Agriculture developed a Model Marketing Act for the states in 2002. The Act permits direct sales by farmers, provides for contract farming and incorporates other provisions to liberalise agricultural marketing. States are being encouraged to replace the APMC with the model Act and some states such as Karnataka, Maharashtra, and the Punjab are either proceeding to or already have amended their current Acts. However there is considerable resistance at the state level fully to adopt the new Act. This is mainly due to concerns about loss of state revenue from purchase taxes.

At the producer end of the chain, small-holder farmers are handicapped because of the fragmentation of their holdings, their limited market surpluses, and the perishable nature of many high-value food commodities. Food retailers have developed elaborate standards relating to pesticide residues and traceability, of which small-holders are usually ignorant. Small-holders also lack information on the prices, grades and standards required by supermarkets, and of the sanitary and phyto-sanitary measures required under the World Trade Organisation guidelines. These factors substantially raise transaction costs and market risks for both retailers and small-holders in their joint efforts to tap the opportunities presented by high-value agriculture.

Agriculture is a state subject in India and the main agency responsible for extension services is the state's Department of Agriculture (DoA). Every state has a separate DoA. There is sometimes a separate department for horticulture which offers extension services. The Department of Agriculture and Co-operation of the Central Ministry of Agriculture has a separate Division of Extension which lays down major policy guidelines on extension. In the 1980s, the World Bank-funded Training and Visit

---

[1] Agmarknet.nic.in — website of scheme of Directorate of Agriculture Marketing and Inspection, Ministry of Agriculture, Government of India.

(T&V) system of extension supplemented these efforts, but over time, as the Finance Minister himself stressed in his budget speech of 2007, the extension services system including T&V has lost its effectiveness.

Besides the government extension services, some services are also provided by agricultural universities, commodity boards, such as those for spices, rubber, coconut and coffee, non-government organisations and agri-business companies, such as those dealing with seed, fertiliser, pesticides, farm machinery and so on. While the quality of these services is in some cases exceptional, there are issues of sustainability, scalability and the fact that some services are tied to the marketing of products such as fertiliser or seeds.

Working capital is also of course an important issue, for vegetable and fruit farmers as for most others. Vegetable and fruit farming usually involves quite short production cycles but requires high-cost, good quality inputs.

It is estimated that between $2,000–$2,400 million worth of fruit and vegetables in India are wasted every year, and there are further losses of

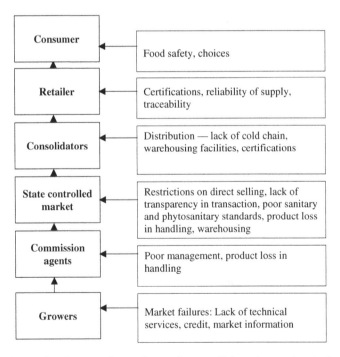

Figure 1: Constraints along the traditional supply chain.

Source: (ICRIER, 2007).

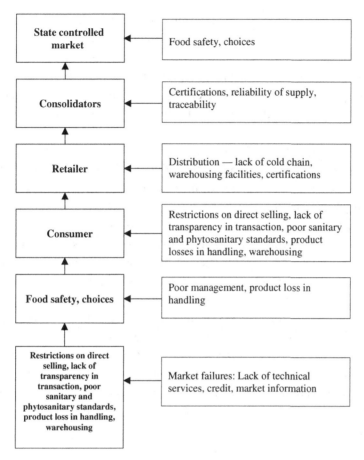

Figure I: (*Continued*)

up to as much as 80% of the most perishable fruits and vegetables. In addition to extension and working capital, small-holder fruit and vegetable farmers also need infrastructure, such as irrigation and cold storage to minimise post-harvest losses, and other storage and warehouse facilities. They need timely and adequate supply of inputs and credit, and efficient and competitive retailers.

CREATING VALUE THROUGH INTEGRATION

It is clear that for any value chain model to work with small-holder farmers, it must provide extension services and market information such as pricing, grading, certification and traceability, and must also deal with factor constraints such as finance and technology. Until recently retail development has focused on the front end of the chain and has resulted in no intrinsic changes in the supply chain. This is because procurement of fresh produce has been largely dependent on purchasing from *mandi* agents or, in the case of large farmers, in spot transactions.

ITC's pilot, on the other hand, attempted to offer an integrated solution. At the time of writing the pilot is still in its learning phase but it already provides several significant lessons for the private sector. ITC, previously the Imperial Tobacco Company of India, is one of India's leading private sector companies with a turnover of over $4.75 billion. The company is involved in hotels, packaging, agri-business, cigarettes, packaged foods and confectionery, information technology, branded clothing, and other products, including the "Mangaldeep" incense stick business which is described elsewhere in this book.

ITC decided to take part in this initiative because they realised that the number of large farmers was limited and that it was necessary to secure supplier loyalty as competition increased. At first ITC started with only three retail points, in addition to working with other retailers with a "shop within a shop" approach. This limited the potential scale of the operation, and ITC is reworking it's strategy in order to take advantage of economies of scale.

In September 2004 ACDI/VOCA, supported by USAID, started the Growth Oriented Microenterprise Development Program (GMED) in selected states and sub-sectors in India. The programme was intended to end in December 2007 but was extended up to September 2008. The goal is to develop commercially viable, sustainable and scalable approaches to fostering the growth of micro and small enterprises. The project focus is on linking small-holder vegetable and fruit farmers with higher value organised wholesale, retail, processing and export markets and on helping to build the capacity of farmers to meet the requirements of those markets. The GMED program is based in Rajasthan and offers technical services in a number of states including Rajasthan, Maharashtra, Punjab, and Andhra Pradesh.

(Continued)

(Continued)

GMED focuses on building the technical, financial, and policy institutions and systems to create an enabling environment for growth-oriented micro enterprises. These are enterprises which can grow and provide jobs, which is critical to India's development. They fall between traditional micro-enterprises, which are generally defined as a form of household income support, and small businesses (www.acdivoca.org). The programme supports these enterprises by improving their access to markets and to financial services, and by improving the policy environment.

The programme focuses on the key constraints to enterprise growth in agri-business and urban services. The agribusiness component is focused on fruits and vegetables, organically certified food products, maize value chain improvement, integration of HIV/AIDS-affected communities into commercial supply chains and the development of technology-enabled, cost-effective private sector agricultural extension services. The urban services component is concerned with improving municipal solid waste management by outsourcing to medium-sized businesses. GMED is solely a technical service program and does not provide grants or subsidies.

The broad strategy of the agri-business pilot was to organise 1,600 small-holder farmers into clusters, to train field extension specialists to deliver a package of production and post-harvest techniques and to link the clusters to organised retail markets. This case covers the Malerkotla cluster in Punjab where the GMED project covers 299 farmers out of the total of 1,600.

Similar programmes were used in clusters in Andhra Pradesh and Maharashtra. In Maharashtra services such as extension, crop processing and finance for farmers and for marketing of produce were provided through the Nandini Cooperative.

GMED's survey found that as many as one-third of the farmers reached through the programme in the three states have landholdings of less than three acres in size. Very few private sector companies were willing to work with small and marginal farmers; this was one of the key constraints in initiating this program with a larger number of private sector agencies in the beginning. A GMED staff member said "ITC was the only one that really came forward as the others were not willing to invest in setting up procurement from many small-holder farmers."[2] Including more small-holders in the project remains an area of concern, but this initial pilot has provided some key lessons in improving outreach to relatively poorer farmers.

In Punjab the first step was to mobilise the farmers. Due to the short production cycle of fresh vegetables, farmers can earn a quick return on their investments. Malerkotla was traditionally a source of vegetables, but because of earlier bad experiences in dealing with private business, the farmers were initially reluctant to work with ITC. Their reluctance was gradually overcome when GMED and ITC started to offer extension services.

Initially the Malerkotla farmers said they would limit their risks; they would only grow vegetables according to the methods which GMED suggested on one-half of their farms. On the other half they would follow regular methods to grow vegetables. Gradually, as they began to see greater returns and received consistent technical support, they switched their entire holdings to vegetable cultivation as GMED suggested. While many farmers were at first not convinced that this was the way to go, the experience of the initial phase and increasing returns to participating farmers will encourage more farmers to become involved in the future.

The GMED India Deputy Chief of Party, Deo Dutt Singh said, "The farmers did not understand the concept of free extension services. They were so used to bad quality government extension services or to private services which were conditional on input purchases. After one season however their trust grew. In fact extension services became the key incentive for farmer loyalty."

The GMED staff introduced a series of simple but effective changes in production techniques. Tray nurseries ensured a uniform crop, and improved seedling survival rates and productivity, and raised beds and shade nets for crops such as tomatoes and cucumbers were also introduced.

---

[2] GMED India staff member.

Figure 2: Map of India showing Malerkotla in Punjab.

The project also brought in improved seed varieties and other inputs. The farmers were trained how to use expensive inputs such as seeds more judiciously; this sometimes helped to cut the cost of operations by as much as one-third.

For example, the farmers were sowing 900 gms of cucumber seed per acre, at a price of Rs. 12,000 per kg, while the recommended seed rate is only 300 gms per acre. The farmers were also using twice as much fertiliser as was needed. They were wasting irrigation water, thus using more electricity and labour than was necessary, and they were using more pesticides than required. After testing the soil the extension staff recommended appropriate fertiliser applications, and the farmers were trained to improve their pest and disease management in order to reduce their use of fertiliser and pesticide.

The farmers were not told which suppliers to use. They were informed about the advantages and disadvantages of the different varieties and suppliers so that they could choose what suited them best.

The GMED-assisted farmers also earned more because they were able to supply early and late in the season and to get better prices. They harvested their crops 15 days ahead of other farmers in the region because seedlings from plug nurseries took only 21 days to be ready for transplanting while seedlings from traditional nurseries took around 30 days. The traditional seedlings also take about one week to get established in the soil after transplanting because their root systems are disturbed during transplanting but this is not the case with seedlings which have been raised in plug trays.

The GMED extension staff also taught the farmers how to stake their plants, and how to use integrated crop management and integrated pest management (IPM) techniques. This prolonged crop production so that the farmers could supply vegetables late into the season.

One of the key changes was the grading of vegetables such as tomatoes. Because it took time, and they believed that grading would lead to lower returns, the farmers consistently resisted grading their produce. ITC and GMED trained the farmers to grade their tomatoes into three categories A, B and C. ITC regularly bought the top two grades while grade C could be sold in the regular *mandi*. As the farmers came to realise which grades fetched the highest prices they made greater efforts to bring the quality of their produce up to that level. Farmers who had started with only 30% of their produce in grade A, reached a level of 90% after following the advice of the GMED extension staff.

Local market prices are often used as the standard for farmers and retailers alike. However the traditional market system is overcrowded and chaotic and has no transparent mechanism for price setting. Several auctions often take place simultaneously. The farmers rarely understand them, and the intermediaries effectively control the prices.

ITC's price discovery system is also based on local market prices, but because the crops are graded, the producers are guaranteed a minimum price, and as there is less need for handling and multiple intermediaries, the farmers earn higher returns. The farmers earn 15% more than local market rates on grade A produce, and grade B produce is bought at local market rates. This is a major incentive for farmers to be loyal suppliers to the company.

ITC provided colour-coded crates to farmers to segregate produce by grade, which facilitates grading and tracing of the crops. The company also organised transport, storage and distribution, thus integrating all the functions of the value chain. The initial results have been positive. The farmers have themselves taken responsibility for value-adding tasks such as grading. The pilot has on average increased farmers' net incomes by one third.

The cost:benefit ratio of the gross returns to the cost of cultivation was compared to understand how returns have improved for the 40 farmers who had the longest experience of working with ITC, out of the total of 60 farmers in the Malerkotla cluster, over the two year period from 2005–2007. Their cost:benefit ratio shifted from 3.9 to 4.8 across the two years. This was for commodities such as tomatoes, onions, cucumber and brinjal. The improvement is attributable both to decreases in costs from better use of inputs as well as to higher returns. The ratios for both years compare favourably with similar figures based on data used by the National Horticulture Mission (ICRIER, 2007). The ratios for tomato and brinjal farming in Karnataka and AP respectively were between 2 and 1.9. The cost of transport is excluded from these calculations because ITC picks up the farmers' produce at the farm gate.

Figure 3 compares the traditional and the modern market systems, and shows how the returns to the producers are increased.

Figure 4 shows the distribution of farmers by the percentage increases in the profit they earned.

The following value chain map (see Fig. 5) shows three key channels in the domestic retailing of fresh fruit and vegetables. The map shows that farmers' returns have increased because of an average of nearly 16% reduction in their costs. It also shows how ITC creates value by taking over key functions like consolidation, wholesale, distribution and retail. While the ratio of ITC's costs to its additional earnings, based on gross sales and operating expenses, is currently 1.0, this will probably improve as the programme expands and its retail end is better organised. This conclusion is made on the basis of sales made through ITC's own sales outlets but also through arrangements between ITC and other retailers such as Foodland. The cost figure does not include GMED's programme costs. These start up expenses amounted to about half of ITC's own investments, which was mainly spent on providing model extension services to farmers to demonstrate the methods to ITC's extension workers.

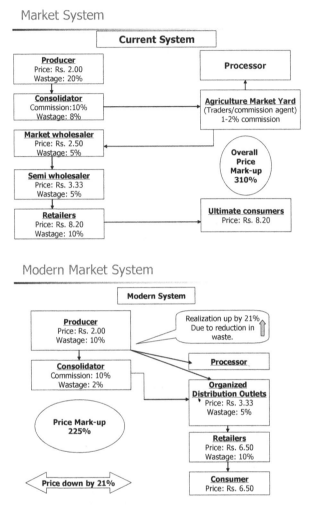

Figure 3: Comparison of the traditional and the modern market systems.

Source: S Raghunath (2004). Delivering Simultaneous Benefits to the Farmer and the common man. Time to unshackle the agricultural produce distribution system.

FINDING THE RIGHT SERVICE DELIVERY MODEL

From the very beginning the project staff found that extension services were a key rallying point in discussions with farmers. GMED trained ITC's extension staff so that technical support could be provided directly

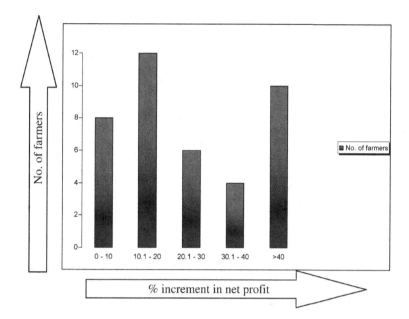

Figure 4: Increment in net profit.

by the lead firm in the value chain. This was to make sure that farmers had access to good quality services from a source that had a stake in their performance. GMED made only one grant, for a total of Rs. 1.2 lakhs, to cover the costs of four extension agents who worked with the ITC staff for six months. GMED's role was to supply extension services and facilitate the lead firm, ITC, in providing these services. The provision of these services through a firm which was itself a part of the value chain ensured that private sector actors such as the ITC extension agents were not displaced by a subsidised project.

ITC and GMED also experimented with training school and college drop-outs to foster a new cadre of extension workers. Four of these joined ITC as junior extension staff, but most of the trainees either got jobs with other companies or went on to further studies. At one stage ITC merged its procurement and extension services, but as the program grew, they were again divided.

ITC's focus is to develop lead farmers, who serve both as sub-collectors for produce and as mentors for local farmers. Approximately 50 farmers are organised under each lead farmer. The produce is transported from the

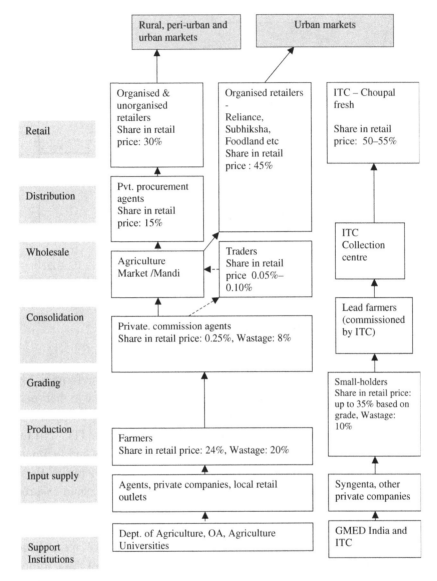

Figure 5: Value chain map domestic — Fresh vegetables.

lead farmer to ITC collection centres where it is re-sorted and tagged for further transportation to Choupal fresh stores.

The cost of the extension services is approximately Rs. 60,000 per annum for every 50 farmers. This excludes the supervision costs and the cost of specialised services and technology. A similar amount is expended on buying from the farm, which demonstrates how expensive it is to provide extension services at the initial stages. ITC's current operational profit is 12% on its sales, and the initial investment of about Rs. 2 crores in developing this value chain and its associated retail chain will not start to be recovered until the programme scales up.[3] The farmers' enthusiasm for the extension service suggests that extension services provided through the lead firm are a key way of ensuring supply, without the need for contract farming as such. ITC has been working with the lead farmers in other ways in order to find how to provide extension services in a way that is sustainable, of high quality, cost-effective and scaleable at the level at which the number of farmers are expected to grow. ITC is focusing on rationalising its costs and expanding the retail chain, while reaching out to more farmers in the existing clusters.

MOHAMMED RAFIQ

Mohd. Rafiq from village Himmatana, Malerkotla in district Sangrur has always grown vegetables such as cabbages, cauliflower and egg plant on his two-acre plot. When he first attended a meeting in the village in February 2006 where GMED was explaining the ITC model, farmers were reluctant to get involved. However, he decided to take the risk of participating in the GMED project. He took a loan from the local cooperative bank and started to grow carrots, okra, tomato, bitter gourd, and cucumber. He also received interest-free inputs from ITC. His profits from vegetable cultivation have been gradually growing, mainly because of his reduced costs. He feels the ITC linkage has definitely brought better market linkages and more transparent terms of doing business, unlike the commission agents he had to work with earlier. However he wants ITC to buy larger amounts of vegetables. This is not yet possible since ITC has only a few outlets that retail fresh vegetables.

---

[3] *Source*: GMED India.

MOHAMMAD ASHRAF

By the middle of 2006 word about the ITC initiative with GMED had spread fairly widely and Mohammad Ashraf found that most of the farmers in Jamalpur, a village quite near to Himmatana, were interested in getting involved. It was not easy to raise the initial investment and he had to eventually take a loan from his relatives. He has leased an additional acre of land which makes a total of 2.2 acres, and has sunk a borewell. Mohammad Ashraf feels motivated and confident about the ITC linkage and states that he is keen to be a loyal supplier to the company on account of the regular extension services the company provides.

CHAIN GOVERNANCE

The relationships between the actors in a value chain critically influence the chain's sustainability.

The Malerkotla farmers were very wary of working with large businesses when GMED first approached them. A few years before GMED's offer, a number of the farmers had had a bad experience with contract farming when a private company failed to honour its commitment to purchase produce as promised. This made it virtually impossible for ITC to use contract farming as a way of ensuring predictable supplies and costs. Contract farming involves forward contracts between growers and buyers, and the key to the success of such arrangements is the commitment of the producer to provide a commodity of a certain type and quality, at a time, price and quantity required by a known and committed buyer. One major reason why this has not been the relationship of choice in India is the fact that such contracts are generally unenforceable by either side.

A market-based arms-length relationship has thus far worked well for the Malerkotla farmers. Their returns are to a great extent assured, but they can also revert to the traditional *mandi*, or to any other buyer if they so choose. This is an important lesson in relation to findings from elsewhere in the world. Research on the UK-Africa horticulture chain for example, suggests that small-holder growers of vegetables such as asparagus, artichoke, snap peas and beans were marginalised when there was a contractual relationship between them and a large corporate buyer. This finding is relevant whether the lead firms and suppliers are local or domestic. In the Indian context for example, initiatives such as grading and sorting are still new to farmers. They have been introduced by the lead firms because they are influenced by the expectations of consumers, NGOs and government agencies with regard to safety and environmental and labour standards (Dolan, Humphrey and Hariss-Pascal, 1999).

Pricing and procurement are decided within the framework of an arms-length relationship, but the lead firm has gone one step further and actually supports the producers with technical services. This is unlike most arms-length market-based relationships, and its success suggests that extension services can be an effective alternative to contracts as a way of ensuring supplier loyalty.

Information technology can be used to develop a platform for exchange of information and data in order to facilitate greater transparency and to improve the bargaining power of farmers. ITC's earlier e-choupal initiative has shown how this can be done. Infosys and GMED have now started to design an ICT-enabled technical horticulture farmer information and supply chain management service program.

CONCLUSION

ITC started with three Choupal Fresh stores in Pune, Hyderabad and Chandigarh. The company now plans to open 500 new fresh produce retail shops and 100 cash and carry outlets in 50 Indian cities over the next two years. ITC is also entering into partnerships with other retailers to supply their fresh produce, such as Food Bazaar and QMART.

The GMED India project has created a prototype business model to integrate very small producers into fresh produce value chains. It has shown that effective extension services can, even in the absence of contracts, encourage and sustain relationships in the value chain, and it has also created a market for its own technical services. which are essentially catalytic in nature.

GMED India and ITC's experience in the fresh produce market shows how small-holders can benefit from organised retail. Other retailers such as Reliance Fresh are also beginning to see the importance of this approach and there is a strong possibility that GMED may itself be privatised to meet the need for developing relevant strategies and embedded service models.

While the most challenging aspect has been organising the delivery of extension services cost-effectively and sustainably, the ITC and GMED pilot is showing what forms of services and market relationships provide a level playing field and increased returns for small-holders. GMED projects that over the next three years in the current program areas of Punjab, Andhra Pradesh and Maharashtra, over 125,000 small-holder farmers can be integrated with ITC's initiative alone. As India is increasingly integrating with global markets this provides an important window of opportunity to ensure that small-holders are included in the process.

REFERENCES

Dolan, C, J Humphrey and C Harris-Pascal (1999). Horticultural Commodity Chains: The Impact of UK supermarkets on the African Fresh Vegetables Industry, IDS Working Paper, No. 96. Brighton: Institute of Development Studies.

Economic Survey of India (2006–07). New Delhi.

Lusby, F and H Panlibuton (2007). Value Chain Program Design, Promoting Market Based Solutions for MSME and Industry Competitiveness. Washington D.C.: Office of Microenterprise Development, USAID/G/EGAD/MD.

Taylor, D and Z Jones (2005). Fresh Fruit and Vegetable Supply Chains in India, Growth Oriented Microenterprise Development Project, ACDI-VOCA. Jaipur.

Case Study **3**

INFAM in Wayanad, Kerala

Jacob D Vakkayil

Yohannan looked with mixed feelings at his stock of the year's produce of black pepper from his four-acre farm. There were at least five quintals of the "black gold" in jute sacks. It was important to keep the moisture level below 11% to ensure good quality pepper. The product inspector from "Organic Wayanad" dipped his electronic moisture meter in to the sack and drew out a scoop. The LCD display showed 9.8%. "The moisture is well within the accepted limits", he said. "You might find it difficult to store this during the monsoons. You can give it to the company now and storage will not be a problem."

Yohannan thought deeply. "I'll see", he said. It was only the previous month that he had received payment for the previous year's sale from the newly formed Indian Organic Farmers' Producer Company Limited (IOFPCL). The price they offered was approximately 30% above the market rate for the non-organic variety. "But what if I need money urgently?" he thought. He postponed the difficult decision and talked about the pros and cons of organic farming. "I have been at it for four years now. There is no marked decrease in the yield compared with

Note: Units of measurement in the Indian numbering system: lakh = 100,000; crore = 10,000,000. Indian Rupees (Rs.) where appropriate are converted into USD at a rate of approximately Rs. 50 = $1.00; Rs. 1 lakh = $2,000; Rs. 1 crore = $200,000.

the time I was using chemical fertilisers and pesticides. In fact, there are fewer instances of diseases such as the deadly "quick wilt" that affects the pepper vines."

Yohannan is one of around 2,000 pepper farmers in Wayanad district in Kerala whose produce has been certified as "organic" by INDOCERT — the only organic certification agency in India. He had been introduced to organic farming by "Organic Wayanad" — a farmer's cooperative that promotes organic farming in the district and helps in cultivating and marketing the product. The organisation collaborates closely with IOFPCL and INDOCERT. A tiny one-room building in the compound of the "Pastoral Center" of the Catholic diocese of Mananthavady in Wayanad district functions as the office for Organic Wayanad and INFAM (Indian Farmers' Movement). There are many common office bearers in the three bodies. These three closely linked organisations cater to the key areas of certification, production and quality control, and marketing in the value chain for organic products. They thus constitute the initial crucial links in a network of institutions which aim to function as the support system for an inclusive chain for agricultural products in the district.

This system of organisations was triggered by one of the more prominent farmers' collectives in the country — INFAM, a Kerala-based institution which campaigned for many different interests of the farming community. INFAM proposed and popularised an alternative way of farming to counter the ill-effects of the agrarian crisis that affected Kerala and particularly the Wayanad district in the state during recent years. There was, however, no simple solution. INFAM worked in Wayanad and elsewhere, and tried a variety of activities, moving in a number of different directions. The development of these attempts to get a better deal for the primary producers is presented below as three tracks in the evolution of the movement and its facilitating role. The primary focus of the chapter is on the district of Wayanad in northern Kerala, in part because the District has become nationally well-known as one of the most seriously distressed agrarian districts in India.

ACTIVISM

The farmers of Wayanad enjoyed relative prosperity in the latter part of the 1990s with the prices of pepper, ginger, coffee and tea, the chief crops cultivated in the district, reaching very high levels. This apparent prosperity led to many opportunities for private financiers and nationalised and cooperative banks who offered loans to finance further increases in production. Many farmers took loans which were beyond their repayment capacity in view of the possible fluctuations in the prices of the commodities. According to one of the prominent banks, the average credit-deposit ratio in the district was 188% against a state average of 46% (Krishnakumar, 2004).

However, three developments jolted the farmers of the district out of their complacency. First, beginning in the year 2000, the prices of farm commodities in the state began rapidly to decline. Pepper, for example, which sold for Rs. 260 per kg in 2000 had fallen to Rs. 78 in 2004. The price of coffee beans fell similarly, from Rs. 70 to Rs. 17 a kilo. Many farmers began to be concerned about these falls in prices, but the situation still seemed redeemable. They were not prepared for the second blow, the severe drought which struck the area in 2004. Finally, all hope seemed to be lost when an epidemic of plant diseases, especially the "quick wilt" disease affecting pepper, decimated the remaining plants.

Elsewhere in Kerala, farmer discontent was already brewing by the late 1990s. One of the main causes of this was the large-scale importation of palm oil from Malaysia and Indonesia with reduced tariffs resulting from India joining the WTO. Palm oil began to be widely used after 1998. This adversely affected coconut farmers in the state who claimed that the reduction in import duty for palm oil had been made at their expense in order to gain favour from countries such as Malaysia in other areas of cooperation. Local organisations resorted to ingenious ways of fighting the influx of palm oil. In 2000, the village of Koorachundu in neighbouring Kozhikode district was declared "palm oil-free" by the farmers who decided to boycott the product. Although many others followed this example, such measures failed to re-instate the supremacy of coconut oil and the advantage that local farmers had enjoyed (Venugopal, 2007).

Faced with these aggravated developments, many farmers began to lose hope. In the first three months of 2004, out of the 19 farmers who committed suicide in Kerala, 13 were from Wayanad (Krishnakumar, 2004). "The farmers were so desperate and they had no one to approach during those days. The major political parties did not seem to be interested in their plight." said Fr. Robin Vadakkencheril — the former Director of INFAM unit in Wayanad, and Joint Secretary of Organic Wayanad, and INDOCERT. Many farmers committed suicide because they could not pay back agricultural loans. The magnitude of their psychological distress can be gauged from the fact that the crisis management cell operated by INFAM from their office in Mananthavady in Wayanad received nearly 300 calls in the first two days of its operation (Nair, 2004).

The Catholic Church in Kerala had some isolated experiences in setting up institutions for marginal and small-scale farmers. Driven by these experiences and prompted by the worsening condition of farmers who constituted the majority of their flock, a few dioceses deputed priests to engage with the farmers. This led to the formation of INFAM in the year 2000. The Chairman and General Secretary of the organisation were Catholic priests. Many of its offices operated from the premises of churches all across the state of Kerala. Within a year of its formation INFAM had a presence in most districts of Kerala and was spreading fast in the farming areas. Membership was open to all farmers irrespective of their religious or political affiliations. Kerala is a highly politicised state, but INFAM tried to be apolitical and to advance the cause of the farming community at all possible forums.

For the farmers of Wayanad, who were mostly Christian settlers from southern Kerala, it was encouraging that the church supported their struggle. A few members of the organisation, including the designated district president of INFAM, Fr. Vadakkencheril, began to visit the farmers in the villages. This led to increased membership of INFAM in the district. Each person who attended these meetings pledged to bring in ten others and eventually, committees were formed at the village level. But given the scale of the problem, especially in districts such as Wayanad, there were no readymade workable solutions that were proven. "We had no solutions initially. All we could do was to listen to their problems" said Fr. Vadakkencheril.

The initial objective was to inform the public at large about the farmers' plight, and in particular the government. Subsequently, a massive INFAM rally was held in the district headquarters of Kalpetta and this caught the attention of the media. Reports about the problems of Wayanad farmers started to appear in local newspapers, and other high-visibility events followed later. These included the symbolic but illegal cutting down of a tree, and a hunger strike. Debt relief for farmers was one of the foremost demands of INFAM. In 2004, they organised a siege of a bank at Kalpetta in Wayanad and declared that the farmers of Wayanad were "on their own writing off their bank loans" (Krishnakumar, 2004). Belatedly, four years later in March 2008, this demand was met by the central government in India which decided to write off small farmers' debts in the annual budget. Debts worth approximately Rs. 60,000 crores were proposed to be written off, benefiting 40 million farmers all over the country.

As the farmers' problems and INFAM itself as an organisation became better known, some criticisms were made of the way INFAM operated. Some of these stemmed from political parties in the state. It was a challenge to remain politically neutral and to be apolitical. On various occasions, INFAM was even accused of being anti-political and a saboteur of the democratic system. The INFAM leaders pointed out that the promises of the political parties to farmers during elections were never honoured. Finally, the INFAM Wayanad unit decided to enter the political arena itself by openly supporting a candidate in the state assembly elections in 2006.

Although, quite predictably, their candidate did not win, INFAM claimed victory. Their aim — the defeat of the sitting representative of the ruling coalition — was achieved because some critical swing votes were cast in favour of the INFAM supported candidate. "The aim was to use one's vote to make a difference and to send a message to the political parties who had ignored the farmers for so long", said Fr. Vadakkencheril. Predictably, the organisation was criticised heavily for this step, because it had deviated from its original apolitical stance. It was also pointed out that farmers who had strong political affiliations were forced to make a choice between INFAM and their own parties.

Aggressive activism for a fair deal for farmers often antagonised other interest groups. In 2002, when state government employees went on a massive strike all over the state, INFAM activists challenged the strike enforcers in many places. The farmers felt that the employees' demands were unjustified given the economic situation and their own predicament. INFAM also demanded a reduction of agricultural labour rates as this was one of the biggest costs which farmers had to bear. This in effect worked against the demand of agricultural labourers who claimed higher wages. In some areas INFAM members resorted to working on each others' farms in order to reduce the cost of labour.

INFAM's early enthusiasm for aggressive activism mellowed over time. Apart from recent increases in commodity prices, one of the main reasons for this seems to be that the non-ecclesiastical leaders of the movement were small-scale farmers who lived off their land. Many of them could not take up full-time activism that earned no immediate financial return. Unlike political parties, there were no regular mechanisms to generate funds. The leaders of INFAM often had to personally bear the cost of their activities. To survive, they had to devote less time to INFAM and to work on their farmsteads. The organisation re-focused its efforts on making farmers more aware of their rights, and on various schemes that could benefit them, or on technical information for better productivity and the promotion of organic agriculture. INFAM does this through a number of means, such as the monthly newsletter called "INFAM Voice" which is published by the district unit.

ALTERNATIVE MARKETING CHANNELS

Together with activism, which aimed at influencing policy makers, many farmers realised that they had to help themselves by finding alternative ways to market their products. Thomaskutty — a banana farmer — described how he sold the product from his farm to the local trader at the market. "I had to sell the bananas at Rs. 12 a kg. The shop keeper almost immediately tied up one of the ripe bunches in his shop. While I was collecting my money a customer walked into the shop to buy bananas. A kilogram was sold to him for Rs. 26! I almost cried there and then." This was a typical experience for many farmers. Traders controlled the prices and they often refused to buy at all because of low demand. For farmers such as Thomaskutty, who grew perishable produce, the system seemed unfairly weighted in favour of the middlemen.

The farmer members of INFAM came up with their own solution to the problem. They set up "Farmers' Shops" where farmers could display their products. If they were sold, they were given the market retail price after a 10% reduction. This provided a fair price mechanism that satisfied the farmer. However, demand and production often fluctuated unpredictably and problems were created when large numbers of farmers harvested their crops at the same time.

Retail shops which sell only farmers' produce are difficult to sustain. In Kerala most farmers produce crops such as coconut, rubber and tea, or spices such as pepper and ginger. Much of the food grains and vegetables that are used in the state have to be sourced from elsewhere, and the local farmers' production exceeds local demand. In these conditions it is difficult to sustain a "Farmers' Shop" purely on local farmers' products, and they have to stock other essential items that are not locally produced. In many cases, they look almost identical to the other nearby grocery shops. They sell products ranging from Palmolive soap to locally produced elephant-foot yam. A Farmer's Shop store keeper said, "We do not keep Coca Cola, Pepsi and palm oil." This was the limit of the anti-multinational stance that could be practically maintained.

At the village level each INFAM unit organises a number of self-help groups, which include some women's groups. They collect weekly deposits, and members who are in need of cash take loans from the groups' accumulated savings. Some of these groups also produce simple items such as snack foods, soap and so on, which are also marketed through the INFAM retail outlets.

These outlets typically have a daily turnover of Rs. 10,000–15,000. The goods are sold at prevailing market prices. The stores are managed by a committee elected by shareholders. All the shareholders must be members of INFAM. After deducting the expenses, the profits are equally shared among the shareholders every year. At one store, the previous year's profit was approximately 30% of the invested amount. The outlets do fairly good business. One reason is that the local consumers who are mostly farmers feel a sense of ownership and buy their provisions from there. They also expect higher quality from the stores. "We are sure to get unadulterated items here", said one of the customers.

Another alternative to these stores is the "Sunday markets" which are being tried out by INFAM in some places such as Chevayur in Kozhikode district. Farm products are brought to temporary facilities on Sundays and are sold to the general public. These markets are mainly located in urban areas where there is a good demand for fresh farm produce. Non-certified organic products are often sold at these facilities. They are priced at approximately 20% above the market rate of their non-organic counterparts. These weekly markets have been fairly successful. "The bottleneck now is that we do not have enough production to cater to the demand", said Fr. Antony Kozhuvanal, one of INFAM's more prominent leaders. Attempts have also been made to organise sales stalls at cultural and religious events where a large number of people congregate. These are however sporadic, and do not function on a regular basis.

INFAM has also appreciated that it is counter-productive to attempt to remove traders altogether. "The initial attempt was to remove all middlemen. Slowly we realised that many of our distribution systems are quite efficient as they have evolved over years of experience. We learned a lot from these experiments", said Fr. Vadakkencheril.

VALUE-ADDED PRODUCTS AND SUPPORT STRUCTURES FOR ALTERNATIVE CHANNELS

As shown, the predominance of cash crop cultivation meant that retail outlets set up for marketing farmers' products could only have a limited scope. Much of the local produce has to be processed, stored and marketed elsewhere. Hence, the farmers had to primarily depend on traders.

In 2002, INFAM made a serious attempt to enter into trading. They bought large amounts of coffee by offering a premium price to producers. The initial capital for this was collected through Rs. 100 loan certificates to which members subscribed. The target was to collect $40,000 from 20,000 members. The actual amount collected was only $9,000 and this led to difficulties in paying the producers at the time of collection. Initially, when the price of coffee beans was Rs. 24 per kg, INFAM paid Rs. 26 by adding the trader's commission to the farmers' share. This could not be sustained for long as prices soon dropped to Rs. 18 per kg. INFAM alleged that this was deliberately manipulated by the traders' lobby and carried on collecting coffee beans for another month at Rs. 22.50 per kg, a premium of 25% over the traders' price.

This intervention may have had some indirect positive effect on the level of prices as INFAM claims that the market price rose to Rs. 23 as a result of its efforts. However, INFAM's management soon realised that in the long-run, the products they offer have to be competitively priced. INFAM's emphasis on nature-friendly, traditional farming methods provided a way to achieve this.

ORGANIC WAYANAD

INFAM realised that to be successful they not only needed to evolve alternative marketing channels but alternative value-added products as well. While INFAM had already been promoting sustainable forms of agriculture, it was primarily a campaign institution and could not freely engage in economic activities or make effective use of the various financial schemes offered by the government and other bodies. It needed smaller, more focused institutions to do this. To facilitate this, the members of the organisation floated a non-profit charitable society and called it "Organic Wayanad".

One of the main objectives of this society was to evolve an internal control system to facilitate organic certification and to ensure that farmers met the necessary quality standards. This was necessary because the certification agencies only provide information to enable farmers to comply with organic standards. In order to avoid conflicts of interest, they are not allowed to provide consultancy services to applicants. The Organic Wayanad Society therefore conducts awareness and training programs for farmers during the process of organic conversion. It also supports the collection of the certified products and functions as a liaison agency between the farmers and the other players in the value chain.

At present there are approximately 2,000 organic farmers in the district who are certified or in the process of certification. Many other organic farmers who are not ready for certification also make use of the services of the society. There is a mandatory transition period of three years from non-organic to organic status, after which farmers' land is judged to be clear and becomes eligible for full certification. The society aims to help more than 500 farmers every year to enter the certification process.

INDOCERT

The second aspect of the value-addition process was to obtain certification recognised by export markets in the West and elsewhere. However, the cost of certification by Western certifying agencies is prohibitive for most farmers in India. Occasionally, government agencies such as the Spices Board can absorb the costs, but this is only possible in special cases and is not sufficient to cover the large number of farmers who want to convert to organic farming. Thus there was a need to make certification accessible locally through a certification agency. This prompted the formation of INDOCERT (http://www.indocert.org) through a joint effort of various NGOs and farmers' groups such as Organic Wayanad. The INDOCERT trust allows institutions and individual trustees to be members. Membership is not a condition or guarantee for getting certification, and members do not receive a share of the potential financial gains of the trust.

This body collaborates with FiBL, the Research Institute of Organic Agriculture, a Swiss-based international institution which helps INDO-CERT in its efforts to ensure quality in the certification process. It also collaborates with bio.inspecta, the official Swiss certification body, by representing it in India, and with SECO, the Swiss State Secretariat for Economic Affairs. INDOCERT is itself accredited by DAP, the German organic accreditation system, to offer certification. It is also accredited by the Agriculture and Processed Food Products Export Development Authority (APEDA) of the Government of India. Bodies certified by this national agency can use the label "India Organic". This in turn is recognised by the United States Department of Agriculture as conforming to their national organic standards.

INDOCERT can certify agricultural crops, livestock products, honey, and the processing of farm products. Inspection is generally done once a year. Additional inspections are conducted wherever necessary. It can also issue "transaction certificates" for consignments certifying that the goods are derived from production and processing systems that are themselves certified as organic. It also certifies organic inputs such as fertilisers, soil conditioners, organic pesticides, repellents and so on, for the National Standards for Organic Production (NSOP) section of APEDA. The certifications are normally valid for one year and are renewed after yearly inspections.

IOFPCL

In 2003, the Indian parliament approved an amendment to the Companies Act of 1956 which recognised the incorporation of "producer companies". This was done at the recommendation of a committee headed by the economist Y. K. Alagh. A producer company is in effect a hybrid between a private limited company and a cooperative society. This change in the Companies Act aimed to allow the incorporation of the unique elements of cooperatives within the regulatory framework applicable for companies. Only primary producers are allowed to be shareholders in these companies. The shares are not transferable and thus cannot be traded on any stock market.

The first Producer Company formed in India was IOFPCL (http://www.iofpcl.com). It is supported by Organic Wayanad, as well as a few like-minded organisations. It was incorporated in the year 2004 and by 2008 it had approximately 1,200 shareholders. Each share is sold at a face value of Rs. 1,000. Normally only shareholders can sell their products to the company. The surplus is distributed to the shareholders as "bonus" after any development plans have been financed.

The company sources products such as pepper, ginger, turmeric, vanilla, cashew, and cocoa from different parts of Kerala. From Wayanad, it chiefly collects organic pepper in coordination with Organic Wayanad. The company collected 65 tonnes of organic pepper in the 2007–2008 season. Out of this, 32 tonnes had already been exported by July 2008. The farmers were paid Rs. 165 per kg, as against Rs. 118 for non-organic pepper in the open market. The farmers also save on transport costs as their produce is collected from their premises. However, full payment is not made immediately. The farmers receive 30% of the price of the products when it is sold to IOFPCL, and the balance is paid after a few months as the goods are sold by the company. Many farmers still have outstanding dues from last season as the company is waiting for all the stock it bought from its members to be sold and paid for. This creates a dilemma for farmers such as Yohannan who have to decide between higher earnings with cash tomorrow, or lower prices with cash today.

The company's finance has been provided by bank loans and borrowings from the funds of the local government body which is known in Kerala as the "*Jilla Panchayat*". The company also makes use of the government's warehouse facilities to store produce. "We can succeed if sales are steady. For this, we need to assure guaranteed supply to our customers. Given the uncertainties in production, and the switching of loyalties of the farmers, this is difficult to do", said Chackochan Pullanthanickal — one of the Directors of IOFPCL who is based in Wayanad. He was referring to the fact that farmers tend to sell where there is an immediate gain, often ignoring the long-term goals and collective interests of their own company. As open market prices are increasing, it is difficult to convince the farmers of the long-term advantages of supporting their company. The company is trying to overcome some of its handicaps by offering innovative services to its members. For example, it is negotiating with banks for special financial services for its members such as sanctioning loans against its warehouse receipts.

The value chain functions are shown in Fig. 1. Organic Wayanad and INDOCERT provide direct value addition to the chain through information and certification. Coordination between IOFPCL and Organic Wayanad effectively removes the need for middlemen in the collection process. This coordination has been possible mainly because of the facilitative role of INFAM and those associated with the movement in the establishment and advancement of these entities.

"I do not use even approved organic fertilisers or pest-repellants", said Dominic — a farmer in the remote Padichira area of Wayanad. "I have not noticed any marked fall in the quantity of production as a result of this. I think that if we are good to the earth, the earth will be good to us." It seems that for farmers like Dominic, the switch to organic farming is much more than merely obtaining certification and the associated marketing advantages. They are aware of the value of sustainable agricultural practices. This is also shown in the other activities of INFAM such as soap production, production and marketing of traditional savouries and snacks, promoting tender coconut as a healthy alternative for soft drinks and so on. The farmers and local people seem to be becoming aware of the advantages of going back to traditionally proven ways of living and farming.

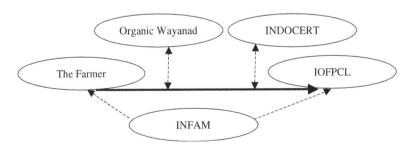

Figure 1: The value chain functions.

Dominic and others believe that the wide incidence of diseases such as "quick wilt" that fatally affects pepper plants is the result of indiscriminate use of fertilisers and pesticides that destroy the plants' innate resistance capabilities. He appreciates the support given by Organic Wayanad and INFAM in making him and his colleagues aware of this.

Apart from pepper, Dominic also cultivates ginger, and he needs to pay weekly labour charges that can be as high as Rs. 4,000. He is fortunate in that he has no outstanding bank loans to service. However, he foresees that next year he will have to run down his savings as his teenage son is going to college away from home. He is disappointed that he cannot sell all his produce to IOFPCL, because he cannot afford to wait for his money for an indeterminate period. He sold half of 2008's produce to the company and has received a 30% payment. Like many others he is holding on to the other half of his production to sell in case any unforeseen emergencies arise when he might immediately need money. He believes that the price premium of 20–30% that the company offers is significant for farmers such as himself. "There would be many who would like to shift to organic farming and sell to the company. But the delay in payment makes them apprehensive". The smaller farmers who do not have any significant savings to meet contingencies are most likely to be excluded.

The effectiveness of these efforts illustrates that it is possible to leverage on the membership and resources of existing institutions, even non-economic ones such as the church, to promote inclusive growth. "The church has deputed priests and made its premises available for coordinating these activities. This was because agencies such as the government were not playing a similar facilitative role during the crisis", says Fr. Vadakkencheril. This seems to have been effective because the large network and infrastructure of the church in the area has made coordination and information dissemination comparatively easy. It is not simple for other agencies to do this. But, the role of the church may also have prevented farmers with other religious affiliations from becoming active members of INFAM. Some people have alleged that INFAM is functioning as a short-cut for the church's ambitions for power. The emergence of entities such as "Organic Wayanad" with less active involvement by the church staff may be the beginning of more inclusive efforts.

It is remarkable that INFAM emerged and remained highly decentralised, in contrast to the hierarchical and centralised organisation of the church itself. Its activities differed widely from place to place, depending on what was relevant for their products. INFAM in Wayanad district itself has evolved systems to deal with coffee, pepper, and ginger as these are its primary products. Other areas have evolved different systems. The lack of centralised control has resulted in many over-enthusiastic or questionable attempts by those associated with certain units. For example, in its monthly newsletter, the Wayanad unit distanced itself from a marketing attempt for rice by another unit which functioned on the discredited "money-chain" model, raising deposits in a pyramid scheme which could only survive as long as it kept on growing (INFAM Voice, 2003). On the whole, however, the decentralised model with few controls seems to have worked in generating local systems which effectively serve local needs.

REFERENCES

Infam Voice (2003). Infam Kuthari Company. *Infam Voice*, 16, p. 2.

Krishnakumar, R (2004). Driven to death. *Frontline*, 21(9). Retrieved 3 May 2008 from http://www.hinduonnet.com/fline/fl2109/stories/20040507002904000.htm

Nair, MR (2004). Need for suicide prevention strategy. *The Hindu*, 8 April 2008. Retrieved 3 May 2008 from http://www.hinduonnet.com/2004/04/08/stories/2004040803430500.htm

Venugopal, PN (2007). The decline and fall of the Kerala coconut. *Infochange*. Retrieved, 10 May 2008 from http://infochangeindia.org/200702105688/Agenda/Cost-of-Liberalisation/The-decline-and-fall-of-the-Kerala-coconut.html

Case Study 4

Spencer's Retail

Sukhpal Singh

BACKGROUND AND PROFILE

RPG Enterprises, controlled by the RP Goenka family, is one of India's largest business groups and one of India's leading retailers with a retail business turnover of $155 million in FY2005. The retailing arm of RPG Group accounted for only 7% of the overall turnover of the RPG Group in FY2005, with the remaining 93% of Group revenues coming mainly from companies operating in vehicle tyres, power and transmission equipment, communications, entertainment, life sciences and other specialised industrial applications. The stated mission of Spencer's, the retail part of the Group, is to provide high-quality and healthy food to customers with trust and transparency by building relationships. This case study focuses on fresh fruits and vegetables which are of high-value and are particularly relevant for small farmers as they are labour-intensive and provide regular income.

RPG entered retailing through the acquisition of Spencer and Company in 1989. Spencer's was founded in Madras (now Chennai) in 1865 to sell imported items to the large British expatriate and military population. By 1897, it had grown to become the largest store in India with 65,000 sq. ft

Note: Units of measurement in the Indian numbering system: lakh = 100,000; crore = 10,000,000. Indian Rupees (Rs.) where appropriate are converted into USD at a rate of approximately Rs. 50 = $1.00; Rs. 1 lakh = $2,000; Rs. 1 crore = $200,000.

of shopping space. At the peak of its performance in 1940, Spencer's had 50 retail shops in most of the major cities in India. The company had also integrated backwards into producing some of the products that it sold such as soft drinks and cosmetics. After independence in 1947, Spencer's sales dropped significantly. Because of its deteriorating performance and poor sales, Spencer's was put up for sale by its owners. The ownership changed once in early 1970, and in 1989, RPG purchased Spencer's and established it as a separate division. At the time of its acquisition, Spencer had nine retail stores, and was still the largest retail chain in India.

RPG entered the modern retail sector in May 1996 by setting up the Food World chain of supermarkets, through a division of its subsidiary Spencer's. In August 1999, Food World was hived off as a separate company, Food World Supermarket Limited, as a 51:49 joint venture with Dairy Farm International (Hong Kong), a member of the Jardine Matheson Group. In 2001, RPG Enterprises entered the hypermarket business under the Giant fascia. Renamed as Spencer's Hypermarket in 2004, the hypermarket chain is managed by Great Wholesale Club Ltd. (GWCL), a wholly-owned subsidiary of Spencer and Company. In 2005, the hypermarket division operated three outlets with a turnover of $48 million and the supermarket division operated 94 outlets with a turnover of $82 million. In May 2005, RPG parted ways with Dairy Farm International. This company took the chemist and pharmacy chain, Health & Glow, and nearly half of the outlets of Food World, the supermarket brand, and is now RPG's competitor. RPG, on the other hand, accelerated its pace of expansion to protect its sliding market share. The Food World outlets that were transferred to RPG Enterprise were re-branded under the Spencer's banner in 2005.

SPENCER'S RETAIL OPERATIONS

Spencer's Retail has 490 stores across Indian cities. They operate under five different formats, each with its own merchandise mix:

Spencer's Fresh: caters to daily fresh food needs and is stocked with a large variety of fresh fruits and vegetables. These stores have a trading area less than 2000 sq. ft.

Spencer's Express: is a small neighbourhood food and grocery store.

Spencer's Daily: is a larger neighbourhood store and stocks groceries, fresh food, chilled, frozen products and much more. These stores have a trading area of 2,000–7,000 sq. ft.

Spencer's Super: is a larger supermarket or "mini-hypermarket" store, with a trading area of 8,000–15,000 sq. ft.

Spencer's Hyper: is a combination of a supermarket and a department store, with a trading area of more than 15,000 sq. ft.

In February 2008 there were 139 Spencer Dailies, 7 supermarkets, 10 hypermarkets, 43 Express and 2 Fresh stores, making a total of 201 stores. 130 of these stores were in South India, although the company also has a presence in Delhi, Haryana, Uttar Pradesh, West Bengal, Maharashtra and Gujarat. In 2006, there were 68 stores across 17 cities which rose to 119 in 2007. The retail stores stock over 25,000 products to suit varied customer needs across the different states and regions. In early 2008, Spencer's Retail employed more than 2000 people in eight states. The stores are located in Chennai, Hyderabad, Visakhapatnam, Bangalore, Aurangabad, Pondicherry, Coimbatore, Salem, Kodaikanal, Trivandrum, Kochi, Secundarabad, Trichy, Noida, Gurgaon, Ghaziabad, Faridabad, Delhi, Mumbai and Pune. Many more stores are scheduled to open in late 2008. The monthly turnover of fresh fruits and vegetables from these outlets is $1 million.

The RPG Group follows a cluster method for expanding its food retail chain, in order to achieve economies of scale in sourcing, logistics and promotional activities. It does not have a very significant presence in the northern part of the country. One important reason for this is that it operates through a hub and spoke distribution system, where the hub services the requirements of the outlets. To optimise costs, a number of outlets are, therefore, linked to a hub and cannot be located too far away.

When RPG Spencer entered the retail food sector in 1996 through the Food World retail stores, it started by providing store space to fruit and vegetable vendors. These vendors paid rent to the retail store for using the space and sold the products at a suitable price margin. The Spencer's retail stores had little or no involvement in the procurement, profiling or merchandising of the food items that were sold. This model was far from ideal since the vendors did not have a customer-oriented approach. They offered limited varieties and poor service, and they did not present the food items attractively. More importantly, the customers did not get any significant price advantage over other alternatives like local hawkers. This model also failed to make any difference to the condition of the farmers who supplied the produce. The large number of intermediaries enjoyed most of the benefits and the real value of the sale was never transferred to the farmers.

When RPG Spencer started retailing, the company aimed to provide total satisfaction to its customers through a wide variety of food items, right pricing, pleasurable ambience, excellent service, best quality and attractive presentation. In order to achieve this overall objective, Spencer's adopted the strategy of what they called "sourced buying". It decided to eliminate the vendors and to bring the sourcing and merchandising of food items under its own control. This meant that the company would be responsible for procurement from wholesale markets, and for storing, grading, transporting, pricing and in-store merchandising of the food items.

At the same time, Spencer's realised that it was a new entrant in the agri-retail sector and that it was not recognised as a very big player in wholesale markets. The wholesalers bought aggressively in large quantities and they completely controlled the market. Spencer's sales volumes were initially quite low and, as a result the company could not gain any advantage and bargaining power in wholesale markets. They therefore decided to adopt a compromise by appointing sourcing agents to buy on their behalf from the wholesale markets, while Spencer's themselves handled the merchandising.

These agents were traditional commission agents or wholesalers in officially approved markets, and Spencer's chose them after carefully assessing their efficiency and capability. They had an in-depth understanding of the wholesale market, they understood market trends, they could provide good quality and the required quantity on time, and they were also capable of sorting, grading and packaging the food items according to the specifications given to them by Spencer's. In short, RPG out-sourced the job of obtaining ready-to-retail producers to the sourcing agents and called it "sourced buying". These agents were able to fulfill the requirements of RPG as they bought from a number of different wholesale markets.

For example, tomatoes were bought from markets in Bangalore, Madurai and Chennai.

This "sourced buying" proved significantly better when compared to the conventional model of providing retail space to individual vendors because it gave a lot of control to RPG Spencer in deciding what was sold, how it was sold and the price at which it was sold. Spencer's could understand the requirements of the customers and provide food items of the desired quality and variety. But the company soon realised that this was not the best solution and that the supply chain could be further improved. For example, the sourcing agents used to buy cauliflowers from the wholesale market for Rs. 7 per piece. But, the farmers sold the same vegetable in the wholesale market for just Rs. 2. Spencer's was paying unnecessarily high costs in the wholesale markets, they were not getting the best possible quality and the farmers were not getting a good price either. The intermediaries cornered most of the five rupee margin.

RPG Spencer realised that this was an opportunity to devise a clear win-win supply chain strategy for the company and for the farmers, by arranging direct procurement from the farmers. Simple calculation showed that if the intermediaries were removed, then both the company and the farmers could gain tremendously. The farmers could get Rs. 3.75 per piece if they sold cauliflowers direct to Spencer's. At the same time, Spencer could save Rs. 3.25 per cauliflower. Both parties could make a significant gain.

The three key elements of Spencer's supply chain strategy are to have a minimum number of suppliers, thus gaining economies of scale, reduced overheads and control requirements, and easier vendor development, create regional hubs to facilitate centralised distribution of up to 90% of their products and daily replenishment; and to minimise the number of intermediaries by buying from as far "upstream" as possible in the supply chain in order to reduce losses and increase margins for the company.

In order to have a healthy relationship with the farmers, Spencer's has adopted a completely new concept known as "contact growing", which is different from contract farming. Contract Farming is a very tight process where both parties have to enter into a formal agreement. It is generally used for a single crop for several years. In contrast, "contact growing" is a totally independent process in which the company only provides specifications to the farmers and there is no agreement. It is used for multiple crops which have a short shelf life. The company tries to "pay higher, buy lower", by paying higher than market prices to growers but still procuring at lower than the wholesale market cost.

In addition to working with individual growers, the company also works with some women's self-help groups where the average household's land holding ranges from about a third of a hectare to one hectare. Also, when farmers who normally supply to its centre have more crops than Spencers' stores need, Spencer's introduces them to other buyers. This ensures that the farmers remain loyal to Spencer's as their preferred buyer.

SPENCER'S PROCUREMENT SYSTEM IN GUJARAT

Spencer's first distribution centre was set up in Ahmedabad in July, 2007 when the chain started operations in Gujarat. It served five stores, and by 2008 it is serving 13 stores and one supermarket in Ahmedabad. There are also four stores and one hyper market in Vadodara. Thus, there are a total of nine stores in Gujarat which sell 10–12 tonnes of fresh vegetables every month, accounting for 12% of the total sales of the stores. Half of the sales are in Ahmedabad. The distribution centre in Ahmedabad gets fruit and vegetables from the Chandrala Collection Centre near Prantij and the Padara centre in Vadodara. The distribution centre also gets fruit and vegetables procured from wholesale fruit and vegetables markets of Kalupur, Vasna, Naroda and Jamalpur. The market *mandi* buying is managed by the *mandi* buying team. The company procures 80% of its supplies from the market and 20% from farmers.

The stores sell 120 different collections of fresh produce which are known as Store Keeping Units (SKUs). Twenty of these are procured and supplied by the collection centre. The vegetables are kept in the stores for a complete day after delivery from the farmers, and the stores have to place orders with the distribution center two days before they will actually be offered for sale. The distribution center in turn conveys these orders to the farmers one day before they have to deliver. Once the material reaches the collection centre from the farmers, it is graded and about 4% is rejected. Sometimes, whole lots are also rejected, especially cauliflower.

If rejections are too high on a particular day, the necessary vegetables are bought from the market. Material which is found to be damaged at the distribution centre is used to make cut-vegetables which are only 1% of the total sold. The material is sent from the collection centres to the distribution centre by each evening and is then sent to the stores the next morning. Some vegetables such as cauliflower are priced at high margins at the store level due to grading losses which can be as high as 30%. In general, however, most vegetables are priced 40% above the Spencer's buying price, as shown in Table 1.

Chandrala is located 15 km from Chiloda in Gandhinagar district and 3 km from Majara Chokdi in Sabarkantha district where Reliance has collection centres, and 45 km from Ahmedabad where all the major fruit and vegetable markets are located (see Fig. 1). Prantij in Sabarkantha district which is the local fruit and vegetables market is 15 km from Chandrala. Gandhinagar and Ahmedabad are the major vegetables markets for vegetables grown in this area. The Chandrala Centre was started on 26 February 2008. The major vegetables procured are chillies, ladies finger, bottle gourd, brinjal, cauliflower, cabbage and tomato, and procurement ranges from half a tonne to two tonnes per day. The farmers generally deliver every other day.

The collection centre level costs Spencer's 33 paise for every kg of produce, which is an average of about 4% of the cost. The company charges the farmers 50 paise per kg for transport, which is deducted from the price they receive. Table 1 shows the difference between Spencer's

Table 1: Procurement and retail prices of Spencer's in Gujarat (Rs./kg).

Vegetable SKU	Procurement price at collection centre	Selling price at retail Store	Difference between procurement and retail prices (%)
Chillies	15	21	40
Ladies finger	25	35	40
Cauliflower	11	21	90.9
Brinjal	7.5	11	46.7

Source: Spencer's collection centre and store in Ahmedabad on April 24 and 25, 2008 respectively.

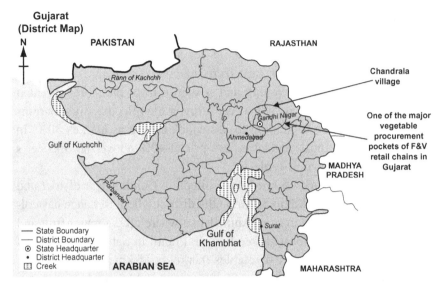

Figure 1: The districts of Gujarat and location of Spencer's collection centre (Chandrala village).

buying costs and the retail prices for the main vegetables in Gujarat. The company buys less than 5% of the supplying farmers' total production. The farmers sell the rejected produce in the local market. This is about 4% of the produce they bring to the collection centre. The grading at the collection centre is done manually; it involves checking for diseases, cuts, size, shapes and colour. The collection centre has five staff — four labourers and one supervisor. The distribution centre employs two fruit and vegetable supervisors, one data entry operator and 10 labourers. Altogether, Spencer's procures less than 1% of the total vegetable production in the Prantij area. The modern new format retail chains together buy a total of about 30% of what is grown in the area.

The Spencer's collection centre at Chandrala village serves about 25 farmers. The company rents the godown from the Chandrala Co-operative Society for Rs. 2,500 per month. Each "SKU" is supplied by two or three of them. The farmers deliver direct to the collection centre and sell their top-grade fruit and vegetables there, at prices which are based on the auction prices at the official markets the previous day.

The actual payments are made to the farmers by a farmer vendor who is appointed by Spencer's. They are relatively large farmers, and they invest between $10,000–$12,000 of their own money in order to provide this service. They are paid a 3% commission on the value of the materials for which they pay, as remuneration for this service. The farmer vendor at Chandrala also supplies his own produce to Spencer's and is paid commission on these supplies as well. He grows a fifth of the material procured by the collection centre, and works under a three-year written contract with the company.

The prices paid to the farmers are fixed according to the market price, which is the auction price at the public market from the previous day, less the transport cost to Ahmedabad. Spencer's agrees on this price with the farmers the day before they sell. The Distribution Centre checks the quality, and allocates and dispatches the materials to the stores. The appointed vendor farmers and vendors at the *mandis* do any necessary retail packing.

Rejections at the distribution centre are around 10%, and a further 2–3% is rejected from the farmer vendors. When buying from the market, Spencer's has to pay 6% commission to the local commission agent and 1–2% market fee. By buying direct from farmers through its own centres, the company gets fresher produce at lower prices. The cost of buying from the *mandi* is 10% over the auction price, because of the 6% commission, the 1–2% market fee, 1–2% for transport, 2% for packaging and 1% for grading. The distribution centre costs a further 7%, which makes the total cost of collection and dispatch as high as 17%.

The farmers benefit from having an assured market, lower transport cost, lower labour cost, timely payment and fair weight. There is no price assurance, and Spencer's prefers this loose "contact growing" system over contract farming as it is more economical. The farmers are also not compelled to sell to Spencer's. The company saves the *mandi* commission by procuring directly from farmers, and it also gets better quality produce with lower losses. During the summer 70–80% of the vegetables are bought from outside the State whereas in winter 80% are locally procured.

Most of the suppliers are small farmers, except for potatoes which only large farmers supply to Spencer's. The average farmer supplies between two and three tonnes of other bulk vegetables to the company and between

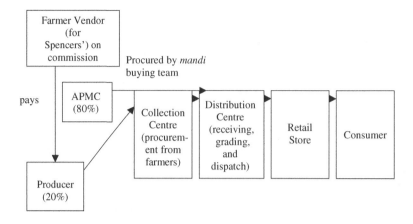

Figure 2: A diagrammatic presentation of Spencer's procurement and marketing operations.

50–100 kg of leafy vegetables per day. More than half the farmers are fairly large, owning more than four hectares of land, about a third of them have about three hectares, a fifth have two hectares and the remaining 10% farm one hectare or less.

About a quarter of the farmers who supply Spencer's also supply to other chains such as Reliance and Shubhiksha which have collection centers in the same area. Only the "farmer vendors" are exclusive to Spencer's.

On a typical day in April 2008, 18 farmers delivered their produce to the Centre. The smallest delivery was 80 kg of ladies finger, supplied by a farmer who owns just over one hectare of land and grows vegetables in a small part of it. The largest delivery was 157 kg of cauliflower by a farmer who has three and a half hectares and grows vegetables on about one hectare of this. All the farmers were upper-caste Patels.

A number of farmers with different acreages who supply at the Chandrala Centre made the following comments about Spencer's as a buyer:

> *"The major benefits of selling to Spencer's are, saving on time and transport cost. But, Spencer's does not accept low-quality produce and purchases only small quantities. Further, their rejection rate is 30–40%*

which is very high. The net prices I get at Jamalpur (the local mandi) are lower, but every grade of produce can be sold there."

— Nareshbhai Patel, who owns 9 hectares,
including one hectare of vegetables

"Delivery to Spencer's takes less time and there are no deductions. These add up to about 8% in the official market. Besides, there is cash payment here. But, the problem is that Spencer's does not buy all my produce and I have to take away the material which is not needed by them. To help the farmer, Spencer's should buy all produce of the farmer during the entire season and should not bargain with farmers on the price."

— Ramanbhai Patel, who owns 9 hectares,
including 4.5 hectares of vegetables

"Earlier I used to sell my ladies' finger at Jamalpur Market every alternate day and now I sell my entire produce to Spencer's. They pay cash and there is no loss of my packing material. Further, I save my time due to the nearby location. I used to spend Rs. 100 on marketing costs at Jamalpur Market. There are no deductions here and no unloading charges but I get the same price as I used to get in Jamalpur Market."

— Rajnibhai Patel, who owns just over one hectare,
including a quarter of a hectare of vegetables

"I save time and cost by selling here. It used to take a full day to sell in Jamalpur and the total cost of selling there was Rs. 140 per day including Rs. 10 transport cost at Rs. 0.5 per kg, Rs. 50 for the 10% fee, Rs. 50 for the loss of a day's labour and Rs. 30 for food. By selling here, my farm work does not suffer as I can get back to the farm immediately. Further, there is no risk of transport to a distant place and packing material worth Rs. 15 per pack is returned here which was not the case in Jamalpur. Transport costs only 20 paise per kg and if the quantity is small, it can be transported by bike or scooter. Thus, I save 30 paise per kg on transport by selling here. I agreed to a 10% lower

price from Spencer's than I could get at Jamalpur market as the cost here is lower for me."

— Pankajbhai Patel, who owns two and a half hectares,
including one and a half hectares of vegetables

A number of different customers were also interviewed at Spencer's:

"I come to Spencer's as the vegetables are fresh and prices — especially of onions and potatoes — are lower than outside. All the products are available in one place here and the staff are quite friendly."

— Sonal R Shah, 45, a homemaker

"Fruits and vegetables are cheaper here than outside. Besides, there is plenty of choice especially in the morning when produce is also fresh. I get all the things here most of the time. Above all, the staff at the store are very friendly".

— K S Chandran, 55, a small business owner

"I come to Spencer's as one gets all the things in one place. Besides, onions and potatoes are cheaper here. The vegetables are also fresh even in the evening."

— Asha Shah, 45, a working woman

Spencer's has been a leader in introducing best practices in modernising the agricultural produce distribution system in India by dealing direct with farmers, rather than through intermediaries, by grading and packing the produce with the appropriate equipment in order to ensure global standards of hygiene and quality, by ensuring that the prices paid to the farmers are commensurate with the value they have added and the risks they run, by minimising wastage at each stage of the supply chain through improvements in handling, packing, transportation, and storage, and by establishing freely accessible information on the prices paid and the qualities required of agricultural products.

The small and marginal farmers are included in the supply chain for vegetables. Thus far, the requirement is small. Therefore, Spencer's buys mainly from small growers. But this is changing, and one farmer was observed who is already supplying 150 kg of tomato and of cabbage daily. Spencer's does not buy the entire produce of a grower and buys only the highest grade produce; the grower has to sell the rest elsewhere. As a result, some farmers end up selling both to Spencer's as well as in the open market, which involves high costs.

It can also be argued that it is not in the producers' best interest to fix prices on the basis of the prices in the local APMC markets. These fluctuate daily and even within each day, and market prices can sometimes be below the cost of production. Nevertheless, the farmers are happy to be paid at prices which are based on the *mandi* price, because they do not choose to sell to Spencer's or to any other chain merely for a price advantage. They appreciate that their total transaction costs are lower with the chains, because they save time and money by supplying to them.

Chapter 4

Inclusive Value Chains in Commodity Crops

Introduction

The case studies in this chapter are about commodities, crops which are produced by enormous number of farmers, world-wide, and which are widely traded. These crops are generally undifferentiated, and they are in no way as perishable as the fresh fruit and vegetables which were the subject of the cases in the previous section. Hence they can be conveniently stored and traded, nationally and internationally.

Two of the cases are about cotton, one is about potatoes and one is about rice. They describe how four very different organisations have attempted to differentiate these crops in order to increase their value, and equally important, to make them less subject to the wide price fluctuations which usually beset the producers of crops of this kind.

Three of the four cases are about organic crops. This is unsurprising, because organic cultivation in many ways matches the strengths of small-scale farmers, and reduces the significance of their weaknesses. It is labour intensive, because the farmer's labour can replace many of the manufactured inputs which conventional farming requires to be purchased from external suppliers. This reduces the need for cash and thus for credit, whose supply to small farmers in India is still very inadequate, in spite, or perhaps because, of many decades of costly attempts to make more agricultural credit available.

Organic cultivation does however need special skills. Although many of these are actually little different from traditional farming techniques, most farmers have to "un-learn" their more "modern" knowledge of chemical pesticides and fertilisers, and re-learn farming methods which depend more on the resources of the land itself. It is also necessary to be able to trace every product back to the farm where it was grown, in order to confirm its organic pedigree. It is obviously easier to train one large farmer, and to trace a crop back to a few large producers, than it is to work with a multitude of small-holders and small holdings; the case studies show how the problems of working with small farmers have been overcome.

Two cases are about cotton. This is as it should be, because cotton is the crop which is most intimately associated with the severe agrarian distress that is presently affecting Indian farmers. Over a quarter of a million Indian farmers have killed themselves in the last 10 years; there are many reasons for this, but one common feature has been that many of them grow cotton. There is a desperate need for new approaches to cotton cultivation and marketing, and these two cases show how small-scale cotton farming can be sustainably profitable.

Rice is the staple on which most people depend, and in particular the poor. The government has therefore played a major role in the production, distribution, pricing and marketing of rice and other staples, for many years. Well-intentioned regulations such as the Agricultural Products Marketing Act, however, can actually increase the share of the price of paddy which is taken by "middlemen". The Kohinoor Basmati rice case demonstrates that these barriers can be overcome, and it shows how costly and time-consuming it is to do this.

The chapter also includes one intervention which achieved temporary success with several hundred farmers, but which was discontinued after a few years because of disagreement between various parties in the value chain. BASIX attempted to link "tribal" farmers from Jharkhand, who are perhaps among India's most marginalised people, with PepsiCo, one of the world's largest and most powerful multinational corporations. These two parties typify the opposite ends of the global value chain, and the experience of trying to link them holds many lessons for any institution trying to do the same.

Case Study **5**

Contract Farming of Potatoes: An Attempt to Include Poor Farmers in the Value Chain

*Braja S Mishra**

BACKGROUND

The experience of the last 50 years suggests that India will remain a nation of small and marginal farmers and agricultural labourers, despite spectacular economic growth in recent years. Agriculture is the main source of livelihood for around 60% of the population, though it accounts for less than 20% of GDP. High growth in manufacturing and services has not translated into high employment. Therefore, economic growth is unbalanced and is not nationally sustainable. Those worst hit by the decline of agriculture are rural agricultural labourers and small and marginal farmers.

* The writer acknowledges the valuable assistance received from Mihir Sahana and Arijit Dutta, and other inputs from Sishir Ranjan and Vikas Kumar.
Note: Units of measurement in the Indian numbering system: lakh = 100,000; crore = 10,000,000. Indian Rupees (Rs.) where appropriate are converted into USD at a rate of approximately Rs. 50 = $1.00; Rs. 1 lakh = $2,000; Rs. 1 crore = $200,000.

The paradox is that agriculture is struggling while traders are profiting, and food prices are also rising. The beneficiaries from high demand and high agricultural prices are large farmers who can achieve economies of scale and can afford to hold their stocks, and traders at different levels (Bhattacharya, 2008).

Two decades ago corporate businesses were only interested in investing in manufacturing and, later, in the service sector. They had no interest in agriculture. However, with the rising demand for biofuels and cash crops, large businesses are now getting into agri-business. International grain stocks are going down because of the shift from food production to biofuels, and there is a booming market for grain (Sivaramakrishnan, 2008). Changes in food consumption habits such as the increasing popularity of fast food, the expansion of supermarkets and of international trade in fresh and processed food have made agri-business more attractive for big business.[1]

Although farming has been the main source of livelihood for millions of Indians for centuries, there are nevertheless very few ways in which small farmers can market their produce at remunerative and assured prices. Small and marginal farmers, who are chronically short of cash, have always had to resort to distress selling, especially of perishable produce. As large Indian companies and multinationals have come into the agricultural sector, a number of contract farming systems have been started, which have the potential to be win-win links between the farmer and the market.

Contract farming is defined as a system for the production and supply of agricultural/horticultural produce under forward contracts between producers/suppliers and buyers. The essence of such an arrangement is the commitment of the producer/seller to provide an agricultural commodity of a certain type at an agreed time and for an agreed price, and in the quantity required by a known and committed buyer.

Source : National Institute of Agricultural Extension Management (MANAGE) (2003), *Spice*, 1(4), Govt. of India.

---

[1] FAO: Agriculture Services Bulletin-145, 2001.

A number of large and diversified companies such as ITC, Cargill India, Escorts, Hindustan Lever, Nestle India, Pepsi Foods, Suguna and others have been involved in contract farming in different parts of India for some time, starting with cereals, pulses, oil seeds, fruit and vegetables, poultry and cotton. The experience has been mixed, and there are many arguments for and against contract farming as a route to secure livelihoods for small farmers.

In principle, however, it must be good for poor farmers to be linked to a modern value chain through which they can get an assured and reasonably remunerative price for their produce. BASIX, as a livelihoods promotion agency, was naturally interested in contract farming as a strategy for promoting livelihoods, and they proposed a contract farming solution for chip-grade potatoes, to link the Kolkata chipping plant of PepsiCo's Frito-Lays subsidiary with a number of very poor small-scale farmers in Jharkhand, Orissa and Bihar.

BASIX is a livelihoods promoting agency, known for its innovative business models to promote livelihoods for poor people. BASIX started as a micro-finance institution in 1996 and has grown to become a progressive livelihoods promotion business spread across 13 states and covering more than 100 blocks in the country. It started operating in Orissa in 2000, in Jharkhand in 2001 and in Bihar in 2007. Following a UNDP sponsored study of livelihoods in Jharkhand, BASIX realised that the good rainfall, fertile soil and favourable climate in the State meant that a large number of livelihoods could be improved through the development of vegetable cultivation in Jharkhand. BASIX identified a number of problems in the vegetable sub-sector which would need to be addressed.

The markets for vegetables were under-developed, and prices fluctuated widely, but the farmers themselves were ill-equipped to take advantage of any improvements. Their productivity was low, they used poor planting material and other inputs, and they lacked knowledge of modern farming practices. Their costs were high, and the supply of credit and other financial services such as crop insurance was inadequate. Lack of agri-inputs was one of the key reasons for low productivity.

In Jharkhand many small- and medium-scale farmers grow potatoes, for their own consumption and for sale, if they have any surplus. Rainy season potato, which is planted in July and August, commands very high prices when it is harvested in October and November, when potato is not commonly available in other parts of eastern India. Hence, potato is considered to be a valuable cash crop in the state. The market, however, is highly volatile in terms of price, demand, and supply. The local market price is mainly decided by middlemen and small-traders.

BASIX identified the potentiality and scope, and they concluded that it could become a major source of livelihoods if the whole sub-sector — from the farms to the final market, could be addressed.

PepsiCo was already growing potatoes for its Frito-Lay factory in Kolkata with a very small number of farmers in Jharkhand, on a very limited scale. The company needed a credible organisation which could facilitate large-scale potato farming. PepsiCo's management heard of BASIX's initiative and started to discuss contract farming of potatoes with them. BASIX decided this was an ideal opportunity to start its work in the vegetable sub-sector, and negotiations began.

The Frito-Lay division of PepsiCo India Holdings needed chip-grade quality-fresh potatoes for its chip factory near Kolkata, especially during the lean period when potatoes are generally not available in eastern India. The Company had been trying to meet the demand with supplies from distant states such as Haryana and Punjab, which incurred heavy costs because of transport and wastage. The farmers of Bankura, Purulia and Bardhaman districts of West Bengal were able to supply what was needed during their harvest season, but it was difficult to get enough chip-grade potatoes during October, November and early December to keep the factory running. Jharkhand is the only place in eastern India where potatoes are harvested during these months. PepsiCo needed the potatoes and the farmers needed a market; BASIX aimed to facilitate the various backward and forward linkages that would bring them together.

When BASIX started to discuss the benefits of cultivating chip-grade potato in dialogue with the farmers, there was great enthusiasm. A number of meetings took place between PepsiCo, BASIX and the farmers. The negotiations went on for almost a year before the farmers and PepsiCo agreed to enter into a contract. BASIX was the facilitator and was also to provide financial and technical services. The aim was for BASIX to create a revenue model which would cover all its own costs and would also allow the deal to be profitable for the farmers and for PespiCo.

THE CONTRACT SYSTEM

PepsiCo selected certain locations which they estimated could meet their demand for potatoes at an agreed price. The company then entered into a procurement and input (P&I) contract with the newly-formed Potato Growers Association which BASIX had helped the farmers to start. The contract detailed the obligations of each of the three parties, the growers, BASIX and PepsiCo.

PepsiCo agreed to provide the specialised Atlanta variety potato seeds to the Growers' Association in carefully identified areas, under supervision from BASIX. The Association bought the seed at previously agreed prices, and delivered it to its members at their own cost, and BASIX provided credit to the growers for this purpose. PepsiCo agreed to purchase the growers' potato crops, provided they satisfied certain conditions, at a price which they declared at the beginning of the season.

BASIX was to pay 75% of the seed value in advance on signing the agreement, on behalf of the Growers' Association, and the balance would be adjusted against the amount payable to the Growers' Association after the harvest. BASIX had to take proper care of the seeds until planting time, and to show the farmers how to plant and cultivate the seed potatoes as PepsiCo instructed, and PepsiCo also had to supervise the individual growers and provide them with expert consultancy as needed, including advice on whatever insecticides and pesticides that might be necessary. BASIX was responsible for ensuring that the members of the Growers' Association followed all of PepsiCo's advice, from planting through the harvest. These instructions, critically, included the time at which the tubers were to be harvested, to ensure that supplies were available for the Frito-Lays factory as needed. The farmers also had to grade, sort, pack and load the potatoes, again through their Growers' Association and under the supervision of BASIX, and in the presence of a representative from PepsiCo if they asked for this. BASIX also agreed to introduce the Growers'

Association to suitable sources of all the inputs they required. PepsiCo was only responsible for the actual seeds.

VALUE CHAIN

The operation started in 2005–2006 with 83 acres and 424 farmers in the Deoghar and Ranchi area of Jharkhand. It increased to 518 acres and 997 farmers in 2006–07, including most of the original farmers, and in the 2007–2008 season there was a further increase to 585 acres and 1442 farmers, including 37 farmers from Gaya in Bihar. There was also a small experiment in 2006–2007 with 10 acres and 27 farmers in Salepur in Orissa (see Fig. 2).

The farmers were selected on the basis of their willingness to work in a group, their ability to adopt the new variety of seed and the new methods, the suitability of their land for rainy season potato cultivation, along with assured irrigation in case of drought or failure of rain, their financial position and past credit worthiness.

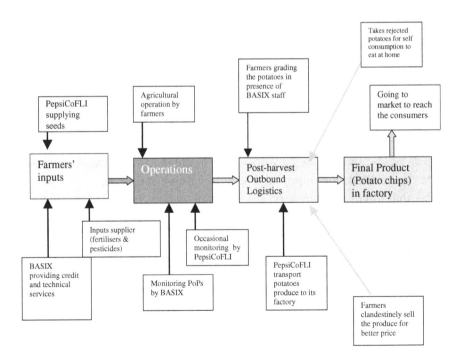

Figure 1: Value chain.

Figure 2: Locations of farming and factory in India.

FINANCING THE VALUE CHAIN

BASIX, as had been agreed, paid 75% of the cost of the seed in advance on behalf of the Growers' Association. The seed cost Rs. 13 per kg in 2005–2006, Rs. 14.50 in 2006–07 and Rs. 19 in 2007–08 because of a shortage of supply. The seed had been treated, and supplies for the first two years were bought from Punjab and Himachal Pradesh. In the third year, because of losses due to rotting in transit, most of the seeds were supplied from the West Bengal cold storage stocks. The cost of rotten and non-germinating seed potatoes was calculated and audited. They were either replaced free of charge or credited to the farmers' accounts after they had delivered their crops.

The total cost of these advances was $14,000 in the first year, $108,000 in the second year and $128,000 in the third year.

Farmers who could not afford to pay for potato seeds or the other inputs received loans from BASIX through Joint Liability Groups (JLG).

A JLG is a group of five to six farmers who are encouraged to come together to form a group, all of whose members take on the responsibility of paying back the loans taken by individual members. BASIX designed a combined cash and kind loan product, with the potato seed supplied in kind and the balance paid in cash for the purchase of other inputs. All the loans were compulsorily linked with life and health insurance, which was offered in collaboration with Aviva and Royal Sundaram. The agreement was that farmers would repay their loans at the end of the season when PepsiCo paid for their crops. If the crop failed, the loan could be extended up to a maximum of 11 months.

BASIX also developed a weather risk insurance product in collaboration with ICICI Lombard, to help farmers avoid severe indebtedness if their crops failed, but the premiums were up to Rs. 5,000 an acre, and the scheme also required complex crop monitoring and data collection. In the event, none of the farmers chose to insure their crops as they thought the premiums were too high.

BASIX provides credit and extension services to its customers, including farmers, through self-employed agents who are known as Livelihood Service Advisors (LSAs). They work on a commission basis, and when they are receiving specific technical services the customers pay BASIX an annual service charge. For the potato farmers this was fixed at Rs. 300 per annum. The PepsiCo staff occasionally monitored these services, and the advisers are guided and managed by BASIX field executives, who are graduates in management and agriculture. The LSAs usually have secondary or pre-university education along with some in-service training in financial, agriculture and business development services. BASIX and PepsiCo worked together with local agricultural scientists to develop an information booklet in the local language about the required cultivation and other practices, which was distributed to the farmers.

The BASIX and PepsiCo staff also monitored changes in the weather which might lead to crop diseases or pests infestation, and advised the farmers on preventive measures.

IMPACT OF THE INTERVENTION

The farmers benefited in many different ways. They started getting assured prices for their produce. All inputs were provided on time without any initial payment. They also learned the basic rules of contract farming and the importance of grading and quality, which will help them to get better prices for their produce in future, and they were introduced to improved farming practices. Some farmers have already adopted these for their traditional crops. They could get seeds at the farm gate and could also sell their produce at the farm gate for an assured price. This eliminated their need for distress selling and reduced the time and cost of transport from the *mandi* to the farm and from the farm to the *mandi*.

The farmers have also realised the advantages of working as a group of producers. This has increased their bargaining power, so they can now buy various inputs delivered to the farms at discounted prices.

Their increased profits and their strength as a group have given the farmers more confidence in all respects. A few of them did not stick to the recommended practices and thus failed to get the expected yield. Despite these setbacks, most of the farmers wanted to continue with contract farming.

The following table (see Table 1) shows the increased yield of chip-grade over conventional potatoes, when planted at different time. There is generally an increase of a tonne or more per acre, or something between a quarter and a third more than the farmers could get from the conventional seed.

In addition to the higher yields, the assured prices per tonne for chip-grade potatoes have been slightly higher than for the conventional potatoes the farmers used to grow. The farmers have also saved transport costs, and even on the few occasions when prices in the open market were higher than those assured by PepsiCo, the effective price was higher than the market price if the higher yields were taken into account. Table 2 gives an account of different prices for potatoes planted at different times.

The price for chip-grade potatoes is for those which are of the required quality. Inferior quality potatoes can only be sold at very low prices, as low as Rs. 2.5 per kg.

Four farmers near Ranchi gave data on their costs and returns at a time when the open market price and the price assured by PepsiCo were the same, at Rs. 9.50 per kg. The comparative table below (see Table 3) shows that the farmers earned better returns by producing chip-grade potatoes.

Table 1: Comparative average yields of chip-grade and check potatoes.

Year	Average yield (MT/Acre)					
	2005–2006/143 farmers		2006–2007/907 farmers		2007–2008/1442 farmers	
	Chip-grade	Conventional grade	Chip-grade	Conventional grade	Chip-grade	Conventional grade
Planting Date						
1 Aug–15 Aug	4	3	4	3	4.5	3.5
16 Aug–31 Aug	4.5	3.5	4.5	3.5	5	4.5
1 Sep–15 Sep	5	4	5	4	6	4.5
16 Sep–30 Sep	5.5	4.5	6	4.5	7	5
1 Oct–15 Oct	6	5	7	5	8	6

Table 2: Comparative price of chip-grade and check potatoes at different planting times.

Planting period	Average market price of conventional grade 2005–06 Rs./kg	PepsiCo price of chip-grade 2005–06 Rs./kg	Average market price of conventional grade 2006–07 Rs./kg	PepsiCo price of chip-grade 2006–07 Rs./kg	Average market price of conventional grade 2007–08 Rs./kg	PepsiCo price of chip-grade 2007–08 Rs./kg
1 Aug–15 Aug	11		11.5	9.5	11	10.5
16 Aug–31 Aug	9.5		10	8.65	9.5	9.5
1 Sep–15 Sep	8	8.5	8.5	7.45	8	8.35
16 Sep–30 Sep	6	7.5	6	6.5	7	7.85
1 Oct–15 Oct	4	5.5	4	5.5	6	7.2

Table 3: Sample cases of cost and return of chip-grade potato by farmers.

Name of the farmer	Yield of conventional (MT)	Cost of production (Rs.)	Approx return (Rs.)	Yield of chip grade (MT)	Cost of production (Rs.)	Approx return (Rs.)
				Cost and return per acre between planted in the second fortnight of August 2007		
Rabi Chatti	3.8	18,000	36,100	5	19,000	47,500
Sukal Oraon	3.4	18,000	30,595	4.5	19,000	42,750
Govind Sahu	3.2	18,000	28,795	4.8	19,000	45,600
Bimal Oaron	3	18,000	28,500	4.4	19,000	41,800

Note: All the figures are approximate.

Table 4: Cost of production for chip-grade and check potatoes.

Particulars	Cost of production of conventional potatoes/acre (Rs.)	Cost of production of chip-grade potatoes/acre (Rs.)
Seed 10 quintals	12,000 @ Rs. 12/kg	15,200 @ Rs. 15.20/kg
Fertiliser and pesticides	3,000	2,000
Labour cost	2,000	1,000
Other costs	1,000	1,000
Total	18,000	19,200

The details of the production costs (see Table 4) show that there is little difference between the conventional and the chip-grade potatoes, and the higher yields and higher prices make them much more profitable.

BASIX as an institution is committed to demonstrating that livelihoods promotion initiatives of this kind can cover their own costs, without need for subsidy from outside or cross-subsidy within the company. They had intended that the operation should be profitable not only for PepsiCo and the farmers, but for BASIX itself. In the first year of its intervention, BASIX earned a surplus of Rs. 45,036 after covering all its costs (see Table 5).

In the second year, however, BASIX incurred a loss of Rs. 10,581. The change arose from a number of causes, including lower production, PepsiCo's more stringent quality demands and some farmers' failure to sell to PepsiCo, or to pay for the LSA services, when they saw that the market price for potatoes was temporarily higher than the PepsiCo price.

One major reason for the lower sales, in spite of the larger numbers of farmers, was the weather. PepsiCo regarded Jharkhand as a supplier of rainy season potatoes, and they needed the harvest to start at the end of October and in early November. To achieve this, sowing has to be completed by mid-August, but since 2006 there have been unusually heavy rains during that time, making it very difficult to plant and cultivate the seeds in the right way. Some farmers also broke their contracts, when they saw that the crops they had planted in early August could be sold at a higher price in the open market than the price offered by PepsiCo. A substantial tonnage of potatoes was sold clandestinely by the farmers in the open market.

Table 5: Income & Expenditure of the intervention (2005–06).

Income	Amount in Rs.	Expenditure	Amount in Rs.
Service charge from PepsiCo for seed distribution @ Rs. 0.75 per kg	56,286	Expenses for sorting and grading	1,700
		Expenses for labor and transport	14,769
Interest accrued for 90 days @ 24% per annum	34,758	Technical services expenses	21,919
		Own staff costs	1,34,225
Service charge received on potato tubers sold to PepsiCo @ Rs. 0.22 per kg	31,372	Commission to LSAs	7,632
		Cost of finance	24,335
Service charges collected @ Rs. 300 per farmer per annum	1,27,200		
Total	**2,49,616**		**2,04,580**
Net (Surplus)			**45,036**

PepsiCo also caused problems. They had paid a high price in the first year to attract more farmers, but when the volume of production increased they started to put very stringent conditions on the quality and size. Produce which did not meet these conditions was valued significantly below the market price. The standard size of potatoes had been set at a diameter of between 45 and 85 mm with a variation of 3% for smaller sized and 5% for bigger sized. Potatoes with mechanical damage, scab, greening, bruising, wet rot, dry rot, infestation and other defects were discarded outright. These conditions had been laid down in the original contract, but they were not strictly enforced by PepsiCo during the initial period when there was a shortage of chip-grade potatoes for the Kolkata

Table 6: Income & Expenditure of the intervention (2006–07).

Income	Amount in Rs.	Expenditure	Amount in Rs.
Service charge from PepsiCo for seed tuber distribution @ Rs. 0.75 per kg	56,286	Expenses for sorting and grading	1,700
		Expenses for labour and transport	14,769
Interest accrued for 90 days @ 24% per annum	34,758	Technical service expenses	21,919
		Own staff costs	1,67,121
Service charge received on potatoes sold to PepsiCo @ Rs. 0.22/kg	32,049	Commission to LSAs	7,632
		Cost of finance	24,333
Service charges collected	1,03,800		
Total	**226,893**		**2,37,474**
Net (Shortfall)			**(10,581)**

factory. The farmers thus came to think that whatever they produced would be bought by PepsiCo. When supplies built up and became more reliable, PepsiCo applied the conditions more strictly. A sizeable number of potatoes were rejected, causing a decline in the price.

The usual procedure had been for BASIX staff to supervise the grading and weighing at the farm gate, and sometimes a PepsiCo staff member would be there too. When the potatoes reached the chip factory gate, however, another round of quality checks was done without either BASIX staff or farmers' representatives being present. This resulted in many potatoes being rejected or revalued, with consequent losses to the farmers. The farmers had not approved of this second check and they registered their objections to it.

Chip-grade potatoes can normally be harvested 90 days after planting, but on occasions the PepsiCo staff insisted that the farmers harvest after only 70 or 75 days because of shortages at the factory. Potatoes harvested early are under-sized and are therefore worth less. There were times when farmers had harvested potatoes on the agreed date, but PepsiCo had not collected them. This happened when they had contracted too much land and the yields were better than expected, or when it had procured potatoes at a cheaper price from other parts of the country, especially during the winter season when potatoes are grown in many places and are available at cheaper prices. While the farmers waited for PepsiCo to collect the potatoes, the weight of the potato crop went down because of decreases due to evaporation from the tubers, resulting in a reduction in price.

PepsiCo's standards seemed to vary according to the availability of produce. They accepted lower quality produce and sold in the open market when prices were high. It is also seen that on the same day when a farmer defaults and sells in a *mandi*, PepsiCo buys the same potato at a much higher rate than they had contracted to pay the farmers from the open market but will not pay higher price to the contracted farmers.

There was also no properly organised grading, testing and weighing system in the field itself, and this created problems between BASIX and the farmers. Some farmers refused to sell to PepsiCo because they considered the price was too low, and they therefore avoided having to repay the money they owed BASIX for seed. BASIX lost Rs. 70 lakhs in this way.

There was also a severe potato blight in 2007–08, and a large amount of potatoes were rejected, which was a severe blow to the farmers. The farmers blamed BASIX for this. Those who joined contract farming never calculated that there could also be some room for loss, in this kind of farming. The farmers tried to shift all negative fallouts on to BASIX.

There were other problems with the quality of seed potato supplied by PepsiCo. Poor quality seeds meant a low yield and poor quality, but nevertheless seed prices increased substantially over the three-year period because adequate supplies were not available.

When the time came to renew the contract for 2008–09, PepsiCo wished to continue, particularly in Gaya in Bihar. BASIX set out some revisions to the conditions of its role as a facilitator. They insisted that the PepsiCo staff should make more frequent farm inspections and that the final quality check should take place at the farm gate in the presence of the farmers and BASIX's staff rather than at the factory gate in Kolkata. PepsiCo did not accept this condition, and BASIX plans in future to deal direct with any farmers who want to contract directly with PepsiCo. If the farmers so wish, BASIX will provide them with technical services, as well as finance and assistance in building their Association, but the relationship will be between BASIX and the farmers, with no contractual responsibilities to PepsiCo.

BASIX nevertheless tried to resolve the issues between the farmers and PepsiCo, and they had meetings at various levels, on the farms, at the Kolkata office and even with PepsiCo management, to discuss quality standards, price, payment and so on. In spite of these efforts, as of August 2008 a number of issues remained unresolved, and the farmers in Jharkhand, as well as those in Orissa, declined PepsiCo's offer to continue farming chip-grade potatoes.

The Growers' Association was one of the major problems. It was formed to take care of all the logistics, from receiving inputs to collecting packed potato for transport, but it only existed nominally, and was actually managed by BASIX staff. This was costly for BASIX, and it meant that the farmers thought that all these tasks were actually the responsibilities of BASIX; all they had to do, they thought, was to grow the potatoes.

PepsiCo needed potatoes quickly, and BASIX underestimated how long it would take to build the Growers' Association as an institution. There was misunderstanding between all three parties, and apparent breaches of contract, so the whole process became mired in an atmosphere of mistrust.

There were also some long-term issues of environmental sustainability which had not been properly considered. Repeated cultivation of the same crop without rotation can lead to a variety of soil infestations. Potato is a thirsty crop which affects water table levels over a period of time. In addition, the chip-grade potato is susceptible to diseases and pest attack and therefore requires more pesticides and fertilisers, which in the long run will have an adverse effect on the environment and on human and animal lives.

The intervention only involved a few hundred farmers, but it did have the effect of increasing local farm wages, although this was later countered by an influx of labour from outside the state. Contract farming is in itself restrictive but it does widen the range of choices available to farmers.

REFERENCES

Bhattacharya, A (2008). Farming Unviable for Small Grower, *The Times of India*, 4 April 2008.

Sivaramakrishnan, A (2008). Food insecurity: A Form of Violence, *The Hindu*, 19 March 2008.

Case Study **6**

Basmati Rice and Kohinoor Foods Limited

Anup Kumar Singh

"All the rice grown in this country possesses a particular quality causing it to be much esteemed. Its grains are half as small as that of common rice, and when it is cooked snow is not whiter than it is, besides which, it smells like musk and all the nobles of India eat no other. When you wish to make an acceptable present to anyone in Persia, you take him a sack of this rice."

Jean Baptiste Tavernier (1605–1689), French chronicler

Such has been the glory of "Basmati" rice — a variety of long grain rice which has for centuries been famous for its fragrance and delicate flavour. Basmati means "ingrained aroma" in Hindi. The subtle aroma and delicious taste of this aromatic fine quality rice has given it a distinct place in the world rice trade. India is the largest cultivator and exporter of Basmati rice in the world. The Basmati rice producers in India, who are mainly in

---

Note: Units of measurement in the Indian numbering system: lakh = 100,000; crore = 10,000,000. Indian Rupees (Rs.) where appropriate are converted into USD at a rate of approximately Rs. 50 = $1.00; Rs. 1 lakh = $2,000; Rs. 1 crore = $200,000.

the Indo-Gangetic plains, have until recently been unable to benefit as much as they should from the success of this world-famous rice variety. Basmati accounts for only 25–30% of the total volume of rice exports from India but constitutes about 45–55% of their total value.

The Basmati rice supply chains are dominated by middlemen and this results in poor returns to the Basmati rice farmers. The area under Basmati rice cultivation has thus gone down in recent years, and this is a major concern for the rice exporters as well as the farmers. In these circumstances, Kohinoor Foods Limited — an Indian global food company dealing in many varieties of rice, supported by the Uttarakhand Organic Commodities Board — a state government agency for promoting organic cultivation, has introduced a programme in order to help to revive *Dehraduni* Basmati rice cultivation in Uttarakhand. This initiative is a good example of how backward integration of supply chains can contribute to the empowerment of marginalised producers and, in the process, create a win-win situation for all the stakeholders.

INDIAN BASMATI RICE INDUSTRY

India is the second-largest rice-producing country in the world. Its annual production of about 85–90 million MT of rice accounts for almost a quarter of the world's rice production. Since rice is a staple food in India, the trade and processing of paddy is to a large extent regulated by the Government of India. The government buys about 20–25% of India's total rice production through a compulsory levy from the rice mills and also by direct paddy purchase through the Food Corporation of India. This regulation aims to protect the interests of rice farmers by offering them a minimum support price and it also replenishes the rice stocks in the central pool from which subsidised rice is supplied across the country. However, premium quality Basmati rice is officially classified by the government as "export oriented", and is therefore not covered under the domestic regulations for minimum support prices and the levy.

The total annual production of Basmati rice in India is valued at some $800 million. The area under Basmati cultivation is about 800,000 hectares. The crop is grown mostly in Haryana, Punjab, Uttar Pradesh, Uttarakhand and Himachal Pradesh. About 1–1.4 million metric tonnes are produced, of which approximately 75% is exported. Haryana and Punjab account for around 65% and Uttarakhand and Uttar Pradesh account for 25% of the total area under Basmati cultivation in the country.

Basmati used to be the main variety of export rice until the late 1980s. General rice exports gained more importance as the Indian economy opened up in the 1990s and increases in the rice stock in the government's central pool led to a relaxation in the rice export rules. Nevertheless, the importance of Basmati rice in Indian rice exports is such that Basmati rice is separately classified in the official export statistics.

Rice exports make up about 15% of total agricultural exports from India. Although the share of Basmati rice in total rice exports from India has come down about 90% in the 1980s to about 23% today, Basmati still earns about 45% of the country's total rice export earnings (see Fig. 1). Figure 2 shows the total value of Basmati rice exports compared with total rice exports during the period 2002–2006.

Because Basmati rice is such an important export commodity, the government of India promotes its export by offering incentives such as exemption from value added tax on Basmati and by exempting exporters from duty on the imported content of goods which they export. In order to protect the interest of Indian Basmati rice in world markets the government

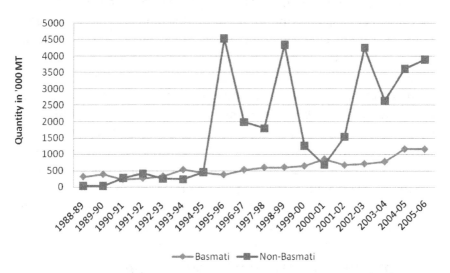

Figure 1: Rice exports from India during 1988–2006.

Source: Director General of Commercial Intelligence & Statistics, Kolkata, Ministry of Commerce, Government of India.

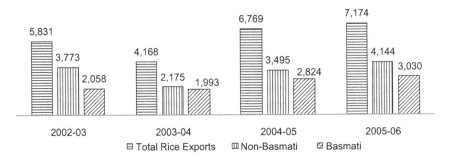

Figure 2: Value of rice exports from India.

Source: Director General of Commercial Intelligence & Statistics, Kolkata, Ministry of Commerce, Government of India.

of India brought a case against RiceTec Inc, a US-based company, to prevent them from using the name "Basmati" for the aromatic rice which they had adapted to grow in American conditions.

The government is also concerned at the high tariffs which are charged on Basmati rice by the European Union. The non-resident Indian community in England has brought pressure to bear on Parliament, and Philip Davies, Conservative MP from Shipley, in the North of England, tabled an early day motion calling for a reduction in the 65 euros per tonne tarrif following several complaints by Indian restaurant owners in his constituency. The UK imports around 200,000 tonnes of rice every year and is the largest importer of rice in the EU.

In 2008, because of the turmoil in world commodity markets and the high rate of inflation, the government took several steps to discourage rice exports. The import duty concession for exporters was withdrawn, a minimum export price of $1,200 per metric tonne was imposed on Basmati rice and non-Basmati rice exports were totally banned. These measures actually make little difference, since export prices are more than the minimum of $1,200 per tonne and the scale of the demand is such that the withdrawal of duty concession does not discourage Basmati exports.

BASMATI RICE CULTIVATION IN UTTARAKHAND

Basmati rice has for many centuries been grown mainly in the traditional areas of North and North West India. The unique climatic conditions found in the fertile plains along the Himalayan foothills contribute to the characteristic aromatic attributes of Indian Basmati rice.

Uttarakhand, meaning "Northern part" in Hindi, is a separate state which was formed in the year 2000 from the hill districts of Uttar Pradesh state, and it is renowned for Basmati rice cultivation. Rice is a major agricultural crop of the state and its "*Dehraduni* Basmati", named after Dehradun, capital city of the state, is one of the most famous Basmati varieties of India. Some experts believe that Basmati rice was traditionally grown only in the Dehradun region, and that it began to be cultivated in other parts of undivided India during the British regime. Today, Basmati is the common heritage of both India and Pakistan, and both countries are planning jointly to claim rights for Geographical Indicator (GI) status for Basmati rice.

Because of the lower yield from traditional Basmati varieties whose productivity is about 1,400–2,100 kgs a hectare compared with 4,500–5,000 kgs by non-Basmati paddy, and also because of the loss of farm land to urbanisation during the late 1990s many farmers almost stopped growing the traditional Basmati varieties in Uttarakhand and switched over to high-yielding varieties of other grains.

MARKETING PRIOR TO THE INTERVENTIONS OF KOHINOOR FOODS LTD

There are three main players in the supply chain of Basmati rice. The farmer sells Basmati paddy to the traders in the *mandi,* the trader supplies Basmati paddy to the rice mills, and exporters market the processed Basmati rice.

At the initial stage, however, there are a number of traditional inefficiencies that make the entire system cumbersome for the small producers. The marketing system, its various actors and the problems it causes for small producers are shown in Fig. 3.

Mandi (The Marketing Yard)

The Agricultural Products Marketing Act requires that agricultural products should be traded in official government-controlled marketing yards which are known as *"mandis"*. Under this act, an Agricultural Produce Marketing Board is set up in every state to develop and regulate the *mandis*. Farmers bring their produce to the *mandis* in animal or tractor-drawn wagons, for

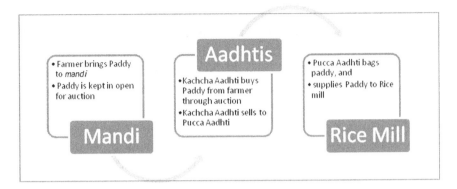

Figure 3: Traditional paddy supply chain.

sale to the government-registered traders. The area covered by a *mandi* varies from place to place but on average there is a *mandi* in every district headquarters town, covering a population of up to 300,000 people.

Aadhtis (The Trading Agents)

Trading in the *mandi* is carried out by agents called *Aadhtis* (brokers who buy and sell paddy). There are two types of *Aadhtis* — *Kachcha Aadhti* and *Pucca Aadhti*. *Pucca Aadhti* are the government-registered wholesalers who own shops in the *mandi* and act as the commission agents for rice mills. In Uttarakhand they are allowed to charge a 2.5% commission on their sales. The *Kachcha Aadhtis* are government-registered petty traders who cannot hold more than 10 tonnes of stock and therefore work as commission agents for *Pucca Aadhtis*. They are allowed by the *mandi samiti,* the *mandi* governing body, to charge a 1.5% commission, but if they finance the trade with their own capital they can charge an additional commission of between a half and one percent to the next player in the supply chain.

Boli (The Auction) and The Sale to Rice Mills

Every *Kachcha Aadhti* is linked to a *Pucca Aadhti* who, in turn, is the representative of a rice mill. The mills supply jute bags for the paddy to the *Pucca Aadhtis*.

Every morning, when the *mandi* opens, paddy is brought on bullock carts or tractors to the designated display area in the *mandi* for visual inspection and grading. The paddy is then auctioned to the *Kachcha Aadhti* who bids the highest price. After it has been auctioned it is taken to the weighing area in the *mandi*. It is unloaded and bagged in gunny bags which the *Kachcha Aadhti* obtains from the *Pucca Aadhti*. After it has been weighed the paddy is delivered to the *Pucca Aadhti*'s store, where four copies of the purchase invoice are made. One copy is retained by the *Pucca Aadhti* and one copy is given to the *Kachcha Aadhti*, the farmer and the *mandi samiti* office, which keeps track of the total 4% *mandi* fee payment to the government. The *Pucca Aadhtis* usually report their daily purchases to their buyers at the end of the day, and they transport the paddy to the rice mills based on an agreed delivery schedule.

Payments

The *mandi* rules require that the credit cycle should be completed within 10–15 days. The transactions between the mills, both types of *Aadthis* and the farmers have to be finalised within this period. The trade is normally financed by the rice mill owners but the *Pucca Aadhtis* sometimes use their own capital as well.

Market Inefficiencies

This process appears to be systematic and foolproof but there are many inefficiencies in these traditional markets which create serious problems for the farmers. The farmers have to bear the cost of transportation to the *mandi*, and they often have to stay overnight in the market-place when sales have not been completed in a day. In some seasons they even have to come to the *mandi* during the night to avoid the morning rush.

The farmers are also unable to benefit from market forces. There is no proper grading system so they have no incentive to produce better quality; this reduces the final quality of Basmati rice. The pricing mechanism is also not well designed. Irrespective of quality, the lowest bid of the previous day is the opening price for the next day's market. The *Aadhtis* tend to keep their bids close to the opening price.

The *Aadhtis* also play various tricks in order to increase their profits. They under-weigh or demand a little extra weight from the farmers to cover what they call "handling loss", and they also hold back stock from the mills and claim that it was purchased at a later date than it actually was, when the prices were higher than those at the real date of purchase. They will receive a high price from the mill but pay a low price to the farmer.

The farmers are not legally required to bear any costs after bringing their produce to the *mandi* but in practice many *Aadhtis* charge the farmers for unloading, bagging, weighing and stitching the sacks, and they also charge the rice millers for the same services.

The *Aadhtis* are also unreliable in their payments to the farmers. The farmers often have to make a number of trips to the *Aadhtis* to collect their payments and they receive no interest on delayed payments whereas the *mandi* rules stipulate that the *Aadhtis* themselves can charge interest at the rate of 1% per month to the rice millers on delayed payments. Some of the farmers complain that the *Aadhtis* will only pay immediately after weighing if they deduct 2% from the total value.

KOHINOOR FOODS LTD — INTEGRATING SUPPLY CHAIN FOR ORGANIC BASMATI RICE

Kohinoor Foods Ltd (KFL), formerly known as Satnam Overseas Limited, is one of India's leading companies in the organised marketing of rice, including Basmati rice. KFL's flagship brand "Kohinoor" is renowned for its quality. Kohinoor started marketing Basmati rice in the Indian domestic market in the year 1990, and today holds a leading position in the branded Basmati rice business in India with about 38% market share. Kohinoor exports Basmati rice to 63 countries, and now has a strong presence in branded Basmati rice markets world-wide.

KFL also sells ready-to-eat and ready-to-cook Indian foods to 25 countries. With overseas offices in US, UK and Dubai, KFL is fast emerging as a global Indian food company. The company's annual revenues are $120 million, half of which is from domestic and export sales of its "Kohinoor" brand of Basmati rice.

In 2003, because of the growing demand for organic Basmati rice from European markets, KFL planned to diversify its traditional Basmati product range. It was clear that the traditional supply chain could not work for organic Basmati, since the organic requirements involved direct interface with farmers. They had to be motivated to adopt organic cultivation, the organic inputs and technical know-how had to be made available, farmers' compliance with organic cultivation practices had to be assured, the crops had to be traceable to the farmer level through proper records at each level, and there had to be a way of ensuring that organic farmers got the premium prices and added benefits over the traditional supply chain, without disturbing the existing supply chains for conventional Basmati and other non-Basmati paddy.

The Basmati rice export business was very competitive, and it would be impossible for the existing trade in non-organic Basmati to absorb the additional costs of organic certification and related extension activities. KFL therefore started to look for farmer groups with whom it would be possible to organise direct contact in order to introduce organic cultivation.

Uttarakhand was the obvious choice for KFL's organic programme. This newly formed hill state was to some extent untouched by chemical farming and the state government had also launched some ambitious projects to develop the state as the "Organic Capital of India". KFL had been buying Basmati and non-Basmati paddy from Uttarakhand through traditional marketing channels since 1998. KFL tried to identify farmers for the organic programme and the company approached various state agencies such as the State Agriculture University, the Rice Research Station and the Rice Seed Development Corporation. They also approached some farmers' groups and in 2004, after some false starts, KFL made contact with a Basmati farmers' federation in Dehradun district. This federation had been organised by the Uttarakhand Organic Commodity Board (UOCB), a state government agency which had been set up in 2003 to promote organic farming and allied sectors throughout the state. The organisation had formed farmer federations in the state under the "Organic Basmati Export Programme" which aimed to facilitate organic certification and marketing for Basmati farmers in Dehradun and Udham Singh Nagar districts. This programme was funded by the Sir Ratan Tata Trust, a foundation established by a member of the founding family of the Tata Group of Companies.

It was not easy to work with farmers who had been organised by the government. There were some positive aspects. UOCB took responsibility for the internal control system and organic certification which enabled

KFL to avoid the pre-operational work of motivating the farmers to adopt organic cultivation. UOCB, with the support of an international organic certification agency, had also developed internal control systems and its team of internal inspectors was ensuring adherence to these in the field. The cost of organic certification was also borne by UOCB.

The farmers' initial experiences with UOCB-supported market linkages during the 2003–2004 season had however not been encouraging. The farmers' organisation was weak because insufficient time had been spent on building the institution, and there were many disagreements among the farmer members. The *mandi* and *Aadhti* system was still being used for purchasing the paddy. The farmers felt that the price they received for organic Basmati paddy was not sufficient to compensate for the loss of income from their second crop of wheat. This was lower than before because the farmers were not allowed to use chemical inputs on the land which was certified "organic", but there was no organic premium for wheat. The farmers did not have enough technical know-how of organic methods of pest and disease control, and they also failed to receive the necessary inputs on time.

PROJECT IMPLEMENTATION

Since the majority of the farmers in Uttarakhand have small holdings, one federation was not sufficient for KFL's requirements. KFL and the first farmer federation therefore identified seven other UOCB-promoted farmer federations, and a total of eight federations, four each in Dehradun and Udham Singh Nagar districts, were prepared to participate in the programme. It took months of collaborative efforts to start the project. A formal contract between KFL and the eight federations was eventually signed in 2005, initially for one year. The Uttarakhand state government was also included at the federations' insistence as the arbitrator and service provider for organic certification. Owing to their prior experiences the farmers were very sceptical about the whole arrangement and they requested a pre-determined price for their organic Basmati paddy instead of KFL's proposal of a 30–40% premium on the market price for conventional Basmati.

KFL asked the federations for a long-term commitment. In return, the federations successfully bargained for a higher base price on which yearly increments were to be added at the time of renewal of the contract. KFL eventually had to offer a price of Rs. 2,100 per quintal of organic Basmati paddy whereas the conventional Basmati paddy prices were around Rs. 1,300 to Rs. 1,400 per quintal at the time.

Modus Operandi

KFL stationed a field coordinator in Dehradun and another in Udham Singh Nagar district on a full-time basis to coordinate with UOCB and the farmer federations. A Basmati rice specialist from KFL's head office managed the technical support to federations such as coordination with various agencies for sourcing organic inputs and supplying them to the federations on an interest free basis, running a seed production programme with selected farmers and providing on-farm guidance.

KFL also undertook various capacity building measures including operational training for the federations. They conducted intensive meetings with each individual federation to finalise the procurement system. The re-designed supply chain for organic Basmati paddy is illustrated in Fig. 4.

Purchase of Paddy

KFL faced a fundamental regulatory obstacle in direct procurement from the farmers' federations. The Agricultural Produce Marketing Act

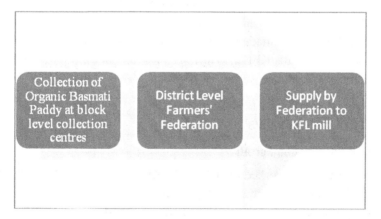

Figure 4: The KFL re-designed supply chain for organic basmati paddy.

prohibits procurement of agricultural produce outside the *mandi*. Therefore, KFL had to arrange for one federation to be registered with an existing *mandi* in Dehradun district. All billings are made through this federation and the *mandi* fee is paid through it for all the four federations of Dehradun district.

The farmers are no longer required to bring their produce to the *mandi*. Their paddy is purchased by the federations on mutually agreed dates at village collection centres. Normally each federation has two or three collection centres. KFL supplies jute bags to the federations. The paddy is packed into the bags and is weighed on electronic weighing machines that have been given to all the federations by KFL.

The weighed bags are sealed and tagged at the village collection centre. The paddy is then loaded into trucks and taken to the Vikas Nagar Mandi office of the Vikas Nagar Federation where the details are entered, and billing is done. The trucks are immediately dispatched to the KFL mill in Haryana.

Payments

KFL and the federation maintain complete traceability of each bag of paddy. Full payment is made by KFL to each individual federation against their invoices on a weekly basis, including the cost of paddy, 1.5% commission to the federation, the 4% *mandi* fee and 1% charge for logistics such as loading, bagging and weighing. Transport and insurance of paddy to the mills is paid by KFL at the time of delivery. Payments to individual farmers are made by the federations and are closely monitored by the KFL field staff. KFL also arranges for annual third party audits of the federations.

Impacts of KFL Initiative

• A Win-Win Situation For All

The new system has worked out to benefit KFL as well as the farmers. The benefits to both parties are summarised in Table 1.

The approximate cost savings of the farmers and of KFL are shown in Fig. 5.

Table 1: Benefits of KFL initiative.

Benefits to the farmers	Benefits to KFL
• Saving on transport cost to *mandi* • Savings on transport losses • Quality inputs available interest free • Technical guidance • Reduced cost of cultivation • Assured premium prices • Saving on weighing, bagging etc. • Weighing accuracy • Reduced transaction time • Ease of transaction • Hassle free assured payments • Community support through federation	• Saving on 2.5% commission to *Kachcha Aadhti* • Saving on transport charge irregularities • Protection from payment of increased prices to *Aadhtis* on account of stock hoarding • Assured supply • Quality guaranteed

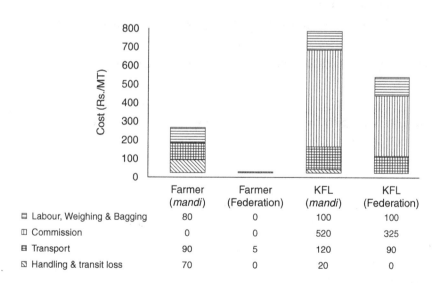

	Farmer (*mandi*)	Farmer (Federation)	KFL (*mandi*)	KFL (Federation)
▤ Labour, Weighing & Bagging	80	0	100	100
▥ Commission	0	0	520	325
▦ Transport	90	5	120	90
▧ Handling & transit loss	70	0	20	0

Figure 5: Cost comparison between *mandi* & federation system.

Source: Based on discussions with farmers and KFL representatives.

Compared to the *mandi* system, the farmers gain approximately Rs. 235 per metric tonne. KFL also gains Rs. 245 per metric tonne, about a quarter of which is spent on providing extension support to the farmers. A subsidy of Rs. 250 per farmer or about Rs. 10 per kg is provided by UOCB as a part of its support for organic certification. KFL is willing to absorb this cost but the UOCB insists on paying this since they have secured external funding up to 2010.

The farmers are also able to make some more money by weighing and bagging their produce themselves, and they are paid for the work. Previously they had to do this for nothing in the *mandi* during the peak times. Moreover, the 1.5% commission to federations not only covers its operation costs but also serves as a cash reserve which can be used to make emergency cash loans to the members. Based on the 2005 data, a comparative analysis between conventional and organic Basmati rice cultivation in Dehradun district (see Table 2) shows a net benefit of Rs. 4243 per acre to the farmers of organic Basmati programme.

• Extended Outreach

The programme was a great success in its first year itself, and the federations then renewed their contracts with KFL for next three crop years. KFL offered an increment of Rs. 50 per quintal per year for the

Table 2: Comparative analysis of conventional and organic basmati rice cultivation.

Particulars	Organic (O)	Conventional (C)	O – C
Productivity per acre (Rs.)	846	720	(+) 126
Cost of production per acre (Rs.)	10,347	10,578	(–) 231
Average per kg sale price of paddy (Rs.)	19.6	17.5	(+) 2.1
Profitability per acre (Rs.)	6,265	2,022	(+) 4,243

Source: Based on analysis of data from Kohinoor Foods Limited and cost-benefit analysis study of organic crops by Centre for Sustainable Development, Dehradun.

Table 3: Programme coverage during the period 2005–2007.

Particulars	Year 2005	Year 2006	Year 2007
Total hectares area under Organic Basmati cultivation	119	310	748
Total number of farmers	190	223	864
Total purchase of Organic Basmati paddy (MT)	107	322	*
Total value of organic Basmati purchase (in million Rs.)	2.25	7.13	11.1**

Source: Kohinoor Foods Limited.
Notes: * Data not available, ** estimated.

renewed period. In addition, KFL also added Rs. 65 per quintal to the base price of paddy as compensation for the loss of income on wheat. Thus, the effective price per quintal of Basmati for the year 2006 was Rs. 2,215. It was Rs. 2,265 in 2007 and Rs. 2,315 in 2008. The wheat incentive became meaningless as the market price for conventional non-organic Basmati paddy reached about Rs. 1,900 per quintal in the 2007 season.

The programme was started in 2005 in 119 hectares with 190 Basmati farmers and by 2007 the coverage had extended to 748 hectares and 864 farmers. The increase in coverage is shown in Table 3.

When UOCB started the Organic Basmati Export Programme in 2003, Kalawati, a traditional Basmati farmer in Swarna Valley in Dehradun decided to convert half of her 1.5 acres land into organic cultivation. Saving fertiliser costs and the assurance of marketing by UOCB were the major factors behind her decision.

Today, she is happy about her decision to stick to the programme even after the relatively bad initial years. Encouraged by the increased income of Rs. 3,060 for her 510 kg production of organic Basmati paddy from 0.75 acres in 2005 she has now converted her entire 1.5 acre plot to organic cultivation.

• Revival of Cultivation of Traditional Basmati Varieties

In 2006 UOCB commissioned a study by the Centre for Sustainable Development, a Dehradun-based NGO, entitled "Cost-benefit analysis of organically produced crops grown in Dehradun and Udham Singh Nagar districts". The study shows that the average productivity of organic Basmati had increased to about 2,100 kg per hectare whereas the yield of conventional Basmati was only about 1,600 kg per hectare. This increase in productivity and the increased sale price have kindled great interest among farmers in Dehradun and Udham Singh Nagar districts. UOCB estimates that the 70–80% increase in the area under Basmati cultivation in the programme area is due to new farmers who have now switched over to Basmati cultivation. This has revived the cultivation of traditional Basmati rice varieties in Uttarakhand state, which was rapidly declining.

Because of KFL's success, several other Basmati exporters have also started similar arrangements with other UOCB-supported organic Basmati growers' federations in Uttarakhand.

MAJOR CHALLENGES

The overall results of the KFL initiative have been very positive. However, there are also a number of major challenges.

The commission agents have not lost a major part of their incomes, because the total volume of rice traded in Uttarakhand state is so large. Nevertheless, it has not been easy to bypass them. It took a great deal of time and effort to register a farmers' federation in a *mandi* in Dehradun district, and KFL was not able to acheive the same result in Udham Singh Nagar. All the activities are coordinated by federations but the 2.5% commission has still to be paid to a *Pucca Aahti* to use his license to pay the *mandi* fee.

The labourers who weigh and bag paddy in the *mandi* have also lost some income. The *mandi* KFL has encouraged the federations to employ the same labourers to do the same job in nearby village collection centres.

Because OBEP is a government supported project, they have placed great emphasis on the inclusion of small and marginal farmers. This meant that a large number of farmers had to be covered to produce sufficient quantities of paddy. It is very difficult to ensure that all these small farmers adhere to organic practices. Every year, UOCB has to expel about

5% of the farmers from the programme because they deviate from organic practices.

Although KFL provides guidance at every stage of cultivation and the quality of Basmati paddy has substantially improved, the farmers are not yet ready for grade-based pricing. KFL grades the paddy at the village collection centres but only to sort out the rejects. KFL is training the farmers in paddy grading and it is hoped that within a year or two it will be possible to start grade-based pricing.

> Ignorance has not been bliss for Bal Singh of Vikas Nagar. He joined the organic Basmati export programme in 2003. However, he did not realise that he had to follow organic practices for all the crops grown on his organic plot, and he applied chemical pesticides on his wheat crop. He was therefore discontinued from the programme in 2004. When he properly understood the requirements, he rejoined the programme in 2005. In order to make up for the loss of the two conversion years he included his whole holding of 3 acres in the programme instead of 1.5 acres taken up earlier.

FUTURE PROSPECTS

"This is a beginning for us" says Mr. Man Mohan Singh, Deputy General Manager at KFL and the man behind this project.

"The confidence of the farmers in KFL and in organic farming in general has increased. We are getting good quality produce as per our choice but the most important aspect of this project is that we are coming closer to the farmers and getting to know their basic needs as well as their difficulties. This understanding will help us in better planning to achieve better quality and increased quantities. We hope to develop this project many fold in the coming years."

KFL is also exploring other ways in which the farmers can get additional benefits. Mr. Umed Fartyal, Deputy Manager at KFL believes that Fairtrade is the way ahead. KFL has initiated the process for Fairtrade certification for the federations so that they can get an additional premium on their produce which they can invest in the sustainable development of their businesses and communities.

Table 4: Kohinoor organic basmati rice: Journey from "farm to fork".

Stage	What it includes	Cumulative price (Rs./kg)	% of total cost
Farm gate	Cost of raw paddy	46.30	30.9
Factory gate	Procurement expenses & Administration costs	62.11	10.5
Ex-Factory	Processing & holding charges	71.79	6.5
Ex- KFL godown	Packaging, Marketing costs & KFL's profit margin	99.14	18.2
Consumer price	Distribution cost & profit margins of supermarket	150.00	33.9

Source: Kohinoor Foods Limited.

Kohinoor organic Basmati rice is sold in the metro cities of India through modern supermarkets such as Big Bazaar, Spencer's and Reliance Fresh. Table 4 shows the price of a 1 kg pack of Kohinoor organic Basmati rice at each stage of its journey from "farm to fork".

Case Study **7**

Agrocel Industries

Anamika Purohit

THE ORIGINS OF AGROCEL

Excel Industries is a leading company in crop protection chemicals, and their Environment and Biotechnical division has done pioneering work in the field of solid waste management and in the development of bio-pesticides.

The late C. C. Shroff, the founder of Excel Industries, and Kantisen Shroff, ex-Chairman of the company and a well-known Gandhian, always wanted to improve the lot of farmers and rural communities in Kutch in Gujarat, the area from which their family originally came. Kutch is subject to long spells of drought, and it was clear that short-term relief work helped only to reduce the hardships of the local people during difficult times. It did not result in any worthwhile long-term solutions to the problem of drought (Galliara and Singh, 2006).

Sustainable long-term agricultural development was clearly the only answer, and in 1978, Kantisen Schroff and a team of colleagues formed the Shri Vivekananda Research & Training Institute (VRTI) with the

Note: Units of measurement in the Indian numbering system: lakh = 100,000; crore = 10,000,000. Indian Rupees (Rs.) where appropriate are converted into USD at a rate of approximately Rs. 50 = $1.00; Rs. 1 lakh = $2,000; Rs. 1 crore = $200,000.

objective of developing agriculture and horticulture in Kutch. The staff of the Institute worked closely with farmers and their experience helped Excel to create a number of agro-products which addressed their real problems. The company had always been concerned with environmental issues and ever since the 1980s they had been active in fields such as integrated crop management (ICM), solid waste management, integrated pest management (IPM) and microbes management.

While working with the farmers, Kantisen Shroff and his colleagues realised that farmer education alone cannot improve agricultural productivity. In order to accelerate their development and to increase per acre production, all the necessary inputs have to be available from one source at the right time, with the right quality and at reasonable prices, along with the latest technical guidance (Galliara and Singh, 2006).

They discussed the issue with the Government of Gujarat and they came up with a formula, which had the potential to achieve a major breakthrough in farming. Gujarat Agro-Industries Corporation, a public-sector business, and the Excel Group set up a joint venture company called "Agrocel Industries" in Mandvi district of Kutch (Galliara and Singh, 2006). This was based on an earlier company called Agrocel Pesticides Limited, which had been set up in order to start a bromine factory in the Kandla Free Trade Zone to produce pesticide formulations for export. This project never started production, but the Shroff family increased their share in its ownership to 89%, it was re-named Agrocel Industries and the Agrocel Service Centre was started in 1989.

Agrocel Industries has two major divisions, for marine chemicals and for agriculture services. The agriculture service division was established in order to provide everything that the farmers needed, at a fair price. It is committed to progressive, regenerative and sustainable agriculture (Mission Statement of Agrocel Service Centres).

The division has two main lines of business; farmer services including agricultural extension, input supply, hiring of equipment, and marketing of organically grown produce through fair trade channels.

The Agriculture Service division was launched in 1988 with a large farmers' seminar which was organised on the basis of a detailed survey of farmers' needs in the Kutch region. It was attended by almost 700 farmers from all over Kutch, and it was clear from the outset that Agrocel's services would be well-received. It was initially estimated that

Agrocel would break even in the fourth year of its operations, but it made a profit in 1991 and has been profitable since that time.

Agrocel set up a number of simple offices and outreach centres were established as close as possible to the farmers/customers. They are staffed with local people who are selected for their enthusiasm rather than their formal education. The staff are trained to get to know the local farmers and to understand their operations in order to identify business opportunities for the company.

Agrocel starts its work in an area by identifying farmers' needs and providing appropriate agronomic advice. Once the farmers take the advice and see that by following it they can get good crops, they then turn to Agrocel for all their input supplies. Most importantly, Agrocel also helps them by providing market outlets for their crops.

All Agrocel's activities are driven by the twin motives of profit and farmer service. Agrocel does not receive any subsidies, although it does implement development programmes for various agencies on a fee basis. They have helped farmers to start producing organic cotton, basmati rice, cashew, oilseeds and other crops, and Agrocel liaises with the organic certification agencies on behalf of the farmers, as well as actually buying and exporting their organic produce.

The core activities in marketing organically grown produce include ensuring that all the registered producers keep to the rules of organic cultivation as well as obtaining organic certification and managing the logistics. At first Agrocel outsourced the organic certification task, but as the business expanded, Agrocel took over this function.

Agrocel charges a 5% margin on its exports of organic produce, and this is clearly explained to the farmers, according to the fair trade transparency norms. The company absorbs a number of risks related to export trade of this kind, such as the possibility that crops will be rejected, (as happened with a consignment of handpicked selected groundnuts) foreign exchange rate fluctuation and many others.

THE GROWTH OF AGROCEL

Agrocel started in 1988 with one service centre at Koday in Mandvi. For the first two years the centre provided agro-input services to farmers, and in 1990 they started to also provide extension services. In 1998 the centres started to market the farmers' organic crops (Galliara and Singh, 2006).

By 2008 Agrocel had a chain of 19 Agrocel Service Centres in eight different states. In addition to the nine centres in Gujarat, where they started, the others are located in Orissa, Maharashtra, Andhra Pradesh, Tamil Nadu, West Bengal, Haryana and Karnataka. They reached a total of more than 25,000 farmers, 7,000 of whom are in Gujarat. Agrocel's long-term goal is to ensure a sustainable livelihood for these farmers in an environmentally friendly way. They aim to structure the entire supply chain so that the farmers can optimise their returns and Agrocel can at the same time maintain itself without subsidy.

Agrocel's business has increased every year, from around \$34,000 in 1988 to \$4.8 million in 2006–07. The growth of the business is shown in Table 1.

The sales figures include Agrocel's sales of farmers' produce to both domestic and export markets. These make up almost 60% of the total of Agrocel's turnover from the Agriculture service division. The remaining 40% is from input sales to farmers.

Agrocel has over 60 customers for the farmers' produce including fair trade buyers. These include some of the largest national and international companies and NGOs such as:

- Bheda Brothers and Mahesh Agro of Mumbai;
- Maral Overseas of Indore;
- Vericott Limited;
- Marks and Spencer;
- Traidcraft of the United Kingdom;
- Oxfam Belgium.

AGROCEL'S COTTON INTERVENTION

During its work, Agrocel came into contact with cotton farmers in Mandvi and Surendranagar districts of Kutch. They were in difficulties because cotton prices were unstable and unremunerative as a result of the United States and European Union dumping cheap and subsidised cotton on world markets. There was also serious overuse of chemical pesticides, which pushed the farmers even further into debt. Agrocel was already

Table 1: Growth of the agriculture service division.

Time	Farmers	Domestic* (Rs.)	Exports* (Rs.)	Total* (Rs.)	Land area in acres (= 4,047 m^2)
Start	500	16.5	—	16.5	6,000
2000	1,150	223	—	223	13,800
2001	2,575	300.99	72.74	373.73	30,900
2002	5,056	533.24	74.4	607.64	60,672
2003	6,098	686.13	75.28	761.41	73,176
2004	9,143	1,198.42	43.69	1,242.1	109,716
2005	12,978	1,171.59	154.22	1,325.8	155,736
2006	15,700	1,307.86	284.45	1,592.3	188,400
2007	25,000	2,130.15	288.84	2,419	240,000
2008	45,000	NA	NA	NA	540,000
2009	60,000			0	720,000
Expected					

Source: Agrocel Service Centre: Company Profile.

* in lakhs

familiar with this issue because it had large sums outstanding from farmers and the dealers who sold to them. These pesticides also degraded the environment and injured the people who worked on the farms.

In order to address these long-standing problems, Agrocel decided to assist the farmers to produce pure high-quality organic fair trade cotton, and to provide a market for them in high-end European markets through fair trade distribution channels.

At first Agrocel bought the organic cotton from farmers and sold it through their existing personal contacts. During this process they met a British fair trade specialist, Abigail Garner. She trained the Agrocel team for 18 months in all the different aspects of cotton processing, and she was then joined by Thomas Petit from France. In 1999 they started a company in England under the name Vericott, being an abbreviation for "vertical integration in cotton", and under their supervision the first consignment of T-shirts was sold under the fair trade label to OXFAM, Belgium. The T-shirts sold well, and Vericott worked with Agrocel to develop a business model that included an integrated farming package and management of the entire cotton supply chain, including ginning, spinning, tailoring and access to the retail market (Galliara and Singh, 2006).

Agrocel maintained its focus on providing agro-inputs and extension services to the farmers. It outsources the task of cotton processing through the various stages of ginning, spinning, weaving and, tailoring to different firms near the relevant service centres, but Agrocel still manages the entire process and the marketing of the final product of each stage. Agrocel offers a range of products made from organic cotton, as shown below (see Table 2).

Table 2: Agrocel's product mix.

Product	Percentage of total product mix
Fibre	40
Yarn	40
Fabric	5
Ready-mades	15

Vericott marketed Agrocel's products to various fair trade organisations, and introduced them to a number of new customers, some of which were fair trade organisations such as OXFAM, while others were purely commercial organisations whose management were beginning to appreciate that organic fair trade products could command a good market. In 2001 their efforts led to an introduction to the Shell Foundation, who started a project called "Straight from the Cotton Fields" in partnership with Agrocel to introduce 500 small farmers to organic cotton cultivation. Shell Foundation provided seed capital to cover the start-up costs of conversion for the farmers, and they also provided business mentoring and other assistance to set up market links and to ensure that the venture was sustainable (Galliara and Singh, 2006). In 2005, Agrocel linked up with the Marks and Spencer retail chain to develop an "Organic Yoga wear" range for their retail stores in UK. This was priced at £58 a set, or over $100, and the range did not sell well, but this was the first time a high street retailer had stocked clothes made from fair trade cotton, and it did bring Agrocel to the attention of a wide range of commercial buyers.

By 2008 the volumes involved had increased and there was a need for more farmers to supply more organic cotton, quickly. Agrocel received orders for more than 8,000 tonnes of cotton, and their main challenge was to increase supply in order to satisfy the growing demand.

THE COTTON VALUE CHAIN

Agrocel's task is complicated by the fact that the production of cotton based goods is both politically and organisationally complex. Cotton passes through several hands and may cross many international borders as it moves from the grower's fields to the retailer's shelves.

The cotton fibre and seed grow in a pod called a boll which develops from the flowers of cotton plants and opens when the cotton plant is mature. After the cotton is harvested, the cotton bolls are taken to a ginnery which removes the fibre from the seed. The fibre is then packaged into bales weighing about 200 kgs, and the seed is pressed into cottonseed oil and is used in processed foods for people or fed to livestock (Product Sector Study, 2005).

A sample of cotton fibre from each bale is tested for strength, length and colour. Cotton spinning mills buy the cotton bales based on these qualities and process the fibre into spun yarn. A textile mill then processes the yarn into woven or knitted fabric.

The fabric will finally be transported to a garment manufacturing shop, which is often in a low-wage country, where it will be cut and sewn into the final garment. This complete range of activities is required to take cotton from the farmer's field to making a garment or other item. Thereafter it must pass through a further stage of the value chain before it reaches the retail shop and the final consumer.

Table 3 lists the main actors in each stage of the conventional cotton value chain.

This conventional cotton supply chain for exports includes traders, or "middlemen" at the level of raw cotton procurement, selling cotton lint to spinners, selling of yarn to knitters or weavers and then selling the cloth/fabric to exporters. Thereafter, of course, further traders such as importers, wholesalers and retailer are involved in reaching the user.

Agrocel is focused at the farmers' end of this value chain, and has been able to shorten the supply chain and maximise the returns to the small producers.

Table 3: The main actors in each stage of the conventional cotton value chain.

Input supplies	Pesticides/Herbicides producers/Fertilisers producers/Seed producers/ Machinery and Equipment suppliers/Land owners (often different from growers)
Cotton and textile production	Cotton growers, ginners, spinners, textile manufacturers
Middlemen: Seed cotton to ginners	Village level trader, main trader
Traders and merchants	Traders and merchants to provide lint cotton to spinners
Marketing	Distributors, wholesalers, retailers

Table 4: Comparative net revenue of farmers from an acre of land.

Inputs/Operation	Cost per acre	
	Organic (Rs.)	Conventional (Rs.)
Land preparation	2272.22	2456.67
Seed	83.33	750.00
Fertiliser	3240.00	4224.50
Sowing	183.33	268.33
Irrigation	2400.00	2900.00
Weeding	840.00	898.33
Plant protection	173.00	1500.00
Harvesting	1888.89	2250.00
Other cost	555.56	666.67
Total cost of production	11636.33	15914.50
Total yield of crop (kgs)	782.22	1100.00
Cost of production per kg	**14.88**	**14.47**
Price gain by farmer	21511.05	29040.00
Other benefit (fair trade premium)	1720.89	0
Total gain by farmers	23231.94	29040.00
Selling price	29.70	26.40
Gross profit to farmers	11595.61	13125.50
Gross profit per kg	**14.8**	**11.9**

The first major change that Agrocel has introduced has been at the farmers' level. Organic cotton involves lower input costs and produces higher yields than conventional cotton, and the profit margins are also higher. Table 4 compares the net revenue of a farmer from an acre of land in conventional and organic cotton.

As the table shows, the yield per acre of land is 29% higher in conventional farming while the cost of production per kg is approximately the same. The gross profit per kg of production, however, is almost 20% more from organic. The figures show the costs of the start-up phase for a farm converting to organic practices. Once the farm is completely organic, after three to five years, the yield per acre of land goes up by almost 10% while the input costs go down by 12–15%. The triple effect of the increase in yield, the reduction in production cost and the price premium for organic, means that organic farmers earn more or less the same as in conventional farming in the long-run. At the same time, the soil fertility is improved over time, while in the case of conventional farming; fertility goes down.

Agrocel has not taken over the middlemen's role in order to maximise its own profits. The motive has been to help the farmers earn a steady, reliable and sustainable income, and at the same time for Agrocel itself to maintain its focus on the area of its expertise, which is agro-input services and marketing. Agrocel outsources the intermediate processes to existing intermediaries, and does not itself compete with them.

Agrocel operates all along the cotton vertical chain, and its operation is unusual in that more than 90% of the farmers who work with Agrocel are small-scale farmers. Agrocel has built up a mutually supportive relationship with these farmers. They have a choice of markets but they also have the benefit of assured demand. They get farm inputs at reasonable prices, advice which is free of cost, and they enjoy the benefits of organic and fair trade certification. At the same time, they can sell in whatever market they chose. Agrocel acts as a buyer of last resort and in principle has accepted the responsibility to buy from the farmers if they wish to sell.

The farmers own their cotton, and are not contracted to Agrocel in advance, but it is usually more remunerative to sell to them because they are able to pay the premium for organic produce, and the fair trade premium.

In the value chain, Agrocel has taken the position of different middlemen, but they can still perform the processes for which they are equipped, at a reasonable price. Agrocel does not replace them, and does not disturb the role of various players in the chain.

While the Agrocel model does displace some of the middlemen who only buy and sell in the supply chain, without performing any physical processing, the impact on these small village traders is not significant.

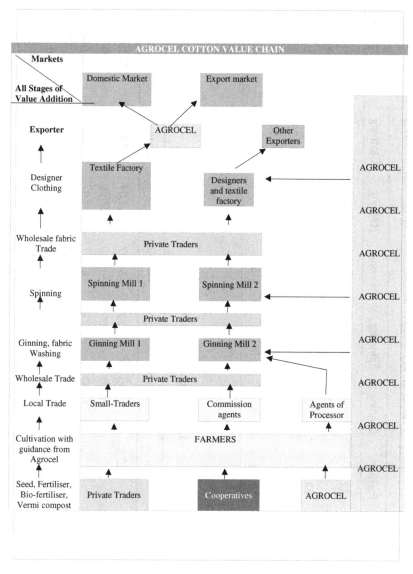

Figure 1: Agrocel value chain.

Their role is very seasonal and does not add substantially to their incomes, since they are mostly farm owners themselves. The following figure (see Fig. 1) shows how the Agrocel value chain works, and illustrates the roles of the various intermediaries.

Table 5: Agrocel model.

Particulars	Farmer	Ginning	Spinning	Weaving	Dyeing	Clothing	Global retailers
Procurement cost (Rs.)	22.00	29.70	38.55	63.82	74.53	114.83	181.79
Processing/Marketing cost (Rs.)		8.00	16.00	7.50	28.00	25.00	210.00
Average cost price (Rs.)	22.00	37.70	54.55	71.32	102.53	139.83	391.79
Average selling price (Rs.)	29.70	38.55	63.82	74.53	114.83	181.79	450.55
Profit (Rs.)	7.70	0.85	9.27	3.21	12.30	41.95	58.77
Profit margin (%)	30–35	2–2.5	13–20	4–5	10–15	25–35	15–25

Table 6: Conventional model.

Particulars	Farmer	Ginning	Spinning	Weaving	Dyeing	Clothing	Global retailers
Procurement cost (Rs.)	22.00	26.00	32.72	56.07	67.07	98.77	151.62
Processing cost/Marketing cost (Rs.)		6.00	15.00	7.50	27.00	25.00	200.00
Cost price (Rs.)	22.00	32.00	47.72	63.57	94.07	123.77	351.62
Average selling price (Rs.)	26.40	32.72	56.07	67.07	98.77	151.62	450.00
Profit (Rs.)	4.40	0.72	8.35	3.50	4.70	27.85	98.38
Profit margin (%)	15–20	2–2.5	15–20	5–6	3–7	20–25	20–35

Tables 5 & 6 compare the Agrocel value chain with conventional value chains and the amounts of value added at each stage, for one T-shirt made out of Agrocel cotton, sold through a retail chain such as Marks and Spencer in the UK.

It is difficult to compare the exact cost at different stages of cotton processing because of difference in batch sizes at each stage of value addition to cotton, but in this table, an attempt is made to analyse the cost at different transaction points along the value chain for a medium size cotton T-shirt of 24 count cotton. The process that is followed to make a T-shirt is the same as has already been described, and the cost price, the processing cost, the selling price and the profit margin at each level have been calculated based on the market prices for cotton fibre, yarn and fabric.

Approximately 1 kg of seed cotton as harvested by the farmer is required to manufacture a T-shirt of this size. The value of the cotton increases exponentially once it leaves the farmers' hands and passes through the different players in the chain. The ginning process removes two-thirds of the weight of the actual cotton boll, and the remaining one-third is retrieved as lint or cotton fibre which goes on to the next processing stage.

Farmers make a 15–20% margin in conventional cotton farming while they make between 30–35% when they work through Agrocel. The ginners' profit margin is only 2–2.5% because ginning is a very simple process. The spinners' margin is higher than that of others in the supply chain because spinning requires a very high initial capital investment. They also enjoy substantial economies of scale as the minimum batch size for spinning at most mills is 15 tonnes. Higher prices are charged for smaller batches. Agrocel is able to consolidate the buyers' requirements and can therefore work on the optimum batch size.

Agrocel charges a 1–3% service charge to cover the cost of its operations and management, but the total value chain is still competitive with conventional systems.

The table also shows that the retailers' costs are more than 100% of its buying cost. They have to incur all the expenses of branding, advertising, merchandising, import duty, value added tax and so on, which in total amount is almost the same as the factory cost of the product.

The conventional trade figures vary from case to case as wages, working conditions, workers' facilities and other costs are not fixed, such as when workers are paid less than the legal minimum wage. The Agrocel fair trade system ensures that all these costs are equitable, that fair wages are paid, without gender discrimination, and that the conditions are reasonable. This can increase the costs, but it also maintains stability as well as serving valuable social objectives.

THE IMPACT OF AGROCEL'S COTTON INITIATIVE

An independent study (Traidcraft, 2005) of the Agrocel cotton intervention, conducted in 2005, shows that the farmers working with Agrocel have on average achieved a 15% increase in their incomes. Another study, conducted in 2004, found that the net earnings per hectare for Agrocel cotton farmers had increased from Rs. 35,332 in 1998 to Rs. 57,940 in 2004 (Dalal Mott McDonald, 2004).

KARSAN CHAUDHARY

Karsan Manji Chaudhary is 50 years old and lives on his 15-acre holding with his wife and their two children. His association with Agrocel goes back to the start of the programme when he attended the early meetings and learned about different crop and pest management practices. He realised the benefits of the new methods, and started organic farming in 1998, with cotton and other crops such as castor, gram and sesame. As a result of these changes, the family's income has risen by almost 30% and he is managing to save as much as 40% of his earnings for his family.

If he wishes, Karsan can sell his entire cotton crop to Agrocel at the current market price plus an 8% premium. The guaranteed market

(Continued)

(Continued)

helps him to plan his cultivation and also to look for the best price in the market. Over time, organic farming also improves his land's performance.

"Now I am 50 years old, but I am doing very well in the field. From the good price of the cotton I am saving for the future development of our family. I have also repaired my home which I built 12 years ago. If we work hard in our fields and we get a better price, then we are happy!"

There have also been a number of clear environmental gains for farmers who moved from conventional to organic farming. Their health is improved, and they are making better use of water, energy and other inputs. There is anecdotal evidence that with the use of appropriate technologies, some young people in the area are choosing to get into farming rather than to migrate to the cities in search of employment, and more parents are able to keep their children in school.

The Agrocel cotton farmers are sure that they can sell their cotton. The buyers provide short-term advance finance through Agrocel, as is required by the Fair Trade norms. Agrocel also sells inputs on credit. Once the produce has been sold the farmers pay back the input cost, without interest. This enables them to buy the seeds and tools they need to cultivate their land.

Based on consumer demand, one of Britain's biggest clothing retailers has launched a major new campaign called "Look behind the label" to inform its customers about the way its products are sourced and made. Companies such as Marks and Spencers and Vericott have benefited by getting authentic organic products, and they have also gained good media exposure because of their pioneering steps in sourcing fair trade goods. These companies want to build close links with Agrocel so that they can benefit from the shared values of good service, high-quality, integrity, respect and social responsibility towards all the stakeholders, from the producers of the raw material to the final customers.

REFERENCES

Dalal Mott McDonald (2004). Agri Impact Assessment Study for Organic Cotton Farmers of Kutch & Surendranagar. http://www.bdsknowledge.org/dyn/bds/bdssearch

Galliara, M and R Singh (2006). Agrocel — A bloom in the desert, Narsee Monjee Institute of Management Studies, Mumbai.

Mission Statement of Agrocel Service Centers. http://www.agrocel.co.in/mission.htm

Product Sector Study-Textile Industries by International Resources for Fairer Trade (IRFT) in 2005 (internal document).

Traidcraft (2005). The development of environmentally and socially sustainable livelihoods for independent small-holder cotton farmers in Gujarat, rural India.

Case Study **8**

bioRe Organic Cotton

Rajeev Baruah

INTRODUCTION

bioRe works with farmers in the Nimar valley in the central Indian state of Madhya Pradesh. The valley lies at around 200–300m above sea level along the Narmada River, and is bordered by the Vindhya hills in the north and the Satpura Range to the south. The valley is part of the central Indian cotton belt.

Farming systems in the region are based around cotton. Cotton is grown in rotation with cereals such as wheat, maize, and sorghum, pulses including soybean, pigeon pea, chickpea, and *"moong"* bean, and other food crops such as chillis and onions.

The climate is semi-arid, with an average annual rainfall of 800 mm in a single monsoon which usually lasts from mid-June to September.

bioRe India was started in 1991 and later became an independent company. It established the bioRe textile chain that links farmers and their families, the textile industry and the trade as equal partners. The aim was to improve the livelihoods of small farmers by introducing and developing organic cotton production and by integrating farmers into the textile value

Note: Units of measurement in the Indian numbering system: lakh = 100,000; crore = 10,000,000. Indian Rupees (Rs.) where appropriate are converted into USD at a rate of approximately Rs. 50 = $1.00; Rs. 1 lakh = $2,000; Rs. 1 crore = $200,000.

chain. The entire supply chain was integrated in 1995 when Coop, a retail company, joined it. Coop is Switzerland's second-largest supermarket chain and Europe's market leader in ecological-social products. Through this partnership, textiles made of bioRe cotton have entered the international market.

The farmer picks and sells the seed cotton but the lint cotton remains after the seed has been removed, and is approximately 33% of the harvest by weight is what is marketed.

HISTORY AND DEVELOPMENT OF THE VALUE CHAIN

bioRe began as the private initiative of an Indian industrialist, Mrigendra Jalan (MJ), and a Swiss cotton yarn trader, Patrick Hohmann (PH), the Managing Director of Remei AG, a Swiss Company trading cotton yarn from India. MJ asked PH to join the board of a new spinning mill, part of Maikaal Fibres Ltd, that was being established in Madhya Pradesh. PH

Table 1: Chronology of bioRe.

Year	No. of farmers	Seed cotton (tonnes)	Lint cotton (tonnes)	Value of lint cotton (Rs.)
1992/1993	Pilot			
1993/1994	223	206	68	47,60,000
1994/1995	568	516	185	1,29,50,000
1995/1996	649	1,366	468	3,27,60,000
1996/1997	688	2,096	713	4,99,10,000
1997/1998	699	1,870	627	4,38,90,000
1998/1999	888	2,043	705	4,93,50,000
1999/2000	1,061	2,584	853	5,97,10,000
2004/2005	1,516	3,127	1,032	7,22,40,000
2005/2006	2,193	4,284	1,413	9,89,10,000
2006/2007	4,991	5,930	2,016	14,11,20,000
2007/2008	7,890	8,500*	2,700**	18,90,00,000

* Estimated.

** The value of lint cotton has been given as an average, although the actual rate varied from year to year.

wanted the new venture to explore the idea of organic cotton growing with farmers who were near to the new spinning mill, with the idea that the farmers could eventually be linked to the market. At that time there was no market for clothes made from organically grown cotton, but PH and his team at Remei AG had seen the potential. The project continued to develop using ordinary cotton until the end of 1990 when the newly-established spinning mill started to have severe financial problems, largely due to poor management. This had adversely effected payments to the farmers and weakened their commitment to bioRe. In 2002 all the work with the farmers was moved to a new company called bioRe India Ltd.

They recruited an organic farming consultant from Emerson College in the UK, and the bioRe team met the farmers to decide how they could be organised, and how they could be advised on changing their systems of farming. At the same time, Remei started to look into marketing what the farmers produced.

This case study describes the production end of the value chain, how bioRe works with the farmers who produce the cotton and what benefits they and the region receive as a result of being part of the value chain.

bioRe aims to be a leading organisation in organic products, by providing the best advice and services to organic farmers of, by linking them to markets and by providing the down-stream customers with good quality products.

LINKING THE FARMER TO THE VALUE CHAIN

The farmers are linked to the value chain through their production of organic cotton. Two organisations work from different sides to achieve the

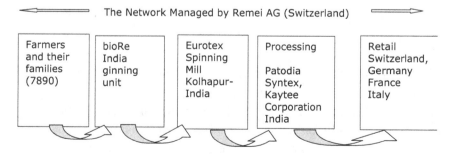

Figure I: Textile value chain.

same objective. They are bioRe India Ltd, a private limited company, and the bioRe Association, a non-profit organisation which is responsible for addressing social issues among the farmers.

In 2002 Remei invested half a million rupees in bioRe India Limited, with the eventual intention of handing over the shares to the farmers in order to provide the producers with a capital stake in the business. The company started to hand over the shares to individual farmers but it became clear that the farmers did not understand their value. It was then decided that it would be better to give the shares to a joint body such as a co-operative, but this stage has not yet been reached. In the meantime, Remei has handed its shares over to the bioRe foundation.

The present shareholdings in bioRe India are as follows:

- 85% held by bioRe foundation
- 11% held by employees of bioRe India
- 4% held by farmers

The foundation and the company carry out different parts of the total undertaking.

bIORE ASSOCIATION — THE SOCIAL ASPECTS OF THE VALUE CHAIN

The bioRe Association was established in 2003 in order to clearly differentiate between the commercial and the welfare activities of bioRe. It is an integral part of the bioRe value chain through which the farming community, which is the first link in the chain, receives benefits from the final customers. The bioRe foundation was established in Switzerland in 1997 with donations from Remei, Coop Switzerland and other retailers, and is the main agency for social development in the farmer community.

One of the first investments made by the bioRe Association was an organic agriculture training center and an experimental farm. This provided a much needed platform for the farmers, where they could voice their problems and look for solutions. The experimental farm shows the farmers that organic farming is not merely good in theory but that it also works in practice.

The vision of the Association is to empower organic farmers and their communities by facilitating education and infrastructure, by addressing local needs and thus leading to a holistic and sustainable development. The Association works in education and training, health and hygiene, the environment, the development of infrastructure related to organic and bio-dynamic agriculture and general social and livelihood development.

Figure 2 shows the number of farmers who attended training and the number of days training that took place at the training center and at farmer field schools in the villages.

The farmer field schools were started in 2007 and about 3,000 farmers have attended them. These schools train "core farmers" who then go on to spread the notion of organic farming in their communities.

India generally has a high rate of illiteracy with very poor educational facilities, particularly in rural areas such as the Nimar Valley of MP. The bioRe Association conducted a survey and found that there was a serious need for schools in the area. They started three schools without knowing whether parents would send their children, but they were well supported and by 2008 there were seven schools with almost 300 pupils.

The first school was started with 32 children in village Narsinghpur, in a farmer's house. The farmer then donated a piece of land for a school building, and the bioRe foundation donated the cost of construction. The new school was inaugurated in March 2008.

The Association also started three adult education centres in an effort to improve literacy in the area, which is only around 50–60%. Over 100

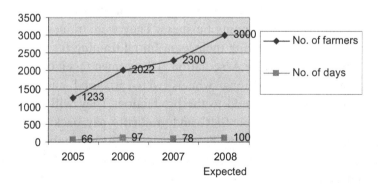

Figure 2: Graph showing the number of farmers who attended the training.

farmers and others have enrolled in them. bioRe has also opened a village information center with the aim to inform farmers and villagers about the programme and the benefits they can get from the various state government schemes that are available.

bioRe works in a remote rural area of central India where there are no effective primary health facilities. In 2006 COOP Switzerland donated a mobile health unit to the community. It is the first unit of its type in the region and is effectively a hospital on wheels. It has its own doctor and an expert staff and during its first year the unit treated more than 5,000 patients. The unit's fees are less than half of those charged by private clinics, and the unit maintains a data base and health profile of all its patients.

The Association also helps encourage farmers to build toilets and provides half the construction cost. A number of small tree plantations have been planted with help from the Association, and the farmers have also installed 200 bio-gas plants to save fuel. The bioRe Association promotes various types of household livelihoods in addition to the cultivation of organic cotton.

They have promoted 61 self-help groups (SHGs), and the members, who include both men and women, are taking loans from the groups' accumulated funds for a variety of purposes. The bioRe SHG program was started in May 2007. These groups consist of 10–12 bioRe farmers, farm workers or women, who save small amounts of money in a common fund every month. Their savings will help them either by inter-member loans within the groups, or by funding an economic activity. A women's SHG in the village of Karondiya has used their capital to start a group spinning business. They were trained by bioRe, and are successfully repaying their loan. Initial training for the women was provided by the bioRe Association. The women received a stipend for 3 months, new spinning wheels were procured and now the women's earnings are related to the production. They will save some money every month in their SHG and gradually pay back the cost of the spinning wheel that they have received. Interestingly after this several young men in the village have been encouraged by this example to take up handloom weaving. The young boys of the village have developed a keen interest in hand weaving and are being trained in this skill.

bIORE INDIA — THE PRODUCT

In 2007 bioRe was working on organic cotton in 460 villages with 7,890 farmers from Madhya Pradesh and part of Maharashtra. This represents a major improvement for the farmers, and is the outcome of five years of activity.

The Central Indian cotton belt is semi-arid, and the farmers there can be divided into two types. The more fortunate are those who farm better quality irrigated land which is located closer to market places. They tend to have relatively large land holdings, they have some education and have better access to credit and other services. These are referred to as "mainland farmers".

The cotton farmers in the interior of the region, where the irrigation facilities are limited, are generally tribals. They have smaller land holdings, poorer access to markets, credit and government schemes and are known as "hinterland farmers".

Both these groups farm in traditional ways. The government does provide some advisory services for farmers, but they are inadequate and do not help farmers achieve sustainable development. The people who actually influence the farmers' lives and their cotton farming are the local traders who sell fertilisers, seeds and pesticides. Some of these traders also buy crops from the farmers, and the seed and pesticide manufacturers are mainly concerned with their own profits. They naturally wish to maximise the sales of their products to the farmers.

The farmers, and in particular the smaller tribal "hinterland farmers", generally borrow from money lenders, and the larger "mainland farmers" are in a better position to access institutional credit with lower interest rates. There is rampant over-use of fertilisers and pesticides, and genetically modified cotton seeds are rapidly gaining ground fast. Out of the $480 million worth of pesticides used in India every year, $300–$320 million is used for cotton.

bioRe works within this context. The primary aim of the company is to promote organic cultivation and to ensure that all the benefits — ecological, social, and economic — are fairly distributed among the stakeholders. bioRe is a profit-making company but it pays no dividends at all. Profits are reinvested in building the business for the future.

bioRe worked mainly with "mainland farmers" at the start, but in 2003 bioRe started working with "hinterland farmers". Initially, there were more "mainland farmers" but now this trend has changed, especially with the arrival of genetically modified cotton. The majority of the "mainland farmers" are doing fairly well and do not wish to change. They can afford to buy fertilisers and pesticides and are less keen to change their agricultural practices. The "hinterland farmers" are more open to change, and they are also in urgent need of higher prices, better markets, and more services.

The primary task of the bioRe team is to identify ways in which these cotton farmers can profitably adopt organic agriculture, and to devise practical steps that can be implemented by the farmers. The team keeps up-to-date regionally and nationally.

The annual routine of bioRe's main operations is as follows:

- February, farmers' registration
- Continuous, farmers' training
- May–September, input supply, mainly seeds
- May–January/February, crop monitoring and on-farm advisory services
- May–January/February, internal inspection for organic compliance
- September–March, raw cotton purchase
- September–March, cotton ginning
- September–June/July, lint cotton and cotton seed sales
- At various times, sometimes unannounced, external organic compliance inspection.

The costs of all these activities are covered by bioRe on a commercial basis, and the Association provides no subsidies for these operations.

bioRe operates in accordance with the European regulations for the organic production of agricultural products (ECC No. 2092/9,1) as applicable in India. bioRe focuses on soil fertility and pest control, the two major aspects of organic cotton cultivation that are different from the normal methods.

Compost replaces chemical fertilisers. The farmers are trained how to mix cow dung with various farm residues to get good quality compost and crop rotation. When a farmer cannot rotate his crops, he is shown how legumes can be grown at the same time as cotton, giving him additional income and helping with food security.

Farmers are trained to manage their crops as naturally as possible. They reduce pest attacks by using compost for fertilisation, which makes the plants less susceptible to pests and disease. They plant trap and border crops, maize and sunflower, and also plant black and green grams which divert some pests away from the cotton. Other crops, such as garlic, chilli and some local plants such as neem also repel certain pests.

TWO INDIVIDUAL FARMERS

Amar Singh is a marginal farmer with four acres of land who joined the bioRe program in 2002. He grows cotton on half of his land and food crops such as maize, pigeon pea, "*moong*" beans or wheat on the rest. He now understands the importance of crop rotation, and he only grows cotton on half of his land. This helps with food security and also maintains soil fertility. He was given financial assistance to build a bio-gas plant which means he no longer uses cow dung and firewood for cooking. This reduces the problem of smoke, which used to lead to health problems in the family, and the cow dung which has been through the plant is more suitable than raw cow dung for making compost. Amar Singh's situation has significantly improved over the last six years. His cultivation costs are lower, but he has maintained without lower yields.

Sadhu Madhav was one of the very first farmers to join the bioRe programme in 1994; he has been an organic farmer and part of the bioRe textile value chain for 14 years. He has been trained in organic farming at the bioRe training centre, in his village and on his own farm. He owns eight acres of land. Half is planted with cotton and half with other crops. He took a loan to build a bio-gas plant and to construct a cow shed so that he could collect cow urine to spray on his fields. The slurry from the biogas plant is also excellent manure.

Before 1994 Sadhu Madhav took loans from money lenders at very high interest rates. This put him under great pressure and he

(Continued)

(Continued)

was heavily in debt, but since 1994 he has been able to gradually pay off his debts because he can sell all his cotton to bioRe at a fair price plus an "organic premium". He has been able to support his son's education, and his son is now studying at the Indore College of Agriculture.

OTHER PARTS OF THE VALUE CHAIN

Ginning is the the first stage of processing for cotton. The seeds are removed from the fibre and the cotton is pressed into bales of 175 kg to be transported to the spinning mills. All the ginneries in India are located in rural areas as they have to be close to where the cotton is grown. Because of their locations and because they are only used seasonally, they have not been well managed professionally. The working conditions are bad, child labour is used, and the statutory taxes are not paid. These issues are now being addressed in new ginneries, but before bioRe set up its own ginnery factory in 2003, it had to sub-contract the process to other firms. The new bioRe ginnery is the only one in India to be SA 8000 certified, and is one of the very few companies in the world to receive such a certification.

There are well established industries in India for the subsequent stages of the cotton value chain, including spinning, knitting, weaving, dyeing and garment processing. Many problems arise because there are too many varieties of cotton and quality is hard to control. There are also many ecological, labour and social issues in the industry, as there are in most industries in India.

Coop Switzerland started co-operating with Remei AG in 1995 when they bought 70 tonnes of organic cotton for processing into yarn and clothing. Together, Coop and Remei AG have developed a major market for organic textiles, and their Naturaline brand dominates the world market. In 2005 alone, more than three million garments were sold, made from over 1,400 tonnes of organic cotton. This long-standing partnership received the "Business Award for Sustainable Development Partnerships" at the United Nations Johannesburg Summit in 2002.

Monoprix of France has sold bioRe garments since 2002, and Coop Italy has sold them since 2003.

The bioRe experience shows that integrated value chains can benefit small producers. There are immense challenges at all levels, in particular with small and marginal farmers, and effective collaboration demands consideration of all the aspects of their lives. The bottom line however is that the smallest marginal producers can be included in modern value chains, if the main participants can mobilise the necessary infrastructure, expertise, and above all, the will to succeed.

FURTHER READING

Eyhorn, F (2003). Organic farming for sustainable livelihoods in developing countries: The case of cotton in India, VDF Zurich.

Organic cotton reduces poverty
www.fibl.org/english/fibl/documents/acitvity-report06/international.pdf

The Impact of Organic Cotton Farming on the Livelihoods of ...
www.fibl.org/english/cooperation/projects/documents/executive_summary.pdf

Cotton Guide mit Cover
www.fibl.org/english/cooperation/projects/documents/cotton-guide-small.pdf

Mid-term Newsletter Maikaal Cotton Research Project
www.fibl.org/english/cooperation/projects/documents/newsletter-cotton-research.pdf

FiBL [Research Institute of Organic Agriculture]
www.fibl.org/english/cooperation/projects/organiccotton2.php

FiBL Tropen
www.fibl.org/aktuell/pm/2007/0830-tropen.php

Organic Cotton Training Manual
www.fibl.org/english/cooperation/projects/documents/cotton-training-manual-text.pdf

Documents annexes sur la culture biologique du cotton
www.fibl.org/english/cooperation/projects/documents/resume.pdf

www.bioreindia.com
www.remei.ch
www.biore.ch

Chapter **5**

Inclusive Value Chains in Fisheries, Honey, Coffee and Poultry

Introduction

All the value chains that are described in this book are inclusive, in that they include small-scale producers whom one might expect to have been excluded by the "modernisation" of the distribution channels of what they cultivated. The producers in the following four cases, however, are in some sense "super-marginalised". They come from groups, and places, which are among the poorest in India, where traditional assistance programmes have typically foundered for want of political will and effective delivery systems. Nevertheless, all the producers are benefiting substantially from the value chains in which they have been included, and many have multiplied their earnings by many times.

They include so-called "tribals", and village women, and fishermen from the coast of the Bay of Bengal. They live in Bihar, Orissa, and rural Madhya Pradesh, and in the "tribal belt" of Andhra Pradesh, close to the border of Orissa. They harvest honey, shrimps and coffee, and they rear poultry. None of them are farmers in the traditional sense, and their traditional livelihoods are in some ways nearer to hunting and gathering than to modern agriculture. The cases describe the processes through which these people have been linked to modern markets, and the challenges which were faced and which still remain.

Three of the four value chains were initiated by "external" agencies which are not themselves members of the chains, and whose initial costs were quite heavily subsidised by government agencies or from other sources. EDA Rural Systems is a rural development consultancy firm, and

PRADAN and the Naandi Foundation are non-government organisations. These agencies aim to withdraw from the field as soon as the producers' institutions which they have promoted are able to stand on their own feet, managerially as well as financially. Such withdrawal is or will be a good indicator of success.

The promoting agencies are facilitators rather than participators, and their remuneration is not directly dependent on the profitability of the producers or of any other members of the chain. Their staff are decently paid, but not at corporate levels, and they are motivated in part at least by their wish to assist people who are less fortunate than themselves.

Falcon Fisheries, the promoters of the coastal shrimp production in Orissa, is a privately-owned for-profit company. The company finances and otherwise assists its small-scale shrimp producers not because of any commitment to "corporate social responsibility", or because it has received government or donor funding to cover the costs, but because they are the most reliable suppliers of good material and hence they are in the long-term the least expensive suppliers. It is good business to buy from them.

These four case studies show that it is possible for even the smallest and most marginalised producers, who live in places which are remote both physically and socially, to be members of modern integrated value chains which sell to sophisticated markets, in competition with powerful large-scale producers. The coffee from Araku Valley commands a premium price partly because of its origins, and it is marketed on that basis. The other three products compete in totally "open" market situations, without any special promotion of features which are linked to the producers. All four value chains are succeeding, and their sales are growing rapidly, because they have been effectively designed, on the basis of painstaking analysis, often over several years of trial and error, and because their development has been well managed.

Case Study **9**

Falcon Marine Exports

Rajeev Roy

Tara Pattnaik, the Chairman of Falcon Marine Exports, is justifiably proud. In 2008, for the tenth consecutive year, the Seafood Exporters Association of India (SEAI) recognised Falcon as the biggest seafood exporter in India. This is no mean achievement for a company which had been started by a first generation entrepreneur and was based in a state better known for poverty and for famine-related deaths.

An important contribution of Falcon is the way they have expanded their supplier base to include small producers. The highly lucrative business of shrimp farming had been the preserve of rich landowners, businessmen and large companies. In Orissa, Falcon was instrumental in facilitating the growth of small, sustainable shrimp farms. Now, all along the Orissa coast, villagers have started shrimp farms in their small land holdings or on leased land. Falcon's support and assistance to these farmers has enabled this to happen.

Note: Units of measurement in the Indian numbering system: lakh = 100,000; crore = 10,000,000. Indian Rupees (Rs.) where appropriate are converted into USD at a rate of approximately Rs. 50 = $1.00; Rs. 1 lakh = $2,000; Rs. 1 crore = $200,000.

ORISSA

The state of Orissa is in north-eastern India and has a coastline of 400 km along the Bay of Bengal. Orissa has been called the land of plenty but of poor outcomes. The plentiful natural resources of the state have not yet been properly harnessed to ensure rapid and sustained economic development. Orissa is rich in mineral resources, it possesses significant industrial potential, and has promising prospects in mineral-based and agro-processing industries. The state's geographic proximity to Southeast Asia, combined with its low-cost labor, could make it an attractive platform for export-oriented growth. Compared to many other parts of India, the state enjoys reasonable political stability and law and order which are critical factors for industrial investment. In spite of these favourable factors, new private sector investment is much lower in Orissa than in other Indian states. The industrial growth rate from 1990–2003 was below 2% in Orissa, whereas the Indian average was over 8% (World Bank, 2004).

In spite of many advantages, Orissa lags behind in industrial development. Orissa's dependence on its rich natural resource endowments and its failure to diversify are evident in its industrial structure. This overall lack of development in Orissa is reflected in its low growth rate and low annual per capita income of about Rs. 10,000. Orissa is one of the poorest states in India, with a development and growth performance that lags well behind all-India averages. Half of Orissa's 40 million people live below the official poverty line. The overall gross state domestic product (GSDP) growth rate at 3.7% falls far short of the 6.2% target set by the state government and the all-India average target of 8% per year (World Bank, 2005).

The state lags behind the rest of the country on most indicators of human development and its performance is similar to that of some of the poorest countries in the world.

THE SEAFOOD TRADE

India has a vibrant seafood export business. In 2006–07, India exported over $1,660 million worth of seafood. In terms of export earnings, frozen shrimp was the largest export item, with 54% of the total value, followed by fish with 17%, cuttlefish with 10%, squid with 7% and others such as live and dried products making up the remaining 12% (MPEDA, 2007).

This is a very fragmented industry. Falcon Marine is the largest Indian seafood exporter and their turnover is a little over $40 million. Most exporters confine their operations to a small geographical region and find it hard to grow beyond their catchment area. Large corporate houses have failed miserably in their attempts at this business. Big Indian business groups like Thapar and Godrej and multinational companies like Unilever and Rallis have met with very little success.

Even smaller entrepreneurs have not met with great success. Since 1979, over 1,000 firms have registered with Marine Products Export Development Authority (MPEDA) to export seafood from Orissa, but by 2008 only 13 remain in business. The situation is similar in other states.

Since 1970, the Indian seafood trade and particularly the Orissa trade has been very dependant on Japanese importers. Large Japanese trade houses like Fuji, Mitsui and Marubeni used to import blocks of headless shrimps, which used to go for further reprocessing in food processing units in Japan, Europe or the United States. More recently, the west has shown more interest in Indian seafood. Many retail chains and traders are directly dealing with Indian exporters and this trade has grown. Even though Japan continues to be the main destination for Indian seafood, the USA has caught up and European countries are not far behind. In 2006–07, Japan accounted for 16.15% of Indian seafood exports and the USA was close behind at 16.03%.

FALCON MARINE

Tara Pattnaik quit his job at a nationalised bank and entered the seafood business as a trawler owner in 1977. He was very successful as a trawler owner and he supplied fish and shrimps to ITC, HLL, Rallis and other multinational companies engaged in seafood exports. This continued for some time and he was able to build up a reputation as an astute business-man. Other trawler owners looked up to him and depended on him to give advice and to lead the way. He expanded his business by buying fish from other trawler owners and smaller fishermen and in turn, selling it to the export houses.

The business was growing but he did not feel secure in his business model. He could see that the big corporations were not able to conduct their business to their satisfaction and it seemed likely that their head offices might decide to leave the seafood business altogether. Also, as a supplier of raw material, he was at the mercy of corporate exporters as the balance of power was very heavily tilted in their favour. Pattnaik's business could easily be severely damaged by the whims and fancies of some key employees of these corporate exporters.

In 1982, Tara Pattnaik decided to start Falcon Marine Exports. He took the necessary clearances from the Reserve Bank of India and the Director General of Foreign Trade and commenced operations. In those days, there were a number of restrictions and regulations and the bureaucratic problems posed significant hurdles to entrepreneurs wishing to do business internationally.

He had managed to nurture some contacts among the agents of the Japanese import houses. He used these contacts to get his first export orders. He leased the facilities of a freezing plant in Puri to process procured seafood. The early days were particularly difficult as the export houses tried their best to discredit Tara Pattnaik and some other local suppliers who had also decided to start their own exports.

On the basis of Tara Pattnaik's impressive track record in the seafood business, a bank sanctioned an export packing credit limit of Rs. 6 lakhs. An export packing credit is a credit limit sanctioned by a commercial bank. It defines the maximum amount an exporter can borrow from the bank, against confirmed export orders. Falcon used this money judiciously and managed to stabilise operations. Starting with a turnover of about $120,000 in the first year, Falcon grew to have an annual turnover of about $0.6 million within two years. The next step was to set up his own freezing plant, and Falcon did this in 1986. Pattnaik delayed setting up his own plant until he had started trading in volumes that justified the investment.

THE ERA OF SHRIMP CULTURE

In the early 1990s, shrimp farming started in India in a big way. Businessmen and corporate houses from the cities flocked to the coastal areas, bought up huge tracts of land and set up large corporate aquaculture

Table 1: **Falcon Marine Exports (all seafood).**

Year	Production (in kgs)	Turnover (in cr Rs.)
1983–84	167,724	3.29
1990–91	422,854	12.38
1993–94	1353,799	32.48
1995–96	1,887,030	55.97
1996–97	2,872,462	84.52
1998–99	2,613,045	114.62
2002–03	3,869,025	153.84
2004–05	5,117,150	165.33
2006–07	5,562,320	200.79
2007–08	6,628,154	210.42

Figure 1: **Map outlining Falcon's network.**

farms. Experienced technicians from Taiwan, Indonesia and Thailand were hired as consultants. The latest aquaculture equipment such as aerators and feeders was imported and installed. Orders were placed for imported feed and aquaculture medicines.

A typical shrimp farm consisted of 8–20 ponds of a hectare each. These ponds were about one metre deep and had mud embankments on all sides. It took about 30 days to pump in the sea water and get the ponds ready for shrimp hatchlings. After that, 20-day-old shrimp hatchlings were released into the ponds. The hatchlings were fed and tended to for a period of about 90 days and then harvested. Theoretically, every four months, a single pond with a stocking density of 15 per sq. m, yielded about two tonnes of shrimp, which could be valued at approximately Rs. 150,000 per tonne at average prices in 1994.

There was a mad scramble to start this business in all the coastal states of India, including Orissa. The foreign technicians carried stories of the astounding successes of shrimp farms in South-east Asia. The economics of shrimp farming were amazing. An investment of $2,000 would generate a surplus of $4,000 in one crop of four months' duration and it was theoretically possible to have three crops in a year.

Even though there were some sporadic successes, on the whole, shrimp culture proved to be a huge failure across the nation. In the initial years, some regional pockets did well. In particular, Krishna, East Godavari and West Godavari districts in Andhra Pradesh were very successful. The towns of Nellore and Bhimavaram emerged as major centres for the trade.

Low investment and extensive culture was successful in 24 Parganas and surrounding areas in West Bengal, Chilka Lake in Orissa, Pulicat Lake in Tamil Nadu and parts of Kerala. Other than these areas, most other regions suffered huge losses. Businessmen in Maharashtra, Karnataka and Gujarat were quick to abandon the business and turn their attention elsewhere.

In Orissa too, the coastline was soon dotted with abandoned, unsuccessful shrimp farms. The business of shrimp farming did not come to an end suddenly. It was more of a gradual process, where occasional successes kept the farm owners motivated for a few more seasons. Very often farms would change hands when a fresh lot of businessmen were allured by the prospect of quick money. In the mid 1990s there was a widespread epidemic of the dreaded "white spot" virus that led to a number of crops being wiped out over a span of a few days. Chemicals were used extensively but were not always effective in containing the disease.

Many problems faced the corporate farmers. The roads were very bad in the coastal regions. Many of the farms were not accessible by all-weather roads, and especially in the vital monsoon period, it was difficult to send four-wheeled vehicles to the farms. Some were not accessible even by two wheelers or tractors and had to be reached by boat. Most of the coast was not properly connected to the regional electricity grid. Lack of electricity was a big problem and most of the farms had to depend on their own generators. These generators were expensive to run and needed huge amounts of fuel which had to be regularly transported. The telephone network did not reach all remote coastal villages and most farms did not have a telephone, and the places where the farms were located lacked the conveniences of city life. There were no opportunities for managers, owners or qualified technicians to have any social life, so instead of living on their farms, most of the staff got into the habit of staying in a nearby city and making frequent trips to the farm.

For many corporate farmers in Orissa, the final blow came in 1999, when the super-cyclone caused widespread havoc across the coastal districts of Orissa. In fact, Falcon too had started their own farm which they operated for a few years. It was also shut down in 1999.

A NEW DIRECTION

Gradually, since the early 1990s, Falcon had shifted its procurement focus and had come to depend on shrimp farms instead of sea caught shrimps for the majority of its raw material. This had worked very well. There was a certain predictability about the quality and quantity of raw material procured from a farm. The product also looked better because of its uniform colour and size, unlike sea-caught material, which was in a mix of sizes and colours. Exporters bought from corporate farms and were not directly exposed to the huge risks that farmers faced. Farms allowed them access to large quantities of raw material which could be procured over a short period of time.

Falcon was facing supply problems because it depended on a few farms and crop failure at these farms would decrease the supplies of raw material. Sometimes, Falcon had to postpone export shipments because of the lack of raw material. Also, many of these farms would divert material to another exporter at the last minute. There was no way Falcon could commit the farm to supplying the material without financing the farming by making advance payments. Falcon did this to some extent but was very wary of committing too much money to a single farm.

Coinciding with the supply side problems, the prolonged recession in Japan led to a decrease in the consumption of shrimps in Japan and the Japanese importers decided to drop the prices they offered.

Falcon decided that it was time to change their business to meet the new challenges. They decided to look west for new markets. Buyers in USA and Europe had always been very particular about quality and Indian exporters found it tedious to comply with western standards. Falcon upgraded their manufacturing units to meet US FDA specifications and started to document and realign their procurement and production processes to meet the requirements of American and European customers.

Falcon was now in a position to cut out the middleman and deal directly with the retailer or wholesaler. Their new client list grew to include companies such as Sysco, Costco and the Darden Group, the owners of the Red Lobster and the Olive Tree chains. In 2003, Falcon set up their own state-of-the-art processing centre where a number of value-added products were also produced. By now, Falcon had moved away from producing the traditional two kilo frozen blocks of shrimps and was producing individually quick frozen (IQF) shrimps, cooked and frozen and marinated and frozen shrimps. Many of these products were cut, de-veined and processed according to customer specifications.

SMALL FARMS

Falcon also made some important changes on the supply side. They stopped giving any kind of financial assistance to the large corporate farms and decided to nurture small farmers. Many villagers on the Orissa coast had been involved in shrimp farming. Some had been employed by the large corporate farms and had picked up the skills of the trade from them. Falcon encouraged these villagers to use small land holdings close to seawater for shrimp culture. Typically, this land belonged to either the farmer or to some other villager from whom the land was leased. A lot of this land was actually unsuitable for growing any other crop. Often, small farmers leased a pond or two from a large farm which had ceased operations. Falcon came up with a value proposition for these farmers and over time, it has been fine-tuned to present the villagers with an exciting opportunity.

Falcon promised to finance the entire shrimp feed requirement and to buy the harvest of the farm. Falcon guided the farmers on how to do the earthwork and make ponds according to their specifications. They also advised the farmers not to have more than one or two ponds to start with. The impact of losses in more than two ponds would devastate a typical small farmer. Falcon did not normally help with the investment in the construction and earthwork but the villagers managed to keep these costs reasonable by voluntary participation of friends and family; labour was the main cost in this work.

Falcon bought shrimp hatchlings from a big hatchery. The main advantage was that the larger hatcheries checked the hatchlings for infections and were able to sell hatchlings which had been tested as virus free. Falcon sold the hatchlings to the small farmer and passed on the benefits of purchasing on a large scale. Normally the farmer had to pay an average price of Rs. 1 per hatchling. With the help of Falcon, it became possible for them to purchase much better quality hatchlings at about half this price.

Falcon recommended low stocking levels. With lower stocking, the margins would be lower but the chances of getting a successful harvest went up tremendously. Also, the total investment in hatchlings, feed and chemicals was reduced. While the corporate farms stocked at the rate of 15–30 hatchlings per sq. m, these farmers stocked around five to six hatchlings per sq. m. They could still expect to harvest about one tonne of shrimps per 100 sq. m pond. A lower stocking density also meant that each shrimp would grow to be relatively bigger, and larger shrimps also fetched a better price per kg.

Falcon tied up with major shrimp feed producers such as CP of Thailand, and Higashimaru and Godrej. Falcon became their distributor for Orissa, and Falcon's wide outreach ensured large sales volumes. In turn, the feed manufacturers agreed to provide trained shrimp culture technicians to advise the farmers who bought feed from Falcon. These technicians also carried stocks of probiotics and chemicals which they used when they came across instances of disease in a pond. Generally, all the feed was sold to the farmers on credit. The outstanding amounts were adjusted against sales when the farmers sold their produce to Falcon. A few farmers paid a small portion of the feed money up front but the majority did not pay anything significant and paid only after harvest. Falcon itself actually got the feed on favourable credit terms from the manufacturers and passed on the credit to the farmers. This was a risky strategy for Falcon, because if there was a widespread crop failure, Falcon would not be in a position to recover the money from the farmers and thus to repay the manufacturers.

These farmers made a saving by not having to pay for the technical advice. As the workers on the farm were the farmer and his family, their labour expense was only a notional opportunity cost. Also, unlike corporate farmers, the local villagers were used to the local living conditions and the lack of amenities.

Table 2 below compares the economics of small- and large-scale farms. It is based on the following assumptions, which are from the actual experience of shrimp farmers:

- survival rate will be 75% for small farmers and 65% for intensive culture.
- feed will cost Rs. 60 per kg and 1.2 kg of feed will be needed per kg of shrimp harvested.

Table 2: Comparison of costs and revenues of small farmers and corporate farmers for a 1 hectare, 100 sq. m pond.

		Small farmer	Corporate farmer
Stocking density	per sq. m	5	20
Total in pond	Nos.	50,000	200,000
Survival	Nos.	37,500	130,000
Cost of seed	Rs.	25,000	100,000
Other costs	Rs.	10,000	25,000
Cost of feed	Rs.	81,000	234,000
Total harvest	Rs.	1,125	3,250
Net profits	Rs.	142,750	291,000

- the size of the harvested shrimp will be an average of 30 gm for the small farmer and 25 gm for the large farmer.

Prices tend to vary. Average expected prices are taken for the calculation.

When the crop is ready for harvesting, Falcon sends ice to the farm and makes arrangements for the farmer to pack and transport the produce to Falcon's closest purchasing centre. Falcon has a network of 11 purchasing centres and processing units across the coast, as is shown in the forgoing map.

The material is weighed and priced at the purchasing centre. In return for all the production support, Falcon pays about Rs. 10–25 or between 3–10% less than the market price. Earlier, some farmers found it profitable to clandestinely sell their harvest to other exporters but some faced problems when they tried to collect payment from these exporters. Most exporters are generally short of cash and, other than Falcon, most have had a very bad record of not being able to pay in time, if at all. Farmers could see that every year a few new companies would enter the market and a few old ones would wind up their operations. Many of these companies left Orissa without settling their accounts with the farmers and suppliers. Hence, the farmers had some sense of security when they sold their produce to Falcon.

Falcon also wants to retain these farmers for many years and they know that if they gave very bad rates for the harvested shrimps, the farmers would sell elsewhere as soon as they had a successful crop. Hence Falcon pays quite reasonable prices. The farmers look to Falcon not just for support in production but also as a dependable customer for their produce.

PHAGU AND CHITTA

Phagu Naik was earlier employed by Navayuga, an industrial group based in Hyderabad which was one of the early entrants into shrimp farming. This company had started exporting seafood in the early 1990s and had also started shrimp farming. Phagu started work for them in 1996 at their shrimp farm in Balasore in Orissa.

(Continued)

(Continued)

He worked in various roles and learned a great deal about shrimp farming, and in early 1999, he was promoted to a supervisor, with a salary of about Rs. 3,000 a month.

Navayuga's experience in seafood was a failure. During the three years in which Phagu was employed by them they only managed one successful crop, and after the super-cyclone in 1999 they decided to close their shrimp farming operations.

Phagu returned to his village in Goda in Jagatsinghpur district. Initially, he planned to go back to the family tradition of paddy cultivation but a very interesting opportunity presented itself. A real estate developer from Bhubaneswar had started a shrimp farm close to his village but the land had been lying unused for the past few years. Phagu approached the manager and offered to lease a pond in the farm. They agreed to lease it to him for Rs. 15,000. Phagu had heard that Falcon finances shrimp farms and went to their procurement centre at Ghanagolia. Falcon was willing to finance his feed consumption but they told him that he would have to pay for the hatchlings in full.

The hatchlings would cost about Rs. 25,000. Phagu had saved about Rs. 30,000. This would not be enough for the lease amount and for the hatchlings. He also needed some money for incidental expenses. He decided to include his cousin, Chitta, who also had a few years experience as a worker in a local shrimp farm. Chitta was interested and decided to come in as an equal partner. Each of them invested Rs. 25,000 and they started the business.

Midway through the first crop, a nearby farm was affected by the white spot virus, so the cousins decided to take preventive measures and spent Rs. 5,000 on medicines. They had to harvest a few days prematurely as they felt their crop was likely to get affected by the virus if they waited too long. They harvested 800 kgs of shrimps of an average size of 22 gms. They sold the crop to Falcon for Rs. 185,000 and made a profit of Rs. 60,000 on their investment of about Rs. 50,000.

(Continued)

(Continued)

Next year, they took an additional pond and were successful again. By 2005, the two cousins had set up independent operations. Phagu continued to lease two ponds in the same farm and was wary of expanding further. He had seen too many big farms fail. He had invested in a light commercial vehicle, which was driven by his nephew and was hired out to local businesses.

Chitta had bought some land nearby and was growing shrimps in two ponds. The cousins helped each other out whenever necessary. Both continue to supply to Falcon. Their success had encouraged some other young people in the village to also start shrimp farms.

The industry has also indirectly benefited many of the poorest people in villages such as those that Phagu and Chitta had their farm. Some were employed as labourers on farms such as Phagu's, and some of the more enterprising poor people also caught wild shrimp seedlings to sell to farms or pregnant prawns to sell to hatcheries. Some of these activities are not strictly legal, but they do help a number of villagers to improve their livelihoods.

Falcon believe in their philosophy of supporting the small farmer and not depending on corporate farms. They started on this path around the year 2000 and by 2008 they were buying from over 1,200 such small farmers along the Orissa coastline. Every year some of the small farmers become big enough to stop needing financial support for farming but they continue to be a valuable source of material for Falcon. In such cases, Falcon pays market rates but gains by not having to bear the repayment risks in case of crop failure.

Shrimp culture requires far higher investment per acre than traditional agriculture. Cultivating paddy on five acres involves a cost of about Rs. 35,000 and the farmer would expect to make a net profit of about Rs. 15,000. Shrimp culture over a similar area of land would cost about Rs. 230,000 but could generate up to Rs. 280,000 in net profits.

VALUE CHAIN

In the following value chain figure (see Fig. 2), the lines in bold represent the parts of the chain where Falcon has worked extensively to strengthen and which differentiate Falcon from most other seafood exporters in India.

There are a few defaulters, but Falcon has been selective in being aggressive about recovering its dues. In India, there is little protection for businesses and business contracts. India ranks 177th out of 182 economies in, "enforcing contracts" (World Bank, 2008). In such a situation it is not surprising that there are rumors that Falcon employees have used strong-arm tactics to recover money that is owed to the company. Such behaviour can be very counterproductive in a industry where there are many buyers and raw material is scarce. According to Pratap Swain, a procurement manager at Falcon, "truly destitute farmers are better left alone because there is actually not much to gain by pursuing them."

There are other advantages in dealing with small farmers. Recently, Indian seafood has been widely criticised because traces of pesticide were found in blocks of seafood from India. Large farms are likely to use pesticides, but small farmers very rarely use them.

RABINDRA KHUNTIA

This was the second roll of the dice for Rabindra Khuntia. After five years as a mill worker in Surat, 1,500 kms away from home, he was back in Kasaphala and was leading the uncertain life of a shrimp farmer. Last year, Falcon financed his crop but freak weather washed away most of his shrimps and he incurred heavy losses. Luckily for him, Falcon did not insist on immediate repayment and in fact, they agreed to finance him for the next year too. If this crop fails, he has decided to run away back to Surat. This time he will take his wife and children with him.

FISHERMEN

The best way for an exporter to eliminate pesticide in seafood is to use sea-caught material. An estimated 1,500 fishermen supply fish and shrimps

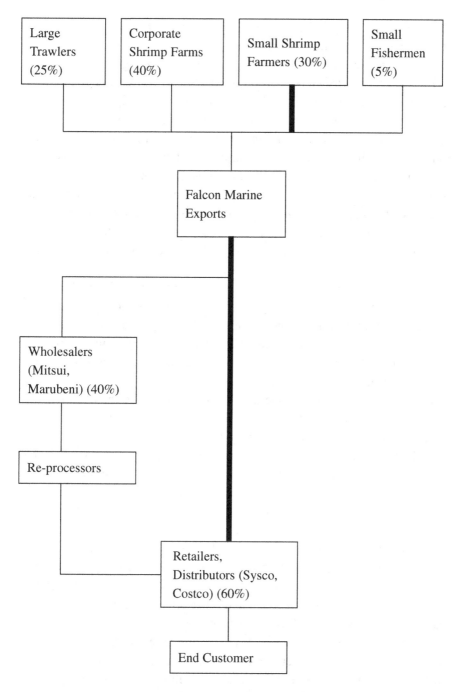

Figure 2: Value chain.

directly to Falcon over the course of a year. There are three main kinds of fishing vessels operating in Orissa.

Large trawlers go deep into the sea and each voyage lasts for about 30–45 days. The trawlers are equipped with deep freezers for storing material during long voyages. The majority of these ships are owned by businessmen who own several such trawlers but a significant number are owned by the captains who man the trawlers. These trawlers operate out of the harbour at Paradip. A number of them have a business relationship with Falcon. The trawlers take advance payment from Falcon in the form of petrol or diesel. Falcon has an arrangement for this with the fuel distributors. On returning from the voyage, they settle accounts by selling part of their catch to Falcon. Falcon is only interested in shrimps. The fishermen sell crabs and other fish to local traders or to other exporters.

Medium-sized trawlers operate out of the nine minor fishing harbours in Orissa. These boats usually go for three to five day voyages. Some of these boats return on the same day if they have been lucky enough to get a large catch quickly. These boats take advance payments in the form of fuel and ice. They do not depend heavily on the advance payments and are likely to change allegiances quickly.

There are a number of fishermen who go out fishing in small, usually non-mechanised fishing boats. They fish close to the coast or in brackish water lagoons and the deltas of river systems. These fisherfolk are not major contributors to seafood exports. They are usually trying to catch sea fish and are thus not of major interest to exporters who are primarily interested in shrimps. For example, in 2007–08, Falcon exported about 6,300 tonnes of shrimps and only about 150 tonnes of fish.

The fishermen need finance, not for business inputs such as fuel but for consumption items. They need food, money for clothes and fuel for household purposes. So, instead of an exporter they have a business relationship with a local merchant or trader who in turn, supplies fish to the markets in Bhubaneswar, Kolkata and other urban centres. These fish are largely consumed by local households, restaurants and caterers.

Sometimes, these fishermen have a large catch of shrimps and they may be tempted to go direct to an exporter but if it is only a few kg, they will not take the trouble and will continue selling to the trader as usual. Different nets are used for catching shrimps and for catching fish. Most small fishermen do not find it worth their while to invest in shrimp nets. Occasionally some of these fishermen come to the procurement centres of Falcon to sell their shrimps but this happens too rarely for Falcon to have an effective relationship with them.

KUNA BEHERA

Kuna Behera had the strange distinction of being the only fisherman from the village of Bagapatia. He managed to catch a few fish which he sold at the nearby village of Gupti. He was not making much money at all and he had seriously thought of selling his boat. On the other hand, he saw his role as the only boat owner in the village as a responsibility. People depended on him if they wanted to cross the river or get supplies from Rajkanika. That did provide him with a secondary source of income too. But still, just a few kilos of fish were not enough; he had to find a way to change his luck. He was seriously considering starting his own shrimp farming business.

THE FUTURE

Tara Pattnaik is a first generation entrepreneur and he had to face all the problems expected to be encountered by someone who is not from a business family. This problem was alleviated to some extent as his brothers joined him in his business. In fact, his younger brother, Pravaranjan, is the current Managing Director of Falcon. The brothers still live in the same house in Bhubaneswar. Tara's other brother, Parthajeet has been educated in the USA and the UK and is expected to play a vital role in Falcon's possible bid to start seafood distribution in USA.

Tara Pattnaik is very clear that it does not make business sense to pursue a relationship with small fishermen at present but he believes that this situation may change in the future. He sees this situation as an opportunity for smaller seafood operators.

Falcon is in the business of frozen seafood but that does not mean that all exporters need to follow the same path. Fresh fish sells for a premium over frozen fish, everywhere. Some small exporters may be able to work with these small fishermen to procure small quantities of fresh seafood for supply to the markets in Singapore and Bangkok. A few have tried in the recent past but have suffered because of regulatory issues and the lack of infrastructure. Tara Pattnaik hopes that with private investment in infrastructure such as air cargo transport and airports, the situation will improve. With small improvements in logistics, he believes it will be possible for fresh fish to be sent directly to markets in Dubai, Hong Kong and even Tokyo. With direct flights from India to New York and London, perhaps the day is not far away when fresh fish can be sent to North America and Europe. He is clear that this is not a priority for Falcon and he does not have time for it right now. He also believes that China and Thailand will soon become net importers of fish and that the international prices of fish will really increase at that time.

Small farmers still do not supply the bulk of Falcon's requirements. About 30% of Falcon's raw material is sourced from small farmers, 25% from large trawlers, 5% from small fishermen and nearly 40% from large shrimp farms. Pattnaik foresees that the future of his company and in fact, that of the Indian seafood industry, lies in developing the smaller-scale seafood producers. Pattnaik wants to grow Falcon by increasing the number of small farmers who supply them from the current 1,200 to about 5,000 in three years.

Pattnaik has been lobbying to persuade the government to release uncultivable land close to seawater. If this land could be leased to small farmers, they would be able to start shrimp culture with a little additional financial support. Even one good crop would be enough to release many such people from the cycle of poverty. He is willing to show the government that this could be more effective than any poverty alleviation scheme the government can think of.

REFERENCES

Marine Products Export Development Authority (MPEDA) (2007). Annual Report 2006–07.
World Bank (2004). Orissa Investment Climate Survey.
World Bank (2005). Investment Climate Assessment.
World Bank (2008). Doing Business in 2008.

Case Study

10

Honey in Muzaffarpur

Ashok Kumar

INTRODUCTION

There are many litchi orchards and other flowering crops in Muzaffarpur and nearby districts of Bihar, and this offers a great opportunity for bee-keeping in the region. The Khadi and Village Industries Commission (KVIC) and the Bihar State Khadi Board recognised this potential, and they have for many years provided bee-keeping training, subsidised financial support and other incentives to local people.

As far back as 1963, the KVIC organised a training programme on bee-keeping in Muzaffarpur in which five persons each from Muzaffarpur and four other districts participated. In the same year, KVIC organised a workshop at Mehsi in East Champaran district to encourage rural people to start bee-keeping. Again in 1964–65, KVIC trained 27 farmers from Muzaffarpur. The training programmes focused mainly on how to domesticate and manage *Indica* bees, which are known as *desi* bees in the region, in wooden bee hives and how to extract honey from the hives.

During the intervening years, most bee-keepers in the region moved to a more productive breed known as Italian bees, or *Mellisfera*. In 1974,

Note: Units of measurement in the Indian numbering system: lakh = 100,000; crore = 10,000,000. Indian Rupees (Rs.) where appropriate are converted into USD at a rate of approximately Rs. 50 = $1.00; Rs. 1 lakh = $2,000; Rs. 1 crore = $200,000.

KVIC provided grants of Rs. 500 along with a Rs. 250 loan to a few bee-keepers in Muzaffarpur so they could expand their bee-keeping. Gradually, bee-keeping started to be seen as a genuine commercial enterprise. Some of the bee-keepers also started to take their hives to nearby Jharkhand each year, to make honey from the *Karanj* or Jatropha tree flowers which grow there. In 1990, KVIC allocated Rs. 14,000, including a 50% subsidy, to a few selected bee-keepers. This was meant to be distributed by the State Khadi Board but, due to a conflict between KVIC and the Board, it was never disbursed and KVIB spent the entire amount meeting legal expenses.

EDA Rural Systems (EDA), a Gurgaon-based development consulting firm working in micro-finance and livelihoods promotion, became involved in enterprise promotion with a sub-sector approach in the late 1990s. In 1999–2000, EDA established an office in Muzaffarpur to promote bee-keeping in Muzaffarpur and Vaishali with grant support from the Small Industries Development Bank of India (SIDBI) under their Rural Industries Programme. At that time there were around 500 bee-keepers in the region with an average of 28 hives each. The majority of these bee-keepers were from the backward *Kushwaha* caste. With an average annual production of around 30 kg per hive, the region produced a total of about 420 MT of honey every year.

Bee-keeping was then considered a part-time activity by most bee-keepers. The market price for raw litchi honey was Rs. 25–30 per kg. The main buyer of the raw honey was Dabur India Limited, a large company that deals in ayurvedic health and natural food products. Dabur bought its raw honey from local buying agents who were paid a commission according to the quantity of honey supplied. There was usually a glut in the market just after the honey extraction, but the beekeepers had no option but to sell their honey and so were at the mercy of the agents who effectively controlled the price.

The major focus of the programme supported by SIDBI was to help prospective and existing bee-keepers to access bank finance to enable them to start or expand their bee-keeping enterprises. EDA continued the programme for three or four years, but the experience suggested that a more comprehensive approach was needed to address the issues which limited the growth of the industry. At this time, EDA's staff made an assessment of the honey value chain by interviewing a sample of bee-keepers and other stakeholders such as honey buyers, input suppliers and promotional agencies. The bee-keepers sold raw honey to agents who in turn supplied private processors such as Dabur. These processors bought different types of honey, including forest honey, from various states, blended them and sold the end product to consumers through wholesalers and retailers. A few bee-keepers sold honey directly to local consumers after sun drying the raw honey in the sun to reduce its moisture content.

The usual situation in the open market for honey is as follows. Consumers buy Dabur honey for Rs. 190–200 per kg (depending upon the package size). The beekeepers get between Rs. 40–45 per kg, which is about 22% of the consumer price. The buying agents get between Rs. 1–2 for each kg which they supply to the processors. A rough estimate suggests that the other costs incurred in procurement, transporting the honey to the processors, and the actual processing, bottling and packaging, including the processing loss, along with selling and distribution account for about 25–30% of the consumer price. The wholesalers, dealers and retailers who sell the processed honey to consumers get about half the consumer price, out of which they have to pay for the operations and any advertising costs.

A number of important issues emerged from the value chain assessment:

The beekeepers lacked any knowledge of scientific bee management, or of disease control, honey extraction methods, quality control or how to store raw honey. They were widely dispersed and were dependent on a small number of agents for the sale of raw honey, and very little value was added at the local level through processing. The existing support institutions and government agencies were doing very little, the bee-keepers had no sources of finance or bank credit to start or expand their bee-keeping, and there were no specialised bee-keeping institutions at the village, block, district or state level to promote the growth in the industry.

In 2002 EDA submitted a proposal to the Ford Foundation for a comprehensive project based on their field experience with the SIDBI initiative and the findings of the value chain assessment. The aim of the project is to enable bee-keepers and other important participants in the value chain to get the business and support services they need to expand their businesses and incomes. The Ford Foundation accepted the proposal in July 2002, and has supported the project since that time. The project operates in about 200 villages of the Muzaffapur region covering the districts

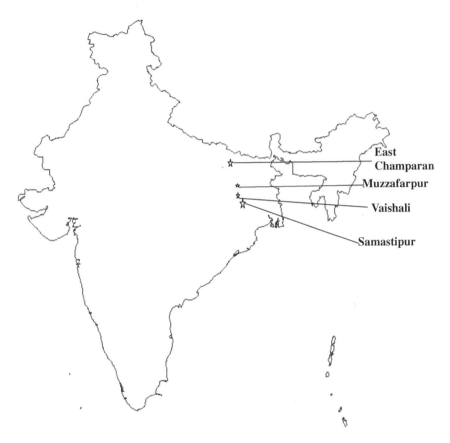

Figure 1: Main honey-producing districts in Bihar State.

of Muzaffarpur, Vaishali, East Champaran and part of Samastipur (see Fig. 1). The project's major activities are summarised in Table 1.

The project initially focused on activities such as mobilising the bee-keepers and forming their associations, capacity building, training on basic bee-keeping, and the development of bank and market links including promoting professional marketing agents. These activities continued for three or four years and were carried out at the same time. Other activities such as forming the bee-keepers' federation, promoting the strategic alliance between a local cooperative marketing institution known as *Timul* and the bee-keepers' federation, the development and launch of the website, efforts to reduce tax on honey trade, and publishing the

Table 1: The project's major activities.

Components	Major activities
• Formation and capacity building of local institutions	• Mobilisation of bee-keepers to form bee-keepers' associations and to build their capacity • Form state level federation of bee-keepers • Encourage collective action by bee-keepers' associations to take advantage of the market and address common business problems • Train bee-keepers to develop entrepreneurial skills, cooperative management, book-keeping, conflict resolution and negotiation skills
• Market development for raw honey	• Develop a strategic alliance between the bee-keepers' federation and *Timul*/Sudha Dairy; encourage *Timul* to sell processed honey • Support collective marketing of honey by bee-keepers' associations • Promote and develop professional marketing agents (PMAs) and the necessary backward and forward linkages • Website development (www.litchihoney.com) to increase visibility of the sub-sector in domestic and export markets
• Training of bee-keepers	• Training on basic bee-keeping and the extraction of by-products • Publish book in Hindi on how to start bee-keeping
• Finance network	• Linking bee-keepers, their associations and others with banks
• Promotion of related activities	• Facilitate establishment of honey processing plants and testing laboratory • Facilitate establishment of related activities such as bee hive manufacturing, foundation sheet making and small equipment suppliers

(Continued)

Table 1: (*Continued*)

Components	Major activities
• Advocacy for policies to create a positive environment in the sub-sector	• Lobby to reduce tax on honey trade in Bihar • Publish bee-keepers' directory to reduce official harassment at check posts during seasonal movement of bee hives to other locations • Workshops with banks to increase financing for bee-keeping enterprises

bee-keepers' directory were carried out two to three years after the project started.

FORMATION AND CAPACITY BUILDING OF LOCAL INSTITUTIONS

At the start of the project, the bee-keepers were working individually with no formal or informal bee-keepers' institutions. EDA encouraged the bee-keepers to form institutions so that they could undertake certain activities on a collective basis.

Forty two bee-keepers' associations were formed with 1,484 members from 128 villages. The associations' members have a total of 82,200 bee-hives with an annual production of over 4,000 tonnes of different kinds of honey, including litchi honey. About two-thirds of the bee-keepers in these villages are members in one of the associations. Twenty-seven of the 42 associations are registered as primary co-operatives and others are in the process of registering. The main function of the associations is to stock the honey produced by their regional members at a common storage place where buyers can come to buy it. It is estimated that the associations sold about 1,500 tonnes of litchi honey between 2004 and 2007. The total amount of honey produced in the region is about 3,300 tonnes. The balance of 1,800 tonnes of honey was sold individually by bee-keepers to various buyers. Of the 1,500 tonnes which was sold collectively, 77 tonnes was sold to the bee-keepers' federation and the rest to outside buyers and marketing agents who had been introduced to the business by the project. The project has not provided any finance to the associations; they meet all of their own expenses. The associations also arrange for the transport of members' bee-hives to other states, and help their members to access bank credit and to purchase inputs.

THE BEE-KEEPERS' ASSOCIATION IN MOHABBAT CHAPRA

A bee-keepers' association with 18 members was formed by the project in Mohabbat Chapra, East Champaran district, in 2002–03. The members started by collecting a monthly deposit amount, which was initially Rs. 30 and was then increased to Rs. 50, which was paid into their account with the State Bank of India branch at Mehsi. In 2003, the association's members sold all their 19 tonnes of honey which they produced through the association to a professional marketing agent who had been promoted by EDA. In this transaction, the members earned an extra Rs. 76 per kg instead of the prevailing market price of Rs. 72 per kg. The members then decided to put one rupee for every kg of honey they sold into the association's bank account. They also deposited Rs. 18,000 they had raised from the sale of containers for storing honey. When the association's funds reached Rs. 25,000, it became eligible for the group linkage programme of NABARD and obtained a loan of Rs. 100,000. The members used this money to expand their bee colonies. In 2003, the association also organised a training programme on basic bee-keeping and quality issue. In 2004, the members again sold all the 20 tonnes of honey they had produced through the association to the same professional marketing agent and received Rs. 45 per kg against the prevailing market price of Rs. 42. In 2004, the association organised two courses on basic bee-keeping and quality issues, and it continues to prosper effectively.

BENEFITS FROM STOCKING AND COLLECTIVE SALE

Raghopur is a small village in Muzaffarpur district, about 20 km from Muzaffarpur. There were 17 bee-keepers in the village in 2002, 13 of whom formed an association with the EDA project's support. They were encouraged to stock and sell honey collectively through the association. In April 2002, nine of the members decided to sell their entire production of 20 tonnes of litchi honey collectively. With EDA's support, they sold it to a local market agent at a price of Rs. 44 per kg as compared with the market price of Rs. 42 per kg. These members therefore realised an additional profit of Rs. 20,000 through collective selling. Since then, the members have continued to sell collectively.

In addition to bee-keepers' associations, the project has promoted 10 women's groups with a total of 120 members, in order to increase women's participation in bee-keeping and to help them contribute to their families' incomes. Several of these groups have received training on bee-keeping and have received bank loans. Some of these women now have their own bee-hives and some work on hives owned by their husbands.

HOW ASHA DEVI STARTED HER BEE-KEEPING UNIT

Asha Devi is 32 years old and lives in Simra village. She is a member of a women's group. Her husband is a marginal farmer and his income was not sufficient to meet the household's expenses. Asha wanted to do something that would bring in more money, so she was interested in bee-keeping and joined a training course. After the training, in 2005, Asha worked for another bee-keeper in the

(Continued)

(Continued)

village, and then, in 2007, she started her own bee-keeping unit. Asha borrowed Rs. 3000 from her group, her husband put in another Rs. 12,000 from various other sources and in December 2007 Asha bought 10 bee hives. By 2008 she has 12 hives and expects to extract about 600 kgs of honey worth Rs. 30,000.

A state-level federation of bee-keepers in Bihar *"Tirhut Madhu Utpadak Swavblambi Sahkari Parisangh"* (Tirhut Honey Producers Self Reliant Cooperative Federation) was formed in April 2005 to help the bee-keepers identify and act on issues hindering the growth of their business, and to act as a catalyst for the industry. With guidance from the EDA project, this federation has undertaken several activities including ensuring better returns on honey, training, developing the market and, strengthening bank links, supplying inputs to bee-keepers in the region and other agencies outside the state, following up with relevant authorities to ensure registration of bee-keepers' associations and policy advocacy, such as dealing with the sales tax issue, the publication of a bee-keepers' directory, and audit and capacity building services for the associations.

POLICY ADVOCACY BY THE BEE-KEEPERS' FEDERATION TO REDUCE TAX ON HONEY

Honey in Bihar was taxed according to an end-note to the list of taxable goods in the state which stated "all other commodities not mentioned in list and not exempt are to be taxed @ 8%". After the introduction of VAT, the tax of 8% increased to 12.5%, which created problems for bee-keepers and traders and prevented external buyers from buying honey from the state. EDA decided to raise this issue directly through the federation and the traders' body. A representation from the bee-keepers' federation was sent to the VAT

(Continued)

(Continued)

Panchayat, which is headed by the Deputy Chief Minister of the Government of Bihar. The move was supported by the Bihar Traders Association. The federation and other people's institutions were encouraged by the project to write letters to the Chief Minister and to other relevant authorities, enclosing supporting documents on the comparative rates of honey taxes in other states. They asked the Deputy CM, the Secretary Commercial for Taxes and other relevant authorities to bring the Bihar state asking for honey tax to come in line with that in other states. As a result of these efforts, the tax on honey in Bihar was reduced to 4% from 1 April 2006.

MARKETING

Before the project started, there was only a small number of local agents who bought local litchi honey for Dabur on commission. The bee-keepers had no alternative but to sell their honey to these agents at whatever price they offered. The agents paid the bee-keepers in installments over two to four months. The bee-keepers had no other customers and they had virtually no bargaining power, so the project tried to build other markets for them in order to improve their position.

Timul is a successful milk marketing co-operative in Bihar, and the EDA honey project saw them as an ideal marketing partner whose well-established marketing outlets might be used to sell honey in the state. The project team approached *Timul* and suggested that they should add honey to their product line. The bee-keepers are often from the same villages where *Timul* procures milk, and some are already supplying milk to *Timul*. By buying their honey *Timul* could help them to diversify and improve their livelihoods. *Timul* would not have to buy honey direct from the bee-keepers but would buy it from the bee-keepers' federation.

The negotiations took some two years, but eventually a formal agreement was signed between *Timul* and the bee-keepers' federation in which the latter agreed to supply *Timul* with processed litchi honey.

Timul, in turn, offered a good price for the honey and would sell the honey in Bihar. This alliance not only protected the bee-keepers from exploitation by agents but it also provided an additional market channel. In 2005–2006, the first year of the collaboration, the honey federation purchased 41 tonnes of raw litchi honey from 13 bee-keepers' associations, with strict quality controls, and had it processed by Ramayna Industries, a privately owned honey processing plant. They supplied the processed honey to *Timul.* The federation paid the bee-keepers through their respective associations, and they added an extra payment of Rs. 21,000 to each association as an incentive to continue the business.

In its very first year the federation succeeded in significantly reducing the exploitation of the bee-keepers. The price of raw litchi honey in April 2005 was quoted by the agents of the corporate buyers as Rs. 18 per kg, but after the federation announced its purchase price of Rs. 45 per kg, the agents increased their price to Rs. 36 per kg, and the price gradually rose to over Rs. 45 per kg. In 2006, the agents quoted Rs. 38 per kg for raw litchi honey, whereas the federation offered Rs. 51 per kg. The agents were again forced to increase their price and as a result, the bee-keepers eventually received Rs. 55–60 per kg for their best quality honey. The price offered by the federation has come to be seen as the support price for litchi honey and the other buyers usually follow it. The project has thus increased the incomes not only of the members of the association which it has promoted, but of all the other bee-keepers as well.

The project assisted *Timul* to launch and market its own brand called "Sudha Litchi Honey". It was launched at the Tourism and Trade Fair in Patna, in September 2005. *Timul* promoted litchi honey by newspaper advertisements and banners, and posters and hoardings were also displayed at milk parlours and other places in Muzaffarpur, Patna, East Champaran, West Champaran and Shivhar districts. *Timul* also sells honey in bulk to institutional buyers, and has thus far sold about 75 tonnes of litchi honey from the bee-keepers' federation. *Timul* is now implementing a new KVIC project in the region and plans to use this to establish a modern honey processing plant.

The project also organised buyer-seller meetings and invited more than 100 honey buyers from all over India. They were taken to the bee-keepers' associations to understand honey production and to see for themselves how the associations worked. EDA also developed and launched a website, www.litchihoney.com, to promote the honey in India and abroad. Some buyers are starting to sell honey outside Bihar and also to export it as a result of this.

Dabur was the only major buyer of honey from the region, and the project staff realised that there was a potential for more buyers to buy the increased production from the bee-keepers. They identified a number of local entrepreneurs with good financial and business backgrounds, and suggested to them that the honey trade was a good business opportunity. Twenty-five potential traders came to a series of meetings, and eventually six of them became what the project called "Professional Marketing Agents" (PMAs). They are good at business and they saw that honey represented a good opportunity. They invested time and money and became successful honey traders. One of them was in the honey trade before, and the other five are new to this business.

These six traders now play an important role in the region. They sell to a number of corporate buyers including exporters, some of whom are based at a considerable distance from Muzaffapur. It is estimated that these PMAs have purchased almost 3,000 tonnes of litchi honey in the last three years from the bee-keepers' associations and individual bee-keepers. Apart from buying litchi honey, they also go to other locations to buy ordinary honey from bee-keepers who are have been introduced to them by the project. The PMAs bought and sold a total of about 7,000 tonnes of honey including litchi honey between 2006–2008. They have sold honey to large buyers such as the Sri Gandhi Ashram, Kashmir Apiary, Kejriwal, Dabur, Punjab Honey, Apis India, and Appropriate Technology, India. The PMAs have good storage facilities in Muzaffapur and can offer the bee-keepers a premium of between Rs. 1–4 per kg over the market rate because they have low procurement costs, they can access large quantities in one place and they have better purchasing and sales networks than other traders.

AJAY KUMAR'S HONEY TRADING BUSINESS

Ajay had a small saw mill and dealt in timber. He was invited to a buyer-seller meeting in Muzaffarpur to introduce him to the honey

(Continued)

(Continued)

market. After several meetings, he decided to start trading in honey in 2003–04. He was helped to get a loan from UCO Bank in Bochaha. The EDA project helped him to visit potential customers in South India to develop trade links and build his confidence, but he paid all the expenses himself. He has been trading in honey since 2003 and is now one of the leading PMAs in the region. In 2003–04, he bought about 90 tonnes of litchi honey from bee-keepers in Muzaffarpur, Samastipur and Motihari districts. He sold more than 80 tonnes of this to buyers in UP, Punjab, Himachal Pradesh and Delhi. His average profit margin in the first year were about Rs. 5 per kg of honey, and his overall profit was between Rs. 300,000–400,000. In 2004–05, he purchased about 180 tonnes of honey. In addition to litchi honey, he also purchased ordinary honey and supplied it to buyers in UP, Punjab, Himachal and Delhi. He invested Rs. 40,000 in a quality testing laboratory, and hired a technical expert to run it. In 2005–06, he purchased more than 250 tonnes of honey, which he sold to a number of large buyers, and by 2007 his business had grown to around 300 tonnes of honey every year.

The project has trained 1,816 people in basic bee-keeping and 117 on by-product extraction, from about 135 villages. Through training and other support, about 730 participants have established their own bee-keeping units and are doing well and expanding them every year. About 260 existing bee-keepers expanded their units after training.

The training programmes have had a significant impact in terms of the number of new units established and the expansion of existing units, which has increased both honey production and profits for bee-keepers.

NAUSHAD'S BEE-KEEPING BUSINESS

Naushad Alam from Amarkh village had just graduated and was looking for a source of income to sustain his family. He heard about

(Continued)

(Continued)

the honey project from association members in the village, and contacted the EDA team for advice on starting a honey business. He joined a training course, and was introduced to the other association members in the village. Since he did not have enough finance, the project helped him to get a bank loan of Rs. 46,000 and he started his business with 20 bee-hives. He now earns around Rs. 45,000 a year from these hives.

The establishment of new units and the expansion of existing units have contributed significantly to increasing the production of honey in the region. About 22,400 bee-hives have been established, and about 1,120 tonnes of honey are being produced from them. The overall quality of honey from the area has significantly improved, and the annual production is worth about $1 million. The average annual production per bee-hive has increased from 30–50 kg due to improved management practices. The establishment of new hives and the increased productivity means higher incomes for bee-keepers.

AJAY KUMAR

In 2003, Ajay Kumar from village Narauli of Muzaffarpur was 30 years old, and worked in a textile shop for a monthly wage of Rs. 700. He was looking for ways of increasing his income. He attended a training course on bee-keeping on the suggestion of one of the ten bee-keepers in his village, and he started his unit with five hives. He soon realised that it was a profitable business, and decided to expand his unit. The project helped him to get a loan of Rs. 176,000 from the Allahabad Bank in Kanahli, in 2004–05. His younger brother joined the business later on. Apart from extracting litchi honey, he takes his bee-hives to Jharkhand every year for jatropha tree honey, to Patna and Chhapra districts for mustard honey and to Samastipur district for *Jamun* honey.

(Continued)

(Continued)

At present he has 275 bee-hives which produce about 14 tonnes of honey every year. Ajay recently started marketing processed honey under his own brand name of *"Piyush"* which means nectar. In addition to his own honey, he also bought 54 tonnes of raw litchi honey from other bee-keepers to process. He participated in two trade fairs, one in Patna and the other in Muzaffarpur, and sold about $2800 worth of honey. He also played a very important role in forming a bee-keepers association in his village. It was registered in 2006 and has 31 bee-keeper members. Ajay is the Chief Executive and helped 22 more bee-keepers to get bank loans. He expects that by 2008 there will be 100 bee-keepers in the village. He estimates that his business made a net profit of about $10,000 in 2006–07.

One very important part of the project is to link the bee-keepers sustainably with banks so that they can access the necessary finance to run their businesses. Several bankers workshops were organised every year, in addition to individual meetings and continuing follow-up with the local branches and regional offices of the banks which are involved. This had to be done to help the bankers understand bee-keeping and to ensure that they would provide finance as needed. The banks lend to individual bee-keepers and to the bee-keeping associations. Over 500 bee-keepers have obtained bank loans for a total of $3 million from five nationalised banks in the area. This figure is based on the initial first-time loans but most of the bee-keepers have taken two or three or more loans. The total of the loans that bee-keepers have received may be well over $6 million.

A BEE-KEEPERS' ASSOCIATION LINKED WITH STATE BANK OF INDIA (SBI)

A bee-keepers' association was formed in village Tarma in 2002–03. The bee-keepers were encouraged to conduct monthly

(Continued)

(Continued)

meetings and to start a savings fund. The project helped them open a savings account with SBI at Kanti branch. The members used their savings for their small credit requirements, and they deposited their repayments back in the bank. In 2003, when their savings reached Rs. 10,000, the EDA team helped the association to approach the branch manager to get a loan under the NABARD scheme. The bank lent Rs. 40,000 to the association, and the entire amount was repaid after the members had sold their litchi honey in April 2004. The bank then provided another loan of Rs. 200,000. The association is now a valued customer of the bank and the loans have become an annual routine.

PROMOTION OF OTHER ENTERPRISES

In order to add more value to raw honey locally, several businesses have been promoted. There were no honey processing plants in the region at the start of project, and the EDA team also helped to establish new suppliers of bee hives, bee broods and foundation sheets so that bee-keepers could obtain the supplies they needed on time.

Two honey processing plants were established, one each in Gaya and in Muzaffarpur, each with a processing capacity of 1,000 kg per day. Two more plants are likely to be established in the future.

SHASHI'S HONEY PROCESSING PLANT

Shashi has been associated with the EDA project since 2002. At first he was a PMA, and then he became a honey processor. Initially he bottled processed honey and marketed it locally as "*Shiva* honey" and his operation was confined to Ranchi, Gaya and adjoining areas. He then developed contacts with bee-keepers in the region and started procuring on a large scale, and

(Continued)

(Continued)

following this experience, he installed a modern honey processing plant. As the processing business grew, in 2004 he incorporated the business as Shiva Agro Natural Products Private
Limited. EDA helped Shashi to borrow $36,000 for the plant
from SIDBI, and in the following year the Bank of Baroda gave
him a credit limit of $34,000 for working capital. Shashi has also
established a honey testing laboratory and his business is very
successful.

Thirteen of the associations have also encouraged village carpenters to
start making wooden bee hives for them. This involves an investment of
about Rs. 50,000, but a carpenter can earn some Rs. 35,000 a year from
this activity.

Businesses have been set up to make wax foundation sheets; the
machinery and working capital for this cost about Rs. 30,000 and it can
earn around Rs. 25,000 a year. Two existing wax foundation businesses
have also become members of bee-keepers' associations, so that six associations have their own foundation sheet units.

Some bee-keepers do not want to keep the new bee broods which
emerge from time to time from their existing colonies and the project has
encouraged them to sell these surplus colonies to bee-keepers who want
to expand their businesses. The sale of bee broods has become a major
source of income for many bee-keepers, and some of them have started
supplying them as far away as Punjab.

PROJECT IMPACT

Since 1999 the project has cost a total of $0.24 million, $14,000 from
SIDBI and $0.2 million from the Ford Foundation. The project has facil-
itated the investment of $0.6 million, 22,500 bee hives have been set up
and about 1,120 MT of honey is being produced every year. This provides
$1 million in annual income to the bee-keepers in the region. The bee-
keepers in the region now have more channels to sell their honey and they

are able to get higher prices because they can sell through their associations and the federation.

The project has generated more competition in the honey market, particularly through the involvement of *Timul,* and the bee-keepers should benefit from this for many years. A total of 8,000 bee-keepers have benefited from the project directly or indirectly, and they also provide employment to many other people. There are 9,000 bee-keepers in the region altogether, with 389,000 bee hives. They have an annual production capacity of about 19,450 tonnes of honey which is worth Rs. 87 crores at the higher prices which the project has helped them to obtain.

MAJOR CHALLENGES

The team has faced a number of challenges during the project. It was difficult to convert the bee-keepers' associations from informal groups to registered legal entities, because of delays in the government co-operative department. In spite of intensive follow-up at each level of the department not all the associations have yet been registered. It also took longer than expected to build the capacity of the associations, because the members were often traveling with their hives to other locations, and disagreements between the members and inadequate support from the larger-scale bee-keepers also delayed the capacity building process.

The bee-keepers' federation also lacked capacity because it was short of money and good management. It was difficult to hire good professionals to manage the federation, and this problem could only be properly solved if it was possible to introduce an incentive-based salary package for the chief executive and to secure the release of the government grants for which the federation is eligible.

In spite of all the efforts to ensure better returns for bee-keepers, the industry cannot be insulated from broader issues. Domestic and international demand and supply of honey, the weather conditions during the flowering of litchi plants in the region, natural calamities such as flood and droughts in the region which can stop the bees reaching the flowers and the washing away of whole bee colonies, unexpected diseases in bees and the adulteration of honey by a few bee-keepers can make a significant difference to the overall returns for bee-keepers.

No activity can be wholly protected from outside events, however, and the project can be said to have made a significant and sustainable improvement to the livelihoods of several thousand people. These issues play an important role in determining honey price, overall returns to bee keepers and the overall profitability of bee keeping enterprises.

Case Study 11

Fairtrade and Organic Coffee

Priti Rao

INTRODUCTION

India has a tribal population of about 84 million[1] people. The majority of them live in remote rural areas somewhat isolated from the general population. Low levels of literacy combined with harsh living conditions have made this section of society one of the poorest and most deprived in the country. Public sector and non-government organisation efforts at poverty alleviation have tended to focus on income redistribution as opposed to income generation.

There are few success stories involving the so-called Scheduled Tribes in India, especially those that reside in eco-fragile regions with minimal infrastructure and means of livelihood. It is particularly unusual to find examples that involve a business model that is commercially viable and at the same time supports poverty alleviation. This case study describes one

---

[1] Census 2001.

Note: Units of measurement in the Indian numbering system: lakh = 100,000; crore = 10,000,000. Indian Rupees (Rs.) where appropriate are converted into USD at a rate of approximately Rs. 50 = $1.00; Rs. 1 lakh = $2,000; Rs. 1 crore = $200,000.

such initiative, involving the Araku tribal coffee farmers in the Eastern Ghats of Andhra Pradesh.

The case starts with a brief background of the region and the history of coffee cultivation. It outlines some of the main constraints the coffee farmers faced that needed to be overcome in order to create an inclusive value chain that was environmentally sustainable, that brought tangible economic benefits to farmers and that created greater prospects for their participation in a global value chain. The case describes the strategy adopted by the Naandi Foundation, an autonomous non-profit organisation based in Hyderabad, in working with 8,000 tribal coffee farmers to build a strong value chain. Finally, it describes some of the challenges inherent in sustaining and scaling up such value chains, and the complex governance structure that is needed to ensure accountability of the various actors involved in the chain.

BACKGROUND OF COFFEE CULTIVATION IN ARAKU VALLEY

Araku valley lies in the picturesque Eastern Ghats of Andhra Pradesh, 90 kms north-west of the city of Visakhapatnam. It is home to three of the most backward tribes in India, the Gondh, the Gadaba and the Poorjas. Their population in the region is close to half a million. The majority of them still live off forest produce and subsistence farming, mainly by growing paddy and millets. Their cash income is extremely low and tends to be in the range of Rs. 550–750 per month. This is largely through the sale of minor forest produce or crops such as niger, pepper, *rajma* (a type of pulse) and seasonal vegetables, and occasional daily wage work. The profits from selling their crops in *shandies* (local markets) are however very small, as tribal people are often exploited on account of their ignorance and low bargaining power. The literacy rate amongst the population is low and maternal mortality is quite high. There is strong Naxal insurgency in the region which is also present in the neighbouring states of Chattisgarh and Orissa, making it one of the most challenging areas in India in which to work.

Coffee offers an opportunity to tribal farmers, even under these difficult circumstances. Coffee was introduced into the Araku region in 1920 by British revenue officers who recognised the potential of the slopes of the hills in the area. After independence, around the 1960s, the Indian Coffee Board and the Andhra Pradesh Forest Department started to make efforts to encourage organised coffee cultivation and production in the area. The movement to grow coffee began in the plantations owned by the Forest Department and later spread to individual tribal farmers. The Integrated Tribal Development Agency (ITDA), an apex institution which implements government schemes in tribal areas, took over the promotion and management of coffee cultivation from the Coffee Board of India from 1995 onwards. By 2008, almost 24,000 hectares in Andhra Pradesh are under coffee cultivation, of which the tribal belt in Araku valley constitutes an important part. This region is also one of the highest altitude coffee growing regions amongst the non-traditional coffee growing regions in India, and the plantations are between 1,500–4,000 ft above sea level. The predominant variety of coffee in Araku is *Coffea Arabica*, commonly known as Arabica.

STATUS OF COFFEE CULTIVATION AND DESCRIPTION OF THE LOCAL VALUE CHAIN

In 2008, an estimated 81,000 farmers are cultivating coffee in the 11 mandals of Visakhapatnam district. The yield of coffee and the resulting income to the coffee farmers is however very much less than it could be. This section outlines some of the main constraints that farmers faced and describes the local value chain as it existed before Naandi's intervention.

Traditionally the tribals used slash and burn cultivation, clearing sizeable tracts of forest lands for agricultural purposes. Several years of this practice have converted large areas of forest land into semi-wasteland. This land, along with some other acreage was leased by the ITDA to tribal farmers for coffee cultivation. On average each farmer was allocated a plot of between one and two acres. In addition the government agencies distributed coffee saplings to the farmers, predominantly of the Cauvery and Selection 5 variety. As the coffee plant takes 4–5 years to mature before yielding any fruits, some financial assistance was also provided to the farmers to cover the cost of nurturing the plants during their initial non-bearing stage.

Coffee cultivation was however new to most of the farmers, who had not been properly trained in the management and care of coffee plants. In the initial years when the plant was still in the non-bearing stage, farmers would often cut down the silver oak trees which provided necessary shade for the coffee plants. They sold the silver oak trees as timber, leaving the coffee plants exposed to a greater risk of mortality.

The soil fertility in the region is also very poor and is one of the main reasons for extremely low yields. On an average, the yields have been less than 400 kg of coffee fruits per year per acre, as compared to three times as much yield from a properly maintained plot of a similar size in a traditional area under organic conditions.

The main reasons for the low survival, growth and yield of the coffee plants were the degraded soil quality, the felling of vital shade trees and farmers' insufficient knowledge of coffee sapling and bush management techniques. The state of coffee cultivation in the region was thus far from achieving its potential.

Unlike other agricultural commodities that can be traded fresh or with minimal processing, coffee, other than when sold as sun-dried fruits, or cherry, has to undergo several processes before it can be sold. The different types of coffee processing value chains are shown in Fig. 1. First, the fresh fruit has to be pulped using special coffee pulpers. This is called the wet processing method as it uses water to separate the skin of the fruit from the bean inside. The pulped coffee beans are then sun-dried or mechanically dried to produce parchment, which is the coffee bean with its original outer husk or cover. This cover is then removed by hand pounding or mechanised hulling to convert the parchment into what is known as clean coffee, which is the dried green coffee beans without the covers. The processing methods and techniques which are used are as important or perhaps even more important than the variety of coffee itself in determining the quality, flavour and price of the end product. Typically farmers in Araku sell their coffee as cherry in the local market. In some international markets this un-processed coffee could command a premium. The modest tribal village's home-drying conditions, however, do not produce high-quality exportable coffee.

The other method of coffee processing is by decentralised home-based processing with hand-operated "baby pulpers". The ITDA has distributed some pulpers to some farmers to help with the first level of processing. This method, however, requires a nearby water source. Once pulped, the coffee is fermented for a couple of days in water using plastic bags, and is then left to dry in the sun. The parchment is subsequently hand-pounded to produce clean coffee.

While this type of decentralised processing adds some value at the local level and is especially useful for farmers in remote locations, it has

**Arabica Cherry   Baby Pulper Coffee   Clean Coffee Centrally
Processed**

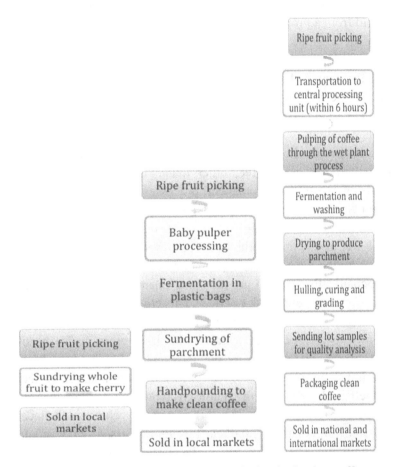

Figure 1: Different value chains in Araku coffee.

several drawbacks. Not all the farmers have access to baby pulpers, and the process requires substantial amounts of water. There is no provision to deal with the resulting effluents that pollute community water sources. The complete process from picking to producing clean coffee is also very laborious for individual farmers and the comparative gains over selling cherry are very little. It is also difficult to maintain the quality of the coffee when using the home processing method. This results in poor non-exportable quality.

Table 1: A comparison of local prices and cooperative prices in Araku.

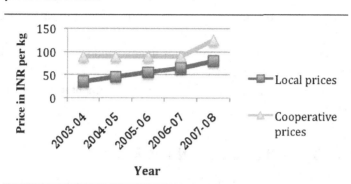

The price that the farmers can get when selling via a middleman at the farm or to traders at local fairs is extremely low in relation to the effort required to produce it (see Table 1). This situation is typical of many "pro-poor" income generation initiatives which never really flourish. While there has been large public sector investment in encouraging coffee plantations, the corresponding facilities for value addition either do not exist, are poorly managed or are inadequate. Similarly little investment is made in branding or marketing that could give higher returns to the farmers by opening up new possibilities for their direct participation in national and international value chains.

Unlike some of the other cash crops grown in the region such as niger, a type of oilseed, or *rajma*, which are locally consumed, coffee is a pure cash crop. It is therefore fully dependent on market linkages, and in the case of the Araku coffee farmers, on having intermediaries through which to sell. Most farmers sell their coffee to local traders during the weekly *shandies*. The price is far below average national prices. The farmers also tend to get cheated by dishonest weighing. In the absence of effective institutional credit mechanisms, many farmers take loans before the harvest from local money lenders. At the time of the coffee harvest the money lenders demand repayment in coffee which they value at prices far below even the locally prevailing prices, thus recovering the principal loan amount at what are effectively very high interest rates.

Low awareness of coffee markets combined with low bargaining power and insufficient buyer competition from outside the region are the main reasons why the farmers end up being caught in an exploitative value chain.

Thus the environmental, technical, financial and social barriers need to be overcome in order to create a new type of value chain that is more inclusive and is commercially viable and environmentally sustainable in the long run.

AN INCLUSIVE VALUE CHAIN IN THE MAKING

In 2001, the Naandi Foundation began to work with the Araku tribal coffee farmers in an effort to build such an inclusive value chain. Several key things had to be put in place. This section outlines the strategy along with the steps undertaken in building this value chain and how it has made a difference to the lives of the tribal farmers.

As mentioned earlier, one of the foremost challenges in Araku valley was to arrest environmental degradation and improve soil fertility. This was primarily done by training the farmers in effective organic methods of coffee cultivation and management techniques.

At the outset, intensive soil inoculation was carried out on the degraded land with organic nutrients in an effort to improve soil fertility. The farmers were encouraged to construct stone boundary walls around their coffee plantations and to preserve the silver oak shade trees. In addition, farmers were persuaded to plant other shade and income crops such as banana, pepper vines which grow on the silver oak trees, pineapple, citrus and ficus within the coffee plantation. This not only shaded the coffee plants, but also provided an additional source of income to the farmers. Plants such as banana also provided excellent compost for *in situ* composting. The bio-diverse plantation also reduces the risks from pests and diseases to which coffee plants are susceptible.

The farmers were then trained to prepare various different organic substances which can be applied as compost or as organic pesticides. One of the distinct achievements of this effort was to secure organic certification through international agencies such as Control Union and IMO. Because of the growing popularity of organic crops this has opened up new international markets for Araku coffee. It also gives the farmers a price edge over conventionally grown coffees. The organic premium for Fairtrade Arabica coffee is 20 cents per pound of green coffee. This translates to approximately Rs. 20 per kg higher price for clean coffee. The yield in Araku for coffee farmers who use organic methods is almost twice as high as for those who are not applying any kind of inputs. Thus while the average yield is around 300 kg per acre, the yield with organic inputs is around 600 kg per acre.[2] This earns more income for farmers and brings greater price benefits, but more significantly the organic method of cultivation using inter-cropping has helped to enhance biodiversity and to create a value chain that is environmentally sustainable in the long run.

Small farmers in India and Araku continue to be exploited because they are fragmented and unorganised and they lack the financial and market linkages that would enable them to have a greater control over the value chains of which they are a part. In order to harness economies of scale as well as to improve the bargaining power of the tribal farmers, Naandi formed the Small and Marginal Tribal Farmers Mutually Aided Cooperative Society (SAMTFMACS) in 2007.

By mid-2008 nearly 8,000 farmers were members of this cooperative with more farmers joining each day. The cooperative helps its members only in the production and sale of coffee, but in the future it may help them to sell other local agricultural products as well.

> "In the process of understanding how to grow coffee organically, we have also developed a greater community feeling and ownership that this is our future and we must take care of it. We are confident now that we can solve our problems and plan ahead for ourselves."
>
> — *Kumbho, Vice President, SAMTFMACS, Araku.*

---

[2] The yield in Araku for coffee farmer who are using organic methods is almost twice as high as those who are not applying any kind of inputs. Thus while the average yield is around 300 kg per acre, yields with organic inputs is in the range of 600 kg per acre.

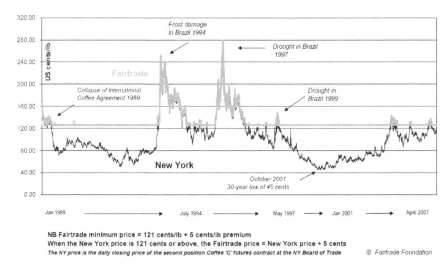

Figure 2: The Arabica coffee market 1989–2007: Comparison of Fairtrade and New York prices.

When SAMFTMACS was registered, it secured Fairtrade certification for Araku coffee, making it the only Certified Organic and Fairtrade Arabica coffee in India.

Figure 2 compares Fairtrade versus conventional trade prices for coffee from 1989–2007. In addition to ensuring that farmers are able to meet the cost of their production, the Fairtrade certification gives a higher brand value for the product. Internationally more and more consumers are beginning to demand Fairtrade products. The Fairtrade label is also useful in other ways. For example, Fairtrade norms mandate that the cooperative has to function in a democratic and transparent manner, thus reducing the chances of political malfunctioning. The Fairtrade premium of US 10 cents per pound of coffee is a good source of income for the cooperative, and cooperatives all over the world are using this premium to develop their communities by building schools, roads, water supply systems and so on (Slob, 2006). Naandi has also been systematically building the capacities of the farmer members of the Society by introducing them to new markets, by exposing them to coffee-tasting events and showing them modern coffee processing facilities.

"The Mulkanoor trip was very good. I had a chance to see the work of the Federations there. After I came back I wanted to motivate the farmers back in my village of Gummaguda. In Tamil Nadu I met farmers who were also poor once upon a time. But they worked hard on their coffee plantations and today they have motorbikes and good houses to live in. I learnt that if we maintain our plantations well, we can develop like them. Today my plantation can be compared to any of the ones in Tamil Nadu. This has inspired other farmers in my village. I am also happy to be part of the MACS as through it we can all develop together. In the future, I want other products to be sold through the MACS."

— Jajamani, Board Member, SAMTFMACS.

The first-hand experience of seeing the success of other farmers and farmers' organisations such as the Mulkanoor multi-purpose society has inspired many of the tribal farmers in Araku.

The next step was to create post-harvest processing facilities that would enable farmers to move further up the value chain. This has been one of the most crucial investments in the region, as very few farmers were able to process the coffee, and fewer still were able to do it to high-quality standards. Selling coffee as mere cherry was not remunerative. The farmers needed a centralised processing facility to ensure coffee processing to the highest technical and quality standards. A facility was needed to collect fresh coffee fruits from individual farmers and to process it in a variety of ways to meet the demands of newer markets, especially the niche speciality coffee markets. Some markets require pulped and sun-dried coffee, commonly known as unwashed Arabica, others prefer unfermented washed Arabica, and yet others need fermented washed Arabica. Producers who can satisfy these different requirements can command higher prices than those who depend on processing facilities which are not under their control.

Naandi started to create the essential physical infrastructure to meet the farmers' post-harvest processing needs. The co-operative bought land for the central processing unit. Naandi raised the necessary finance through grants and commercial debt to create an asset that will ultimately be owned by the community. The land for the asset is registered in the name of the co-operative. The cost of the processing unit is about $50,000. An international organisation provided a grant of $7,500, and the balance was raised from a bank loan to Naandi, which was secured on the processing plant. Once the MACS has repaid this loan to Naandi, and Naandi has repaid the bank, the plant will be owned by the MACS. One strategic benefit of this arrangement is the fact that the co-operative members cannot sell or pledge the equipment, since title to it is in safe custody of the bank. It also allows time for the co-operative to mature and for the members to experience enough positive benefits to prevent the institution falling prey to political maneuvering, as has so often happened with farmers' co-operatives in India, particularly in tribal areas.

> "I will never give up coffee now. The coffee plants are like my children. Just as your children look after you when you are old, these plants will look after my family for many years. Organic didn't mean much to me. I'm not a farmer and I'm illiterate. But I saw the soil was responding to the care we gave it. I've learnt new things about growing coffee. Naandi has also made my work very easy. They pick up the coffee fruits as soon as they are plucked and save me a lot of time and effort.
>
> — *Tiku, Gondivalasa village, Araku Valley.*

Naandi has engaged some of India's most experienced coffee experts to guide the whole process. While only the primary processing facilities, that is pulping, fermenting, washing, drying and a small storage godown, are presently in place at the MACS, high-quality secondary level processing facilities for hulling, curing, grading, roasting and testing have been identified and are being used as sub-contractors to enable the tribal farmers to participate in the global value chain.

Currently, close to 300 tonnes of clean coffee can be processed in the central processing unit in a season. The other advantage of a central facility is that it leaves the farmers free to concentrate on growing and improving yields rather than spending time on manually processing coffee.

Perhaps one of the most important criteria of an inclusive value chain is the proportion of the end-product price which the farmer obtains. Coffee is one of the five most traded commodities on the planet, but less than 10% of the final sale value goes back to the farmer (Fitter and Kaplinsky, 2001). The increasing number of consumers, especially in Europe, who are willing to pay the Fairtrade premium has ensured that this proportion has increased in recent years. Coffee commands different price premiums depending on its taste profile as well as its producer origins. Naandi aims to enable farmers to get even higher prices than the Fairtrade and Organic premiums by creating a brand identity for Araku coffee, both nationally and internationally. Globally coffee is a very competitive commodity and different country producers position themselves in unique ways to get premium prices. One such success story is the way in which some Ethiopian coffee producers who produce some of the finest coffees in the world have created speciality brands named after the regions of Yirgacheffe, Sidamo and Harar. These are sold worldwide as branded trade-marked coffees under special licenses. In India, similarly, the brand "Monsoon Malabar" is famous around the world and sells at a premium.

Naandi intends to follow a similar strategy on behalf of the coffee producers in Araku. While coffee used to be sold at low prices locally without any identity or recognition for the farmers, it will now be sold under the brand name of "Araku Emerald" in speciality coffee markets around the world, giving Araku farmers not only better prices but also due recognition for their labour. Tiku and Kumbho, a tribal coffee farming couple who have achieved very good results, received the "Flavour of India" Award from Jairam Ramesh, the Minister of State for Commerce and G.V.Krishna Rau, Chairman of the Coffee Board of India.

The farmers have realised that well-organised collective marketing of their produce can more than triple their incomes. In 2003–04, the average price realised by Araku coffee farmers was between Rs. 25–35 per kg of clean coffee. In 2004–05 this had gone up to Rs. 90 per kg, and in 2007–08, it had increased to Rs. 123 per kg, one of the highest prices ever realised by farmers in the region. This price was obtained for the supply of fresh coffee directly to the central unit at designated village procurement centres, whereas the low prices previously realised by the farmers were for coffee that they had processed themselves which had taken several days of their labour.

The turnover of the business in 2007/08 was almost Rs. 11 million with the average sales price per kg of clean coffee close to Rs. 175. This is a very good price for coffee from a non-traditional region. As volumes increase with expanded processing facilities, the cost of processing and marketing will come down and farmers will be able to get a greater share of the final price.

Local open market prices for coffee in Araku have also risen. While it is difficult to attribute this directly to the efforts of the co-operative, which is marketing internationally, it has no doubt contributed to it.

Thus not only have the farmers belonging to the co-operative benefited, but hundreds of other farmers in the region now also benefit because the local traders and middlemen have to pay them higher prices. The average per capita income from an acre of coffee cultivation has gone up from Rs. 2,500 to as much as Rs. 8,000 and in some cases is as high as Rs. 30,000 due to better coffee management and yields.

In the future Naandi hopes that the farmers will be able to secure an even greater part of the value chain when they can themselves control the institution that roasts, packages and markets the end product directly to the consumers. It is only too well known that the bulk of the profit in the coffee value chain is made at the top end of the chain in roasting and marketing.

This is the story of a small tribal farmer by the name of Bisoi Arjun living in Malisingram village of Araku valley. Bisoi is around 55 years old. He is married with two wives and five children. "I thought, I was born to borrow money and would drown in debts. I used to walk more than 30 km a day to Gondivalasa and other villages to work in the fields of the money lenders. All we knew was to grow seasonal crops like cabbage or carrots on the hill slopes after clearing the trees. Whatever we grew, we ate", says Bisoi.

(Continued)

(Continued)

"My wife Kamala would dry mango seeds and boil them with water. We would drink this every time we were hungry. Apart from the occasional vegetables grown in our fields, we never cooked other dishes."

But with the introduction of the organic coffee project, thousands of farmers are now looking at coffee farming as a steady source of livelihood. "Initially, we couldn't understand why there were so many trainings for us. We thought we knew how to grow things, but the amount of care that we had to take of the plantations was quite a lot. Making manure, pruning the shrubs in a particular way was part of these trainings. At the time many of us didn't think it was worth putting in so much effort. But now I'm glad we continued, because no one else who is growing coffee the traditional way has ever come near the incomes we have managed after going organic.

In 2001–02 Bisoi had an acre and a half of coffee plantation on lease from the government and two acres of his private land where he grew other subsistence crops such as paddy and millet. His overall annual income at the time was less than Rs. 7,000. The majority of this was from other regional crops such as niger, jackfruit and tamarind. His coffee plantation at the time was only three years old and not bearing any fruit.

In the year 2003–04 Bisoi harvested around 125 kg of clean coffee which he sold in the local market at Rs. 35 per kg fetching him a total income of Rs. 4,375. In 2004–05 with higher yields and the price of Rs. 90 per kg paid by the co-operative he earned close to Rs. 34,000. With this income Bisoi bought a pair of bullocks worth Rs. 11,000 and also a small amount of gold.

In 2005–06 he made an income of Rs. 32,000. With this money Bisoi bought another half-acre of land for coffee and one more acre for vegetables. He also contributed towards the education of his grandchildren. In 2006–07, Bisoi earned Rs. 41,000 from his one

(*Continued*)

(Continued)

and a half acres coffee plantation. He used this money to buy a bicycle for himself and also to help his son build his house. He has leased another acre of land for coffee from the government. In 2007–08 he earned a record sum of Rs. 67,000 from his 1.7 acre coffee plantation.

"For my wife, the fact that we are eating three meals a day coupled with seasoned vegetables, tamarind *rasam* and occasionally chicken is a great sense of pride and security. We are confident that we'll give our children a better life than what our parents could give us", says Bisoi.

— *Bisoi Arjun, Malisingram village, Araku Valley.*

There is a time lag of three to four months between the harvest and sale of coffee due to the various stages of processing. Producer organisations worldwide have always struggled to get working capital so that they can provide rapid payment to their member farmers. This is also one of the most important ways by which such organisations can gain the trust of their members.

One way co-operatives do this is to identify lenders who are willing to make loans to coffee producers at low interest rates against signed buyer contracts. Because there are restrictions on borrowing from foreign institutions, Naandi has had to borrow from local commercial banks at interest rates as high as 13% in order to provide the farmers with working capital at the time of harvest. This has to some degree ensured that farmers do not fall into the hands of money lenders who charge exorbitant interest rates to farmers but who do give them credit when they need it.

In addition to the working capital, adequate storage facilities are also needed to save the farmers from having to sell their coffee at low prices as soon as it is harvested. When farmers have access to affordable credit and storage facilities they become aware of the ever-changing national and international prices for coffee, and are empowered to wait for the right moment to sell.

CHALLENGES AND SUSTAINABILITY

While the Araku experience has shown that it is possible to combine good business and environmental responsibility and at the same time to give the poor a greater share of the ownership of a value chain, there are many challenges. Some of these are beyond local control, such as world coffee prices which are linked to global production levels in a particular season. The four key challenges are basically geographical, environmental, financial and institutional.

The geography of Araku is itself a challenge, primarily because it affects the inclusivity of the value chain. Almost 20% of the farmers live in remote areas, and the nearest road head is sometimes 10–15 km from their farms. Because of this, these farmers are unable to bring their raw coffee to the central processing collection centres themselves. Even if they were to process the coffee themselves and sell it to the cooperative their transport costs would be very high, which would significantly reduce their incomes. Their coffee could be Fairtrade-certified, but they would not be eligible for organic certification, because of the routine malathian sprayings which the public health department carries out around their houses to prevent malaria. The other areas that tend to get excluded are those where the Naxalite insurgents are active. This prevents the coffee trucks from moving around, as the insurgents sometimes seize them or threaten the drivers at gunpoint. Efforts are being made to negotiate with the insurgents through influential community members, and also to improve the farmers' on-farm processing methods, so that they can earn higher prices.

There are also a number of environmental challenges. "Organic" is a core value of the programme, but organic farming alone is by no means a panacea for all the problems of coffee plantations. A coffee bush can yield fruit for up to 25 years, but like other crops it is susceptible to pests and disease. Some of these such as leaf rust do not threaten the life of the bushes, but others such as stem borer or berry borer can wipe out entire plantations. It is vital therefore to work continuously on soil enrichment as well as to preserve biodiversity by intercropping. Most tribal farmers, however, are unable or unwilling to invest even on a minimal scale to get higher yields, as they are not sure of the returns. The co-operative is considering the introduction of collective organic sprays to help the members to improve their yields.

The farmers also need a comprehensive crop insurance scheme for their coffee, which is rapidly becoming the main source of income in the region. No scheme of this kind is available from government or private sources. Naandi may form a partnership with some other institutions to protect the farmers against the huge losses they might suffer from some unforeseen disaster.

There are also a number of financial problems. Presently almost all the direct costs of running the business are being covered by the co-operative from the sales proceeds. Naandi's inputs are subsidised through grant funding from charitable organisations, but this is only available for a limited period. Between 2001 and 2008 Naandi spent close to $0.48 million on the project including overheads. Between 2004 and 2008 the total sales were almost $0.46 million. Processing costs absorbed about $0.21 million of this, and the farmers themselves directly earned $0.24 million. In 2008, the co-operative received for the first time a Fairtrade premium of $11,000 to be spent on community development activities.

In addition, Naandi raised almost Rs. 1.3 crores in 2007 from grants and bank loans which was invested in a new central processing unit with 300 tonnes processing capacity. Naandi plans to spend a further $0.4 million in 2009 and 2010 to further develop the processing unit. This investment will yield substantial results in the future.

Significant investment is required in the initial years for coffee producers to be able to produce high quality coffee that will give them higher returns and enable them to participate in global value chains. The non-profit structure of the Foundation and the youth of the Cooperative, however, make it difficult to raise commercial equity or debt. As operations expand and more farmers supply coffee to the central unit, more working capital and investment will be needed. Alternative institutional structures may be needed to allow the business to grow more rapidly and at the same time to preserve its core values.

It is particularly hard for a non-profit foundation to start and develop an inclusive value chain. It is socially and politically challenging to organise small and marginal tribal farmers into a single institution and to maintain their cohesion. When there are several thousand farmers it becomes even more difficult because of the potential governance hazards that are inherent in most cooperatives. Dedicated and sustained institution building is required. It may also take a considerable time before the farmers can not only benefit but can become actively involved in decision-making, especially in marketing and finance. Apart from the obvious difficulties of language and literacy, these areas require professional expertise. It is to be hoped that the farmers will eventually be able to identify and appoint professionals who will perform these vital tasks and will also be accountable to them.

COOPERATION AND GOVERNANCE IN THE VALUE CHAIN

The development of an inclusive value chain for Araku coffee has involved substantial co-operation between various actors, especially at the producer's end. The concept of governance is used to understand the extent to which producers participate in the value chain, and how and on what terms they participate (Kaplinsky, 2000).

The co-operative and the emerging value chain are very much at a formative stage, but it is already possible to analyse the level of integration in the value chain along with the extent to which farmers are engaged in decision making.

The level of vertical and horizontal integration in a value chain is a direct indicator of the level of producer participation and decision-making capacity, which are important features of successful co-operatives.

In the initial years there was little vertical integration; the farmers' involvement was limited to their coffee farms. They were involved only in the production of coffee fruits, their harvest, and maintaining the basic records which were required for the organic certification process, with the help of community workers. Since 2006, the farmers have taken on greater roles within the value chain. They now handle procurement during the harvest which entails quite complex logistics and planning. They are also involved in coffee processing at the central unit and are gaining an increasing understanding of coffee processing methods and quality standards. Co-operative members have also taken over responsibility for making payments to farmers, which was previously done by Naandi staff or community workers.

The level of horizontal integration in the value chain, that is the extent to which the producers and their co-operative become more involved in the management of the value chain, is also an important indicator of the capacity of the co-operative. This can include acquiring knowledge about markets, making decisions on contracts and buyers, and co-operating with other actors in the chain. This process has only just begun for the Araku Co-operative. Marketing decisions such as price negotiations and buyer contracts, especially for international markets, are primarily made by Naandi, but the farmers are given complete information about the quantity and quality of coffee purchased by the buyers as well as the price. Naandi acts only as an authorised agent on behalf of the farmers as opposed to a trader who would buy and re-sell

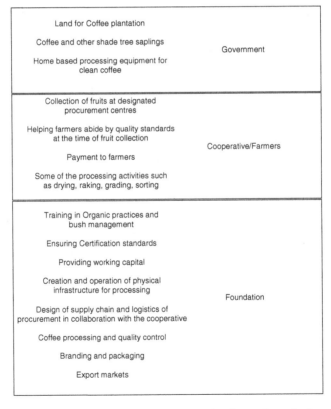

Figure 3: Role of various actors in the value chain.

Table 2: Governance analysis of Araku coffee value chain.

	Exercised by parties internal to the chain	Exercised by parties external to the chain
Legislative governance	• Coffee quality standards set by buyers • Price and delivery schedules set mutually by producer and buyer	• Coffee Board of India sets specifications for Indian coffee as well as export norms • Organic certification standards set by IMO • Fairtrade certification standards set by FLO, Germany
Judicial governance	• The co-operative ensures that farmer member supply fruit of specified quality standards • Naandi on behalf of the co-operative ensures that the buyers' as well as certifying agency standards are met	• An independent quality laboratory monitors quality consistency of pre-shipment and actual shipment samples • Independent auditors evaluate cooperative performance • Fairtrade and IMO conduct annual inspections to ascertain compliance
Executive governance	• The co-operative helps farmer members to supply fruits of specified standards • Naandi trains farmers to meet the organic and Fairtrade standards	• Technical coffee and organic agriculture experts help cooperative and Naandi to understand and meet quality standards

at a profit. The entire sales proceeds, after deduction of processing and marketing costs, go back to the farmers.

As part of running the business, the farmers also regularly meet other actors in the value chain such as technical experts, international buyers, certification agencies and local government organisations.

The development of the Araku coffee value chain has involved working with several different organisations at the local, national and international level. Each of these exercises different levels of authority within the value chain and outside it. These involve legislative governance, which defines the conditions for participation in the chain, judicial governance, which measures compliance with the rules through performance audits, and executive governance, through which assistance is provided to value chain participants in meeting the operating rules (Kaplinsky, 2000).

The combination of internal and external agencies within the value chain ensures a fair degree of transparency and accountability within the system. External agencies exercise a great deal of authority, especially in the case of Certified Fairtrade Organic coffee, and they ensure environmentally sustainable production, price transparency and democratic behaviour in the cooperative. Producers and buyers have to abide by the rules set by these agencies. Producers have limited control in the value chain, but they do exercise some control over prices and delivery schedules, both of which are critical. They must therefore have some knowledge and understanding of the various standards which apply in order to be able to comply with them and thus to benefit from operating in a global value chain.

CONCLUSION

The Araku coffee farmers' case shows that it is possible to build inclusive value chains through business models that are commercially viable, environmentally sustainable and also support poverty alleviation. Such value chains can bring about dramatic changes in the lives of the small farmers. The Araku farmers were landless and their environment was degraded; they have become proud cultivators of sustainable coffee plantations. They were fragmented and exploited and have now become members of a large cooperative; they were selling their coffee in local markets at far below production cost and are now earning a fair price for their labour in the international market; they were isolated and ignorant tribals and they now understand the nuances of coffee processing and marketing.

REFERENCES

Kaplinsky, R (2000). Spreading the gains from globalization, what can be learnt from value chain analysis, IDS Working Paper 110.

Slob, B (2006). A fair share for coffee producers, In *Business Unusual: Successes and Challenges of Fair Trade*, Osterhaus, A. (ed.), Brussels: Fair Trade Advocacy Office.

Case Study **12**

Small-Holder Broiler Farming in Kesla

Anish Kumar

CONTEXT

The Kesla small-holder broiler poultry value chain was initiated by Professional Assistance for Development Action (PRADAN) in 1992. PRADAN is a public service organisation promoting rural livelihoods in the poverty-stricken central Indian region — home to the largest concentration of poor people in India and possibly in the world. About two-thirds of the estimated 280 million poor families in India live in the central Indian states of West Bengal, Orissa, Bihar, Jharkhand, Chattisgarh and Madhya Pradesh.

PRADAN works with 150,000 of these poor families. It organises women into self-help groups and assists families to adopt livelihood activities in agriculture; such as cereal crops, cash crops, vegetables and horticulture; livestock, such as dairy and fisheries; and forest and

Note: Units of measurement in the Indian numbering system: lakh = 100,000; crore = 10,000,000. Indian Rupees (Rs.) where appropriate are converted into USD at a rate of approximately Rs. 50 = $1.00; Rs. 1 lakh = $2,000; Rs. 1 crore = $200,000.

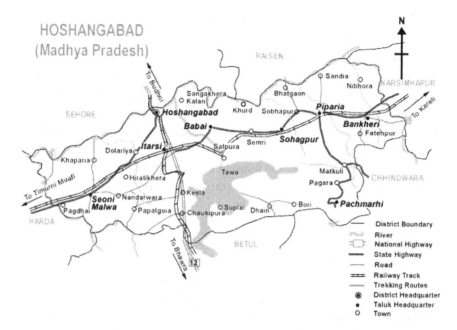

Figure I: Locations of main broiler production and markets.

plantation-based activities including tasar silk and shellac rearing, and leaf plate-making. They also promote the integrated development of natural resources through livelihood-focused watershed development and small-scale irrigation and rural enterprises such as modern commercial poultry, mushroom cultivation and tasar silk processing. The small-holder value chain described in this case study emerged in Kesla block of Hoshangabad district in Madhya Pradesh from PRADAN's experiences of improving the income-earning opportunities from backyard poultry.

About 44% of Kesla's population is tribal and 13% are from scheduled castes. The poultry project is concentrated in the southern part of the block, where 80% of the population is tribal. Villagers in this area have been displaced by a number of projects such as the Tawa Irrigation Project, the Itarsi Ordnance Factory and the Central Proof Range Establishment. The development indicators are abysmal — there are only eight hospital beds per 100,000 people and about 38% of villages are linked by an all-weather road. The area is undulating and less than 9% of the land is irrigated. The agriculture is mainly rain-fed with rudimentary agricultural practices. The average productivity of millet and maize, the principal crops, is barely 40% of the national average. Most families are unable to produce enough grain to last more than six months. People are forced to go into more vulnerable occupations, earning wages as migratory agri-labourers, construction workers or even collecting unused artillery shells in the nearby military test-firing range to sell as scrap metal, putting their lives at risk. The typical livelihood portfolio of a family consists of one-third earnings from low-productivity rain-fed agriculture, one-third from collecting minor forest produce and the rest from wage earnings, in all totalling about Rs. 15,000–18,000. Most of the households with which PRADAN is working are in deficit, hence people reduce their consumption, forward sell their expected agriculture or forest produce at low prices, or, when this is not enough, they borrow money. The prevailing daily wage rate for men in construction or non-agricultural operations is Rs. 40–45, and during harvesting of wheat and soyabean it is as high as Rs. 55–60. Wage-earning opportunities during other times are severely limited.

Most of the poor households in the area rear country poultry. A household typically keeps between 5–15 birds, which survive by scavenging on household waste. This activity, known as "backyard country fowl rearing", uses little of the family's labour or cash resources and provides Rs. 1,000–1,500 in a good year, mainly to meet emergency cash requirements. In addition, about 20 or 30 eggs are consumed by the family every year. The activity is valued by the families, but they do not see it as a significant income source.

There is a long history of keeping poultry within tribal communities, and it is socially valued. It has, however, remained very simple and is not used for commercial purposes. Chickens are kept for festive occasions, for ceremonial purposes and for celebrations and as a special delicacy in honour of visitors. Chickens are sold at times of financial need and when there are no other alternatives. No efforts are made to improve the quality of the flock. The households spend little or nothing on their poultry and keep no account of what they do spend. The chickens are left on their own to scavenge and look for food. They often feed on kitchen leftovers or crop waste, for which they have to compete with dogs, goats and other household animals.

Very few households have built special pens for their flocks and the birds usually stay in the family's main house. Breeding is left to chance and average flock sizes are limited, ranging from 5–15 birds. One hen typically lays no more than 30–60 eggs a year, in three batches of 10–20 eggs. Mortality rates are relatively high.

The marketing chain is informal. Small-scale traders visit people's homes to find out if they have any birds to sell, and they then sell on the birds to purchasers or through brokers either in the same village or in nearby weekly market places. The brokers are small-scale petty traders who do business in two or three commodities, by collecting them from households and bringing them to the local market.

Basically, poultry rearing and its associated value chains are very informal. The chickens are owned by the household and the women take care of them. There is no management as such, and the chickens are basically left to their own devices for feeding. A woman who is winnowing grain or threshing maize will throw the leftovers to the chickens, and they also feed on kitchen waste. Little or no use is made of vets, but some traditional indigenous medicines are sometimes used when a bird is sick or injured. Less than 5% of the households have chicken pens, and most people share their own houses with the birds. Breeding is left to chance and no selective breeding is practised. The flocks are therefore often inbred, and this leads to reduced performance.

The productivity of the birds is very low. They put on no more than about 850 gms of weight in eight or nine months, and although 70–80% of eggs are hatched, which is quite a high figure, chick mortality is very high at about 50%. Around one-fifth of the grown birds die each year, but adult bird mortality is considerably higher during summer due to disease outbreaks; it is not uncommon for whole flocks to be wiped out. The marketing is also very informal. Individual households sell occasional birds directly from their homes to local buyers or at the markets, and the buyers also go round to purchase birds for resale at the weekly markets themselves. There is very little trade in eggs, which are generally consumed at home or kept for hatching.

Table 1 illustrates the value chain of home-based fowl rearing. The starting point of the value chain is the production of birds, and the costs entailed are essentially the market value of the eggs and a notional figure for the cost of care.

It takes six to eight months before the birds are marketable. The total opportunity cost of rearing marketable birds, including egg costs and the time taken by family labour including children for 180 days at a notional figures of Rs. 3 an hour is estimated to be Rs. 20 per bird. The food scavenged by the bird is not included in the cost, as the opportunity cost of this to the family is minimal.

Table 1: Home-based country fowl rearing finances (Rs.).

amount in Rs.

Transaction points	Cost of production/ Buying	Selling price	Gross margin	Transaction costs	Net margin	% Return	% of final market price	% Net margin of total margin	Actors
Home-based country fowl rearing									
Production end	20	60	40	0	40	200	60	63	Individual households
→ Brokering point	60	70	10	5	5	8	70	8	Brokers
→ Primary market/bulking	70	85	15	5	10	14	85	16	Local village *haats*
→ Terminal market	85	100	15	7	8	9	100	13	Traders

The first transaction happens at the house where brokers pick up the birds and bring them to a nearby market, *haat* or *kasba*. Primary bulking takes place at this point, where the brokers congregate and birds are bought by traders from nearby cities for retailing. In this traditional value chain the farmer takes 63% of the price paid by the consumer. This relatively large share is because the farmer's out-of-pocket costs are negligible and the opportunity value of the cost component is very low. It consists only of eggs that are in any case difficult to sell, and the value of the time spent looking after the birds.

The transaction costs include haulage losses and maintenance costs at different points. One key feature of this chain is the scarcity of supply for what is only a small niche market. In the final urban market these chickens only constitute a small portion of the retailers' business. Although the farmer's return per bird is high, the annual return from this activity for a family which has 15–20 birds is only Rs. 1,200–1,800. A typical poor family in the area has an annual income of Rs. 16,000 from their entire portfolio of livelihood activities, thus the share of their income earned from poultry is only about ten percent.

India's growing economy and the increasing demand for animal protein presents new opportunities for poultry producers. In India the poultry industry has been growing at more than 12% a year over the last decade. National annual consumption of chicken in India is 2.2 MT. A CII-Mckinsey report (CII and Mckinsey, 1998), on the sector predicts that production will reach 10 billion broilers by 2015.

The estimates of income elasticity for meat and eggs strongly suggest that consumption of these products can be expected to continue to grow strongly. Per capita annual chicken consumption in India is 850 gm against a world average of 9.5 kg; in rural areas this is just 350 gm. Chicken is the preferred meat for the non-vegetarian population because of its universal usage, its wide culinary adaptability and also for health reasons, because chicken is considered as white meat, while both goat and lamb are red meat which is considered unhealthy. Due to the religious beliefs of the majority Hindu community, beef is restricted to a very small segment of the population; in smaller cities its sale is also strongly discouraged. The market for pork is also limited due to its low popularity in the predominantly non-vegetarian Muslim community.

Most of the opportunities in poultry, with its double-digit annual growth, have been seized by the large breeders. The small farms' share of total production has fallen from 55% in 1970 to less than 10% in 2008.

This concentration of production in the hands of big producers has also been aided by the inability of small breeders to operate in an industry that is increasingly market-oriented and vertically integrated.

This is the context in which PRADAN's intervened in the poultry value chain, starting in 1988 in the indigenous poultry sector and in 1992 in home-based broiler poultry.

The home-based broiler poultry model described in the following section demonstrates that it is possible for small farmers to participate in this growing industry. The small farmers have been able to match the efficiency of large producers and organised integrated value chains. In 2008 the small producers were the largest commercial producers of poultry in Madhya Pradesh and Jharkhand. About 3,700 women poultry farmers who are organised in 14 cooperatives breed half-a-million chicks every month and produce goods worth Rs. 40 crores every year.

The small-holder broiler value chain attempts to adapt the complex broiler production technology to the small farmer's context and at the same time to achieve economies of scale through collective buying of inputs and marketing of produce. The value chain is based on decentralised production, with each family rearing 300–400 birds on their farm, so that the operation fits into their daily life. The producers are rigourously trained to ensure efficient production, and they are supported by technical experts and quality on-call veterinary services. Cost effectiveness is assured by collective procurement of inputs and sale of birds to achieve economies of scale and to integrate the producers into the whole value chain. The problem of volatility in the market has been dealt with by delinking the producers from the vagaries of the market, through collectivisation of the marketing operation. This is key to the success of the enterprise. PRADAN also introduced customised financial and MIS software for decentralised operations, and a system of growing charges was devised to create an incentive for efficiency. The para-vet charges were also linked to production results.

In 1988, PRADAN started work on augmenting the incomes of the tribal poor in Kesla through poultry. In 1992 the monthly traded output of table birds in the area was only 2,500 birds. In 2005, this area — a 60 km stretch between Itarsi and Shahpur — was the third-largest broiler area in Madhya-Pradesh, producing over 200,000 table birds every month. The success of broiler farming among the tribal poor has had a multiplier effect. With the easy availability of poultry feed, vaccines and delivery of chicks to farms, rearing broiler birds has become much easier. Larger farmers have also

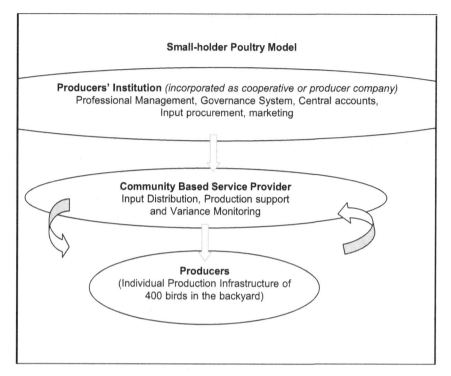

Figure 2: The home-based broiler poultry production model.

found it expedient to set up broiler farms in the area as more traders come there for supplies, and this improves the economies of scale for all parties.

The following table (see Table 2) details the stages of the programme, its salient features, milestones and lessons.

There were many challenges in the technology, the unit size and the institution model. PRADAN took almost 10 years to create a small-farmer-centred model of broiler farming. The total investment in Kesla over the four phases was around $0.42 million, as shown in the following table (see Table 3). PRADAN's implementation costs are not included in these figures.

The first major hurdle was to create a market for broilers. In 1986 PRADAN started by assuming that a large market existed in Bhopal. After a few years it was clear that the production volume and the transaction costs in reaching Bhopal made this unviable. The local table-meat market was dominated by goat meat which was sold fresh-cut in convenient quantities, while the chicken market consisted mostly of country fowl which were sold by numbers not by weight. It took two years to establish broilers as an alternative meat product sold by weight in this market. The success of Kesla

Table 2:

Phase	Salient features	Lessons/Issues
First phase: 1988–1992		
Experimentation		
Introduction of improved breeds in backyard poultry and interventions in the market for better prices	1. Marketing 2. Cage rearing of cockerels 3. Breeding and rearing separated.	✓ Little industry interaction and individual experimentation ✓ High return on investment but low absolute income failed to motivate farmers or to encourage intensity in the business ✓ Trials with 25–30 cage reared birds failed miserably
Second phase: 1992–1997		
Pilot testing and demonstration of broiler farming	1. Broiler rearing on deep litter initiated 2. Breeding and rearing done by the same family 3. Rigorous training 4. Standardisation of production prototype	✓ Adequate financing is vital — units were underfinanced ✓ Criticality of unit size: lower unit size did not adequately provide for debt servicing ✓ Financial implications of market volatility were ignored, there was no risk mitigation system and the intervention was fragile

(Continued)

Table 2: (*Continued*)

Phase	Salient features	Lessons/Issues
Third phase: 1997–2002		
Scaling up		
Expansion, systems design, institutionalising producers' cooperative	1. Rapid expansion 2. Producers organised as cooperatives 3. Intervention in other components of value-chain 4. Establishment of warehouse and wholesaling	✓ Key to success was de-linking of production and business risks ✓ Enterprise ownership needs more than systems, it requires investment in people ✓ Margins are needed to cover establishment costs
Fourth phase: 2002 onwards		
Prototype development Documentation, developing systems for large-scale marketing, lobbying, setting up projects in new locations	1. Modern retail outlets 2. Feed production 3. Replication by other NGOs and by PRADAN	✓ Creating a good governance structure that is able to exercise ownership; professional control of the operating structure is the biggest challenge ✓ Integration of all the cooperatives through a producer company dedicated to the growth of small holder poultry farmers

poultry was closely linked to the growth of the chicken market in Sarni-Pathakheda, which consumed almost two-thirds of the chicken produced until 2000. The townships around Satpuda Thermal Power Station and the Western coalfields at Sarni-Pathakheda are only 60 km away from Kesla, and they

Table 3: Programme costs ($).

Particulars	Phase I Learning & groundwork 1986–1991		Phase II Piloting & demonstration 1991–1997		Phase III Scaling up 1997–2002		Phase IV Prototype development 2002 onwards	
	Grant	Loan	Grant	Loan	Grant	Loan	Grant	Loan
Production infrastructure			9,600	3,900	72,000		54,000	130,000
Working capital				10,000	6,000	20,000		50,000
Capacity building of producers and support infrastructure	18,000		4,000		4,000		33,600	15,500
Total	**18,000**	**0**	**13,600**	**13,900**	**82,000**	**20,000**	**87,600**	**195,500**

have many consumers with high disposable incomes. The cooperative is still only able to sell only 10–15% of its total produce in the Bhopal market.

CREATING INPUT SUPPLY IN A NEW MARKET

In 2004 when PRADAN initiated the small-holder poultry project in Jharkhand, basic inputs such as feed and medicines were not available even in the state capital Ranchi, even though it consumes 20 tonnes of live birds every day. Producers had to compromise on the quality of inputs, so that it was quite common to have to use date-expired vaccines and spurious medicines. The producers collectively negotiated with manufacturers in Kolkata and as the scale of their operations increased, a few showed some interest and started dealing direct with the co-operative. The cost of inputs has now fallen substantially because of the Jharkhand Poultry Federation's collective purchases.

It also took many years to organise the supply of quality inputs at competitive prices while production was still low. Rail transport of chicks by was initially very difficult, in that one in every five consignments was delayed. This is still a problem in any new area when the programme starts.

Bringing producers together in a cooperative with predetermined service norms was another challenge, particularly when there was already a local retail market for the produce that paid a higher price. The service norms of the cooperative initially caused mistrust because the producers had to accept a 60% lower price than the retail prices charged in local villages. The farmers had to learn that marketing and distribution cost money, and that producers cannot expect to get the same prices as retailers. They had to be trained so that they could understand the way in which their cooperative worked.

This was even more difficult because all the inputs were given on credit to producers, and the amounts owed were deducted after the sale of the poultry. The farmers were thus in physical possession of goods with a value that could easily be greater than their entire annual profit margin. Vested local interests and individual farmers' shortage of cash caused some delinquencies, but PRADAN has generally been successful in discouraging side-selling of this kind, mainly by showing that it was possible for the co-operative to earn good profits for its members if they stuck to the rules.

PHOOLWATI BAI — A PROUD POULTRY FARMER OF MANDIPURA

Phoolwati Bai lives in the village Mandipura. Her family consists of her husband and six sons. She is a landless farmer. Prior to starting her poultry business, Phoolwati's only regular source of income was from loading sand in the local quarries, earning between Rs. 10–15 a day. She often migrated to neighbouring districts to get casual labour jobs in the harvesting season. Her husband worked as a wage labourer in Itarsi, 25 km away from Mandipura, earning around Rs. 1,200 a month. Phoolwati started her poultry enterprise in 1997 and she earned Rs. 1,500 with her first batch. She then repaired her house with a loan of Rs. 19,000 from her self-help group, and she successfully repaid the loan with the profits from her poultry business. In 2005 the family then got a loan of Rs. 30,000 from the PMRY, the Prime Minister's Rojgar Yojana, a government scheme to encourage self-employment, to expand her poultry shed. Phoolwati has made regular repayments and is confident that she will repay the loan within a few years. She and her husband have stopped wage labour and migrating for work. They are doing their best to educate their children in order to ensure that they have good careers. One of her sons has completed his higher secondary education and now has a job. Phoolwati has also invested in two life insurance policies and makes deposits of Rs. 883 twice a year. In 2007–2008, Phoolwati earned Rs. 38,000 from her poultry business.

A typical farmer in the value chain is a rural woman from a disadvantaged community, who has hitherto depended on rain-fed agriculture and casual wage earnings. PRADAN's systematic intervention at different points in the value chain has enabled such women to access the skills, the infrastructure, the inputs and the marketing arrangements she needs for a successful home-based broiler unit. All she needs is one cent of land, just over 400 sq. ft, which can be either owned or leased. She can earn between Rs. 13,000–18,000 a year from this, which works out to between Rs. 65 and Rs. 90 a day for 200 days of work. This income is available to her on a continuous basis, and it helps her to meet her need for cash and also to invest in household assets for the family. Table 4 shows the economics of a typical individual farmer's operation in the broiler value chain.

Table 4: The economics of an individual 400-bird broiler unit.

Techno-economics of individual broiler unit (*Unit size: 400 birds per cycle*)

Capital investments/Rs.	36,000	Batches in a year	6	Feed conversion ratio	1.65
Working capital/Rs.	17,000	Days per batch	35	Mortality	5%
Margin per batch/Rs.	3,100	Hours per day	3	Average flock weight	1.5 kg
Annual margin/Rs.	18,600	Days engaged per year	210		

The farmers obtain their finance from a mix of bank loans and subsidies from existing poverty alleviation schemes, such as the Government of India's flagship self-employment programme, the *Swarna Jayanti Gram Swarojgar Yojana* (SGSY), tribal welfare schemes and externally aided projects such as the District Poverty Initiatives Project (DPIP). New producers raise their working capital as individual bank loans or from the pooled capital at the cooperative. The cooperative also raises working capital from banks for its own operations and for its members.

The home-based broiler value chain is essentially a scaled-down version of the modern industrial broiler value chain. The two value chains and the margins earned by the major actors are compared in the following table (see Table 5).

The value chain is centred on the farmers, and this is the key to its success. The smaller size of each producer unit means that the share of the

Table 5: The industrial broiler chain and small-holder based broiler value chain (Rs.).

amount in Rs.

Actors	Share in consumer pie (%)	Realisation	Value increase	Direct cost	Margin	Share of total margin (%)
Industrial broiler value chain						
Farmer	76	38	38	35.5	2.5	33
Wholesaler	4	40	2	1.5	0.5	7
Distributor	6	43	3	1.5	1.5	20
Retailer	14	50	7	4	3	40
			50	42.5	7.5	
Small-holder home-based broiler farming						
Farmer	76	38	38	34	4	53
Cooperative	4	40	2	1	1	13
Wholesaler	6	43	3	2	1	13
Distributor	0	43	0	0	0	0
Retailer	14	50	7	4	3	40
			50	41	9	

Table 6: Home-based broiler farming: Margins and actors.

amount in Rs.

Transaction points	Cost of production/ buying	Selling price	Gross margin	Transaction costs	Net margin	% Return	% of Terminal market price	% Net margin of total margin	Actors
Home-based broiler farming									
Production end →	34	38	4	0	4	12	76	44	Individual Households
Primary bulking →	38	40	2	1	1	3	80	11	Cooperative
Wholesaling →	40	43	3	2	1	3	86	11	Traders
Terminal market	43	50	7	4	3	7	100	33	Traders

return which goes to the producer has to be higher than in the industrial broiler chain. The small-holder value chain introduced in Kesla is more efficient than a large private farmer in the area and is thus able to stay competitive.

The new value chain builds on the low-cost labour which is available in rural households, as compared to more expensive labour in urban and peri-urban areas. The farmer's margin is almost 60% higher in the smaller units, because of the low or negligible opportunity cost of labour. The

Table 7: Comparative features of the value chains.

	Free-range backyard poultry	Modern industrial broiler farming	Home-based broiler farming
Pre-production	Chicks are obtained by hatching of eggs in the household. Birds scavenge.	Chicks are supplied from hatcheries. Feed is bought from compound livestock feed manufacturers or prepared in-house.	Chicks are supplied from a hatchery or from own production. Feed is produced in cooperative's own unit.
Production	No significant labour deployment required in family. No access to veterinary/ technical services.	Outside labour is employed. Veterinary/technical services bought from market.	Family labour. In-house round the clock veterinary and technical services at doorstep.
Marketing	Directly bought from farm by brokers or sold in local *haats*.	Involves elaborate chain of wholesalers and distributors for supply to retailers.	Direct to retailers, wholesalers and cooperative-owned retail outlets.

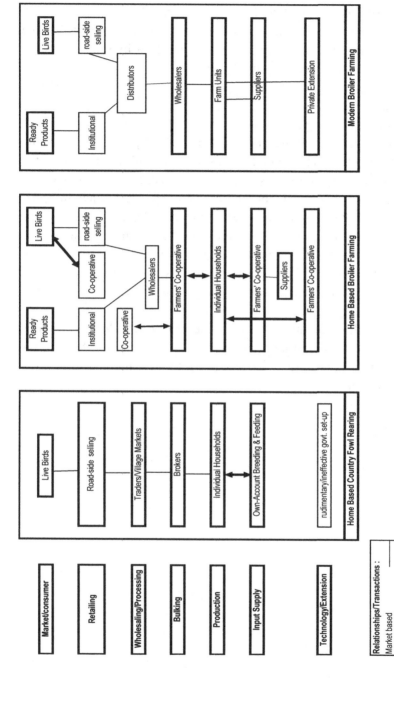

Figure 3: The value-chain map.

co-operative aggregates the production of several small decentralised units to create marketable lots. It has to bear the cost of collectivisation and of the veterinary and management support which is provided to the member farmers, but these increased costs are offset by selling direct to retailers, without any intermediary distributors.

The margins and actors in the small-holder value chain are shown in Table 6.

The producer's margin as a proportion of the total margin in the chain is less than that in the traditional household poultry value chain, as shown in the earlier table. The absolute annual earnings from the traditional value chain are however very low because of the low carrying capacity of individual households using the traditional informal methods. In the PRADAN home-based broiler model, the farmers get all the food and medicines which their birds need from outside sources, via their cooperative, and they are thus independent of the resource constraints of the small farmer. The unit size has been designed to make optimum use of one family's surplus labour. Table 7 compares all three poultry value chains.

Figure 3 illustrates how the home-based broiler value chain gains efficiencies by bringing functions in-house. This increases the margins for the farmers' cooperative, and enables it to meet the increased costs of collectivisation.

REFERENCE

CII and Mckinsey (1998). *Food and Agriculture, Integrated Development Action* (FAIDA), Confederation of Indian Industry.

Chapter **6**

Inclusive Value Chains in Non-Food Artisan Products

Introduction

The two cases in this final chapter of case studies are about non-farm products. Much has been made in recent years about the potential of non-farming activities to absorb rural labour which cannot find a place in modern farming. This is either because new agricultural methods must inevitably be more capital intensive than the traditional methods they replace, or because of population growth.

The preceding case studies have shown that modern integrated value chains can sometimes be inclusive; they need not necessarily employ less people per acre or per unit of production than traditional ones, and they can increase farmers' incomes. But they are exceptions, the overall trend is probably inexorable, and millions of people must move out of farming. The obvious alternative is of course rural-urban migration, either on a seasonal or a permanent basis, but it is generally agreed that every effort should be made to minimise this; it does not always result in improved livelihoods, and even if incomes are increased the general quality of migrants' life is not.

There are large numbers of non-traditional rural non-farm activities, (Mahajan and Fisher, 1997) such as phone kiosks, farm machinery repair and construction, and employment in these is growing far more rapidly than in farming. Many more people, however, are employed in traditional activities, notably in handloom weaving, but also in other fields, some of which have been declining even more rapidly than agriculture.

There have been many expensive attempts in India to protect and assist such industries. Markets have been reserved for them, particularly those involving government purchases, licenses for new competitive industries have been limited, heavy subsidies have been provided, and all manner of co-operative and state interventions have been attempted. These have been partially successful at best, and have often merely delayed rather than prevented the decline and demise of traditional artisanal crafts.

The two examples in this chapter are different. They are about two very traditional activities, hand-made "mojari" leather slippers and hand-rolled "agarbatti" incense sticks. Both have been successfully preserved and indeed expanded, in terms of both incomes and volume. The new value chain for slippers was initiated by a state-sponsored rural assistance agency, and the agarbatti value chain was set up by ITC, one of India's largest and most profitable private-sector companies.

In contrast to most government-sponsored craft support programmes which depend largely on low prices and protected markets to maintain demand, these initiatives are based on an understanding of consumer preferences. The traditional leather slippers have been radically redesigned to suit the tastes (and the feet) of foreign and sophisticated urban Indian buyers, and the agarbatti have been re-merchandised so that they can effectively be distributed and marketed through the company's highly integrated and comprehensive delivery channels. The final prices to the consumers, and the marketing margins to the "middlemen", are higher in these new value chains than in their traditional alternatives, but the village producers of both items are better paid, on a more sustainable basis. Women in particular have benefited, since there is more decorative needlework on the redesigned slippers, and the incense sticks are mainly rolled by women.

The agency which set up the mojari value chain attempted to withdraw after some years, and some of the improvements which had been achieved failed to survive. The state attempted to revive the system with more direct interventions, which seem generally to have failed because they were based purely on technical analysis rather than in an understanding of the crafts-people's view of themselves and their craft.

There is no sign that the agarbatti value chain is similarly vulnerable. It was initiated by the company which markets the products, and there is no reason for any "exit"; ITC wishes to remain in the business. An agency which promotes a value chain for the benefit of the producers rather than its own profit must eventually leave the producers to fend for themselves; the exit may be fatal for the value chain. This difference is in itself an argument for value chains which are promoted purely for profit rather than for the public good.

REFERENCE

Mahajan, V and T Fisher (1997). The Forgotten Sector: Non-farm Employment and Enterprises in Rural India, ITDG, London.

Case Study **13**

ITC Limited and the Agarbatti Industry

Nagendra Nath Sharma

BACKGROUND

ITC's foray into the agarbatti (incense sticks) industry shows that a large company and unorganised producers can work together to transform the landscape of a particular sector, and to create an inclusive win-win situation for major stakeholders in the value chain.

This case study describes the origins of the ITC intervention, the business model, the roles and relationships of the important stakeholders, its impact on the major participants in the value chain, especially the small producers, and the possibilities for scaling it up and sustaining it in the long term.

ITC is one of India's leading private sector companies with a market capitalisation of almost $11,400 million on 31 March 2007 and a turnover of almost $4,000 million during the year 2006–07. ITC employs over 21,000 people who work at more than 60 locations across India.[1] It is a

---

[1] ITC Web site : www.itcportal.com.
Note: Units of measurement in the Indian numbering system: lakh = 100,000; crore = 10,000,000. Indian Rupees (Rs.) where appropriate are converted into USD at a rate of approximately Rs. 50 = $1.00; Rs. 1 lakh = $2,000; Rs. 1 crore = $200,000.

multi-product diversified company making and marketing cigarettes, paperboards and specialty papers, packaging materials, packaged foods and confectionery, clothing, stationery, safety matches, agarbatti and other fast moving consumer goods (FMCG). ITC is also involved in information technology, hotels and agri-business. The company has a number of strong brands and is one of only eight Indian companies in the Forbes A-list for 2004, which lists 400 of the "the world's best big companies". "*The Economic Times*" brand equity listing includes ITC among the 100 biggest FMCG brands. Three of the company's brands are included in the top five brands in India.

ITC is generally regarded as a company with genuine social commitment for sustainable and inclusive development. Its chairman Y. C. Deveshwar calls this "a commitment beyond the market".

Social development is one of the components of ITC's corporate strategy. Its mission to create wealth for its stakeholders by "creating multiple drivers of growth", is intended to ensure the long-term sustainability of its business and to contribute to making India's development more inclusive and equitable.

ITC's major initiatives in rural areas are the e-Choupal trading and information system, live stock development, social and farm forestry, women's empowerment and integrated watershed development, as well as the fresh produce business which is described elsewhere in this book. The aim of all these programmes is to build the company and also to bridge the rural and urban divide and to promote inclusive growth. Its e-Choupal initiative has won international recognition, and it is helping Indian farmers to improve their competitiveness through the application of information technology.

All these initiatives, although they may appear to be no more than "corporate social responsibility", are linked to ITC's business operations and add to the profits of the company.

ITC aims to create multiple drivers of growth by using its core competencies in large-scale marketing and distribution, brand positioning, supply chain management and high-quality management and leadership. Their forays into new business are expected to win a significant share of their chosen markets. The overall sales of agarbatti, for instance, the subject of this case study, are growing at an annual rate of between five and ten percent.

In 2004 ITC started to market agarbatti under its brand name "Mangaldeep", which means "auspicious lamp". The business model is based on outsourcing all the production of agarbatti to small producers through partnerships with self-help groups, non-government organisations and small-scale firms.

ITC aims to enhance the competitiveness and profitability of the small and cottage units with which it is working in the agarbatti business, by providing inputs for product development and linkages for marketing. Before launching the product, ITC conducted a fragrance mapping exercise across the country, and the company's research and development centre regularly evaluates different fragrances in order to suit their consumer's preferences.

V. M. Rajasekharan, who runs ITC's agarbatti business, said:

"ITC's strategy for business growth has been to creatively and synergistically blend its proven core competencies in its established businesses to create multiple drivers of growth in the FMCG sector. It is as a part of this strategy that ITC commenced marketing agarbatti sourced from the small-scale and cottage industries. This business of marketing agarbatti manufactured by micro and household enterprises and continuously enhancing their quality, leverages ITC's core strengths in brand building, marketing and nation-wide distribution, supply chain management, paperboard manufacture and the provision of creative packaging solutions."

OVERVIEW OF THE AGARBATTI INDUSTRY

Incense in its different forms has been widely used for thousands of years across various cultures. The word "incense" is derived from the Latin word "incendere", meaning "to burn". Incense is an aromatic gum or stick that produces a sweet odour when burned. It is used in the ceremonies of all the major religions, such as Hinduism, Judaism, Buddhism and Christianity. Incense sticks are used to combat bad smells and to drive away mosquitoes. Incense is also said to uplift people's moods, to soothe their senses and to purify the environment. Most Hindu households use incense during their prayers.

The scents are made from raw materials such as sandal-wood powder, natural herbs, fragrant materials and aromatic oils.

The incense stick or "agarbatti" as it is called in Hindi, became popular in Bangalore around 1900. It consists of charcoal dust mixed with perfumes which is rolled on to bamboo sticks. The sticks were called agarbatti as one of the raw materials was Agarwood plants. Agarbatti is very simple to manufacture. It consists of a paste of dust from various trees which is mixed with charcoal and Jiggit, an adhesive substance made from the powdered bark of the Maclilus Makarantha tree, which is then rolled on to bamboo sticks. The product became very popular and its production spread widely in the south as it was convenient to use.

Jasmine and sandalwood were readily available in the area, and the Maharaja of Mysore also patronised the craft. During the 1920s and early 1930s, chemicals such as Musk Xylol, Musk Amberette and Crystalose started to be used as substitutes for wood-based raw materials.

Initially most agarbatti was made by Muslim families but later other communities joined the industry. Its production spread to Karnataka, Tamil Nadu and Andhra Pradesh. The manufacturers drew on ancient Ayurvedic books to design new formulations and varieties and by the 1940s the agarbatti had become a popular household article.

Since then agarbatti has grown into a major industry, and many cottage and household businesses have started making it. The industry started in and around Mysore, where it provided employment to thousands of people, and it then spread to Tamil Nadu and Andhra Pradesh. As the process of making agarbatti is very simple and does not need any machinery, the agarbatti firms outsourced the manufacturing to poor households in rural and urban areas. The women from these poor households took on this work very enthusiastically as it could be done at home, interspersed with child care and other household duties, and it provided them with a supplementary source of livelihood. This led to the creation of a very large production base.

An important turning point came in the 1940s (www.msmefoundation.org) when the then Government of India liberalised the import of chemicals and perfumes. This helped the growth of the agarbatti industry, and later on, between 1965 and 1988 many famous firms entered the market and fuelled its growth and exports.

Since the 1980s, the bamboo sticks on which the incense is rolled have started to be made in other states such as Assam and Tripura, as well as in Gaya and Munger in Bihar, and in parts of Madhya Pradesh, Maharashtra, Gujarat and Orissa. Agarbatti is now a widely accepted product and is sometimes known as the "fragrance ambassador" of India.

There is no precise data about the industry, but the All India Agarbatti Manufacturers Association estimates that it has an annual turnover of about Rs. 2,000 crores, and has grown at a annual rate of between 5–10% between 2003 and 2008. About one fifth of the production is exported, and premium brand products account for around 20% of the market. The majority of sales are of agarbatti with simple fragrances with low prices for mass consumption.

It is estimated that there are more than 5,000 small businesses in India which carry out the final process after the unperfumed sticks have been rolled by mainly self-employed women, working at home. These businesses put in the perfume and package the final product, and their main raw material is the intermediate product, "raw" agarbatti before it has been perfumed. 80 or 90% of the raw agarbatti are made by women at their home on a part-time basis.[2] It is estimated that approximately 100,000 tonnes of agarbatti are produced in India every year. This creates about 16 million days of work and provides a supplementary livelihood to about 200,000 people. Over and above that, an additional 10 million work days are used in making the bamboo sticks which are in turn the basis of the raw agarbatti. ITC business buys its finished agarbattis from the small firms which in turn buy their raw agarbattis from women who have been organised into self-help groups (SHGs), facilitated by ITC.

There are over a thousand different brands of agarbatti in the domestic market. Twenty or thirty big firms control around 25–30% of the total business. Their average annual turnover is around $3 million, and the remaining firms are much smaller.

N. Ranga Rao and Sons of Mysore is one of the biggest firms. They market agarbatti under the "CYCLE" brand and have a turnover of about Rs. 160 crores, with about 8% of the total domestic market. Their products are also exported to more than 45 countries. Hindustan Lever and Reckitt Benckiser also tried to enter the agarbatti business under the "Glade" and "Haze" brands but they failed. The main reason of their failure was the high prices of their products. This was acceptable for better-off people, but the main market is in less well-off households. Sales of agarbatti are also highly sensitive to price. These companies also made the mistake of emphasising the appearance of their products rather than

---

[2] Diagnostic Study of Mysore Agarbatti Cluster, www.msmefoundation.org.

their fragrance. Most consumers buy on the basis of the fragrance and flavour of the product. In recent times other large companies such as T-Series, a large multi-product consumer goods company, have entered the market. T-Series sells its products under the "Flora" and "Real Rose" brands.

This industry is fragmented and has a long supply chain from the stick maker to the final consumer. Most of the operations are outsourced as the process is highly specialised and labour intensive. Decentralised production is more economic for the firms who market agarbattis, and is suitable for the people who actually manufacture the product. Village women roll raw sticks in their spare time along with their other household tasks, and this enables them to earn some additional income. This form of production also discourages the formation of trade unions, which makes it more attractive to the businesses.

The agarbatti industry has generally flourished, in growth and employment creation, and this has been achieved without any government support.

PRODUCT AND PROCESS

This industry has a very limited product range. Some of the more popular types of agarbatti are raw battis, scented agarbatti, flora battis, masala battis, dhoops and cones. Raw battis are made by rolling bamboo sticks in a paste of charcoal dust and Jiggit powder. These are not scented and mainly used as the raw material for scented agarbatti.

Broadly, the product classifications are based on the nature of the perfumes and fragrances, such as different flowers and sandalwood, and the thickness and quality of the bamboo sticks and packaging. There are more than one thousand brands on the market.

ITC's range includes twelve different fragrances. The products are targeted at different market segments, and the sticks are available in packets of between 10–40 sticks. The price varies from Rs. 20–40 per packet. ITC has introduced "fragrance-locked" packaging which adds value to the product and also differentiates it from the competition.

The process of making agarbattti is simple and is mainly done by hand. The raw materials used are bamboo sticks, Jiggit and charcoal dust. The sticks are rolled with a paste of Jiggit and charcoal dust. Jiggit dust

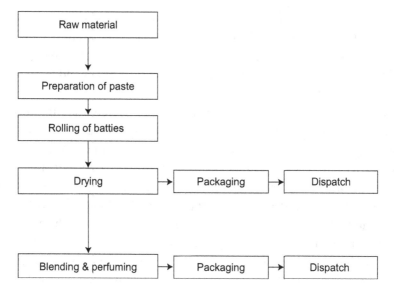

Figure 1: Process of making agarbatti.

is mixed with charcoal powder to make the paste. This is rolled manually on to the bamboo sticks. A powder of red dust is put on to the paste and the stick is then dried in the sun. After rolling and drying, the sticks are dipped into perfume and dried to make the final product (see Fig. 1). The art of making perfumes is kept secret by the manufacturers. In spite of some interventions by the Khadi and Village Industries Commission (KVIC) of the government, and a few big firms such as Hindustan Lever, there have been very few changes to the technology and process of making agarbatti.

ITC'S BUSINESS MODEL

The central principle of ITC's business model for agarbatti is that all the production is outsourced to households, and to micro and small businesses. The raw agarbatti sticks are made by women members of SHGs who supply them to small firms which have been identified by ITC. These firms carry out the perfuming and packaging and complete the final products as required ITC. They are then marketed by ITC under its brand name "Mangaldeep".

The prices at different stages of the value chain and the trade terms between the different stakeholders are negotiated and fixed by ITC. The sources of the raw materials, including the bamboo sticks, the perfume and the packaging materials are identified and their prices and trade terms are decided by ITC.

The main role of ITC is to network with the NGOs and other organisations which form SHGs. Many of the SHGs receive assistance from various government schemes such as the Swarnjayanti Gram Swarozgar Yojna (SGSY). They also take loans from banks which are linked to ITC's operation. In a few places SHGs have been formed solely to manufacture raw agarbatti for ITC's suppliers. ITC collaborates with local NGOs and other organisations which work with SHGs, and the company is thus indirectly able to access the cheap capital and other benefits which SHGs enjoy from government. The SHGs sell raw agarbatti to ITC's identified small-scale suppliers which manufacture the final product. Most of these small firms were already making agarbatti under their own local brands, or for other larger businesses, before they joined the ITC network.

Women who make raw agarbatti on an individual basis and are not associated with NGOs or SHGs are not included in ITC's supply chain, because the company cannot economically coordinate the activities of individual workers.

The technical inputs such as perfume selection, quality improvement, training and packaging are provided by ITC.

ITC has made agreements with a number of NGOs and other institutions which work with SHGs, such as the KVIC, Art of Living, Bangalore, Trust for Village Self Governance in Kuthambakkam near Chennai and a few more organisations which work with SHGs. ITC also collaborates with SEWA and Munger in Bihar, and buys about 10 tonnes of agarbatti every month through them, thus providing supplementary earnings for about 600 women. ITC also works with a small firm in Tripura in the North East, which is a major centre for supply of bamboo sticks.

ITC selects fragrances based on consumer preferences and selects the manufacturers from whom the small manufacturing units are required to procure the material. The specifications given to these manufacturers conform to the recommendations of the International Fragrance Research Association, which ensures that only safe chemicals are used. ITC provides regular feedback to its network partners on safety and other statutory requirements.

ITC's most important role is in brand building and marketing. It advertises in the media and distributes samples on a regular basis. The company markets the "Mangaldeep" incense sticks through the retail outlets which already carry its other products, and "Mangaldeep" has become the second largest incense brand in India.

ITC nominates the sources of supply for raw materials and sets the standards and fixes the prices of the product at every stage of the value chain. ITC does not itself buy or supply the material to the SHGs or the small firms which complete the manufacturing process, but it closely controls the specifications and prices. ITC encourages the raw material suppliers to sell to SHGs on credit in order to reduce the SHGs' working capital requirements. ITC pays the small firms within 10–15 days of delivery and requires them to settle their accounts with the SHGs in the same way.

OUTREACH

By 2008 ITC was providing a livelihood to about 5,000 women who make raw agarbatti, as well as direct and indirect employment to about 1,000 people who work in the small businesses. This amounted to under 5% of the total market, but ITC's share was growing rapidly.

Ten small firms are engaged in finishing the agarbattis and together they supply about 180–200 million sticks per month to ITC. These are marketed through the half-million retail outlets which already distribute ITC's other products. Seven of the small firms have been awarded ISO 9001–2000 certification since 2006, and one firm in Pondicherry has been given the International Fair Trade Association certification. Three of the 10 firms are in Bangalore, and one each in Delhi, Chandigarh, Kolkata, Hyderabad, Agartala, Coimbatore and Pondicherry. During 2007 ITC bought a total of $5 million worth of agarbatti from these 10 firms.

EXTENDING OUTREACH

Kuthambakkam is a village in Thiruvallur district of Tamil Nadu situated about 30 km from Chennai inhabited by 1,095 households mostly belonging to the weaker section of society. R Elango, ex-President of Gram Panchayat started some initiatives with the support of Exim bank and other agencies for providing gainful employment to women and youths of the village. They were trained to make energy-saving kerosene burners, first-aid components, pet houses etc., for big companies. Observing the simple techniques of agarbatti making and support from ITC, he organised and trained 30 women in February 2008 and after about 4 months, the women's groups are supplying about 2 tonnes of raw agarbatti monthly to one SSI unit identified by ITC for making final product. The specifications, price and trade terms are being negotiated and fixed by ITC. A video made by ITC was used as a tool for training. With the support of Indian Oversees Bank and Rotary club, a work shed has been built where these 30 women are working and getting about Rs. 80–100 per day. About 150 women of the same village are willing to join this initiative. Elango is confident that in a year or so, about 600 women from nearby villages will also be part of the value chain.

ITC is just beginning to export agarbatti, but sales have already been made to Singapore, Malaysia, the UAE, Bahrain, South Africa and the USA.

VALUE CHAIN

The major actors in the value chain are ITC, the SHGs and their members, the small firms, the retailers and the wholesalers. The driver of the chain is ITC. The operations of the value chain are shown next.

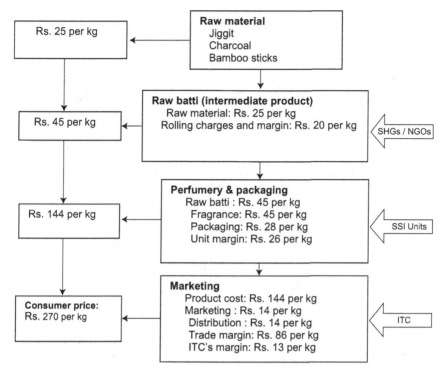

Figure 2: Map of value chain for agarbatti.

IMPACT

This business has provided a livelihood to 5,000 women who make raw agarbatti and has also created additional direct and indirect employment for about 1,000 people who work in the 10 processing firms. These women are mainly from very poor households or are marginal farmers. Before this intervention, they mainly worked as agricultural labourers during the farming season only. Since they started to roll agarbattis for ITC they are getting about 300 days work in a year at around Rs. 80–100 per day. This increases their total earnings by about Rs. 50–60 per day. The impact of this initiative on the life of a typical woman in Munger district of Bihar is described below.

SHAYAMA BEN

Shayama Ben is a resident of Kharagpur block in Munger district in Bihar. Her husband is a mason who earns a very low income since his ill health makes him lose many days of work. They have five daughters and four sons. Her 85-year-old mother–in–law also lives with them.

Their life was shattered when her brother–in–law expelled them from their parental house. They were forced to live in a tent made of plastic sheets.

In 2005, Shyama Ben attended a meeting of the Grama Sabha in her village where details of the "Sunhera Kal" programme implemented by SEWA and supported by ITC were explained to the villagers. One component of the programme provided opportunities for women to form SHGs and roll raw agarbatti.

Shayama Ben joined the programme. She joined an SHG and was trained in rolling agarbatti. Her other family members also learned how to roll agarbattis and now they roll about 175 kg of raw agarbatti and earn about Rs. 2500–3000 per month. One of her daughters is also engaged in sorting agarbatti at a common facilities centre which has been set up for the groups.

Shayama Ben has now built a tiled house with her savings and has taken a loan from the group. She is now confident of her future.

The average annual turnover of the firms which do the perfuming and packaging is $0.4 million and their net profit is about 5% of sales. Three of the 10 firms are start-ups and the other seven were already in the same business but have increased their turnover by about 50% since they started working with ITC. In addition to their increased earnings, these firms have improved their process control, their inventory management, their production planning and their quality control. ITC pays them regularly, as they pay the SHGs which supply them, and their earlier working capital problems have been largely solved.

THE ANANTH AGARBATHI COMPANY

Ananth Agarbathi Company of Bangalore is a small industrial firm which has been in the agarbatti business since before 1970. As is the case in most such firms, the family members managed the whole operation. The firm marketed about 100 different brands of agarbatti, many of which sold in very small quantities. Because of the intense competition and the working capital problems associated with holding stocks of so many brands, the firm's growth was very slow.

The company started to do business with ITC in 2003. Annual turnover was $0.6 million at that time, and by 2008 it had grown to $1.6 million. In the beginning ITC's business made up 30% of the total turnover but this increased to nearly 80%. The firm employs about 150 people and their average monthly wages are about Rs. 4,000.

As a result of becoming part of the ITC value chain, Kashi Vishwanath and his family members are able to concentrate on their core competency in production. The firm has adopted many improved practices and recently acquired ISO-9000 certification. It is now poised to expand.

The value chain has also improved the business of ITCs' existing retailers who sell agarbatti along with other ITC items. ITC's trade margins on agarbatti are between 30–35% i.e., manufacturers offer margins of about 40%, but they say that the ITC product sells faster and is therefore a more profitable proposition.

As ITC's share of the agarbatti market is less than 5%, there is ample scope for growth and the promotion of new manufacturing networks covering more people. ITC also plans aggressively to expand its export sales of the product.

V. M. Rajasekharan is confident that the business will grow, even though big companies such as Hindustan Unilever and Reckitt Benckiser have failed. ITC has learned from their failure. The major reason was the high prices they charged, and ITC is keeping its prices at a level which should meet the expectations of its customers. He hopes to attain a turnover of about $20 million by 2012, and thus to create a regular source of livelihood for about 25,000 poor people, mainly women.

Case Study **14**

Operation Mojari

Vipin Sharma and Mallika Ahluwalia

In the desert state of Rajasthan in western India, over 100,000 families earn their livelihoods by making traditional hand-stitched shoes made out of coarse vegetable-tanned leather, which are known locally as "mojaris". For hundreds of years, these shoes were the footwear of choice for all village residents.

But in recent decades, the livelihoods of this large community of mojari makers were threatened by the invasion of cheaper, more comfortable and more durable factory-made shoes and slippers. An integrated programme to support the livelihoods of these artisans was introduced in 1997. Operation Mojari (OpM) proved to be a successful intervention, which helped to revive the livelihoods of several thousand artisans across the state. It transformed a traditional hand-stitched local footwear into a modern hand-crafted product with a contemporary appeal. It brought in new technology, new designs, new markets and higher incomes to the artisans. Supported by the United Nations Development Program, the project was implemented by the Rural Non-Farm Development Agency (RUDA), an independent agency established by the Government of Rajasthan to support rural livelihoods.

Note: Units of measurement in the Indian numbering system: lakh = 100,000; crore = 10,000,000. Indian Rupees (Rs.) where appropriate are converted into USD at a rate of approximately Rs. 50 = $1.00; Rs. 1 lakh = $2,000; Rs. 1 crore = $200,000.

However, after Operation Mojari ended in 2003, the mojari makers started facing tough times once again, largely due to the fact that the project did not include a plan for a sustainable exit by RUDA, the promoting agency. Although they were still using the new technical inputs, the mojari makers found that, by 2005, they could access neither fresh designs nor the higher-value distant markets.

There are valuable lessons to be learnt from OpM. Firstly, that it is possible to create a large modern market for traditional products, secondly, that the primary producer can be integrated into the value chain, and thirdly, that interventions must be comprehensive to be successful. However, OpM also shows how important it is to ensure the sustainability of market linkages through building local capacity.

Mojaris were once the footwear of choice in Rajasthan because of their heat insulation properties. Air pockets in the leather helped retain body temperatures even as outside temperatures went over 50° Celsius in the day or dropped dramatically at night.

In every village, a small community of low-caste households made footwear for the village. Artisans who work on mojaris are from socially excluded communities, such as the Raigar caste, because working with raw leather is considered impure in Hinduism. Some artisans also belonged to poor Muslim communities. It is estimated that nearly 100,000 families across Rajasthan were once employed in making mojaris.

When communications between villages and towns were difficult, the mojari value chain began and ended in the village. The lowest caste was engaged in carcass removal and flaying. The skin was then locally tanned with vegetable processes. This tanned skin would be used to make mojaris or other leather items. The mojaris were then sold in the local markets. Slowly, mojaris evolved from a coarse shoe to a handicraft with fine embroidery and ornate embellishments, and the finer quality pieces started to be sold in neighbouring towns. Different regions across the state developed their own distinctive styles; the Jaipur mojari, for example, became known for its soft shades, while the Jodhpur mojari was famous for its fine embroidery.

However, demand for mojaris declined dramatically in the last 50 years with the arrival of factory-manufactured plastic footwear, such as Bata slippers and sandals. Not only were these synthetic shoes cheaper, they were also much lighter, more durable, washable and came in many designs and colours. This cheap option was particularly popular with the women and children, who earlier had mostly remained barefoot.

Since there was no longer enough demand to sustain the large number of mojari makers, many skilled artisans turned to other means of livelihood or entered the unskilled labour market. The numbers of mojari makers started to fall sharply and this traditional skill was slowly being abandoned. In Udaipuria, a village near the state capital of Jaipur, a few generations ago all the households were engaged in mojari making. By the 1990s, only a quarter of them still relied on mojari making as their main source of livelihood. Most of them travelled to Jaipur every day to work on building sites and similar unskilled labour activities.

In the 1990s, the National Leather Development Program (NLDP), the government's country-wide initiative to promote the leather industry, noted the declining state of the mojari market and the decreasing livelihoods for the artisans. Given the large number of clusters of skilled artisans, the Government looked for ways of reviving the craft and ensuring sustainability of the mojari makers.

In 1994, NLDP set up a project to aid the mojari artisans in collaboration with the Footwear Design and Development Institute (FDDI) of New Delhi, focussing on artisans at Ramgunj, an urban mojari cluster in Jaipur. The project aimed to revolutionise the shoe-making process by mechanising many of the operations. Costly leather cutting and sewing machines were bought with project funds and placed in the community as a "Common Facility Centre". A designer was brought in from Italy to create a new look for the product.

However, the project failed because it attempted drastically and rapidly to transform the traditional product. For example, the distinctive stitched sole of the mojari was replaced with pasted polymer soles. The artisans were reluctant to abandon their previous methods and move to the mechanised operations. One artisan at Ramgunj said, "I am a master in my own shop, and they wanted us to go there and work like wage labour. I will not be another person's servant." Furthermore, the designs were not created with a view to the market; they were very different from the traditional designs, and they appealed neither to the traditional market, nor could they capture the new urban market.

There were many lessons to be learnt from this project. The top-down approach and dramatic shift in the process was not accepted by the artisans.

The technology was too modern for the leather workers who until then had used only simple hand tools. Furthermore, given that the activity was a home-based household enterprise, the idea of working in a workshop under a Common Facility Centre was misconceived. And it was in any case unlikely that any other artisans would be able to obtain similar expensive modern machinery; the approach was not replicable.

With these lessons in mind, in 1997, NLDP approached the United Nations Development Program (UNDP) to fund a project for leather workers across the country. One of the sub-projects of NLDP was OpM in Rajasthan. The newly-established Rural Non-Farm Development Agency (RUDA) of the Government of Rajasthan was chosen to implement the project.

RUDA was established in 1996 by the Government of Rajasthan as an independent agency to promote sustainable livelihoods in the rural non-farm sector. RUDA aimed to promote rural micro-enterprises by moving beyond narrow scheme-based approaches to more holistic support of identified sub-sectors through integrated cluster-based initiatives. The organisation looked at both backward and forward linkages to make traditional clusters commercially competitive. Apart from leather, RUDA also identified the wool and minor minerals sub-sectors for support. Figure 1 shows the locations of the five districts of the State where OpM

Figure 1: Map showing locations where OpM was implemented.

was implemented, namely Jaipur, Jodhpur, Nagaur, Pali and Jalore. The project was started in 1997 and finished in 2002, it cost a total of Rs. 3.85 crores and it reached about 3,500 artisan households, all of whom were from socially and economically marginalised communities.

OpM was based on the idea that it would be possible to arrest and reverse the decline in the market for mojaris with technology- and design-based solutions. The project aimed to link the artisans to mainstream high value markets.

Development projects centred on handicraft skills often face a tough choice — should they focus on the craft or the craftsman. Often, it is only possible to preserve a craft at the expense of the craftsman, since traditional artisans may be reluctant to expand their scale of production and their livelihoods may be destroyed by the introduction of new technologies and more efficient processes. Similarly, it might be in the best interest of the artisan to ignore his traditional skills and instead to re-train himself and adapt to a more profitable livelihood in a related modern industry. The managers of OpM were firm that their first priority lay with generating livelihoods for the artisans. The managers saw the opportunity to use traditional skills but were open to adapting the mojari as much as necessary to meet new market demands.

In particular, the mojari had many characteristics which reduced its popularity outside its traditional market. The most obvious flaw was that the shoes were the same for both feet. This lack of left-right differentiation can cause blisters and general discomfort. There were also no standard sizes. The artisans used their own wooden lasts or moulds to make the shoes, but there was no system of standardising the size of the lasts. As the lasts chipped and wore out, the sizes of the shoes were also affected. This lack of standard sizes meant that customers would have to try on many pairs to find a pair that fit them.

The traditional vegetable-tanned leather, although it had the advantage of being porous, smelled strongly, and the traditional carcass removal and flaying process caused blemishes on the raw skin that affected the end product. The traditional shoes were also made in the same basic designs, always with a pointed or rounded toe, and a closed heel. The vegetable tanned leather used to make the mojari is usually very heavy, and the heel was always reinforced with a piping that made it bulkier, leading to blisters and cuts on the back of the wearer's foot.

OpM first task was to revise these traditional flaws. Specific technical interventions were introduced to deal with all these problems. In addition, the project also looked at design, markets and longer-term sustainability.

"Initially there was a lot of resistance from the mojari makers", recalls Sanjay Joshi, who was a field coordinator with RUDA. "People didn't want to change their practices, they didn't see the benefit." "The first time I went there with polymer lasts, I couldn't even find an artisan willing to keep one in his house," he recollects. The field co-ordinators had to build up trust gradually; and the UNDP money paid for free distribution of lasts in the initial phase to encourage greater acceptability and understanding of the benefits of using them.

These lasts came in the standard internationally recognised sizes, and had left-right differentiation. This change from wooden to polymer lasts resolved the two main design flaws of the shoes, and made them much more comfortable. The project also introduced new skiving or leather shaving techniques to reduce the bulkiness of the tanned leather.

OpM brought in famous national and international designers, even borrowing from the textile and garment sectors, to create new products. Through a supplementary grant from the UK Government, a few well-known designers from UK were also brought in to introduce designs which would be acceptable in Europe. These designers modified the traditional pattern to make it more fashionable; thus, from one standard toe design, the mojari now had five different toe shapes.

Traditional selling points such as the delicate embroidery were integrated into the new designs. These new designs and patterns, such as the square-toed shoe and the "mule", with an open back, were probably one of the most important contributions of the project as they opened new markets. The changed patterns also helped to overcome traditional problems such as the way the hard leather cut some wearers' feet. The open-backed shoe was particularly popular for this reason.

Machines were distributed free of cost at the village level to mechanise some of the more tedious procedures, like polishing and finishing. This increased productivity. However, the shoes remained primarily hand-made.

The more discerning and demanding clientele outside the local markets demanded that the odour and blemishes on the leather should be remedied. The RUDA managers, therefore, studied the backward linkages in the value chain. The traditional methods used by the flayers for transporting carcasses and removing the skins resulted in many tears and blemishes in the leather; for example, the flayers used to pull the carcasses along the ground. RUDA collaborated with the Central Leather Research Institute to train 500 flayers across Rajasthan in better practices. The flayers were helped to get bank loans so that they could purchase air pressure machines to remove the skins from the carcasses. These machines not only resulted in a neater end-product without cuts but also reduced the time to remove a skin from over half an hour to under 10 minutes.

Similarly, RUDA helped the flayers to get small carts to transport the carcasses. This dramatically reduced the number of tears and blemishes in the leather. The flayers were also trained how to work more efficiently with the skin so that three separate layers could be created from one hide, which in turn increased the number of shoes that could be made from 15–20 to 40–60 pairs. This not only improved the quality of the mojari leather, but the flayers also benefited economically — they could now command nearly double the price for each hide, up to even Rs. 1,200 for one buffalo hide.

The RUDA staff also worked with the tanners to improve their productivity and the quality of the leather. Vegetable tanning can be done at the household level, and does not require large investments. It is also eco-friendly. However, the traditional vegetable tanning process was very labour-intensive as the skin had to be soaked in dye, and hung out to dry. It was also unpleasant because of the smell, the more so because of the social stigma attached to the process. RUDA collaborated with the Central Leather Research Institute to introduce new methods in one district which reduced the tanning time from around 30 days to only 15–20 days and also improved the quality of the finish.

The project also introduced chrome-tanned leather from factories for those markets where the smell of vegetable tanned leather was a problem. This additionally overcame some of the problems with unevenness in the colouring. All these interventions together meant that a household could make and sell more shoes than before.

Mojaris had traditionally been sold in the local village markets in Rajasthan, where they were facing increasingly stiff competition from cheaper factory-manufactured shoes. Therefore, a major challenge for the project was to increase the sales of the newly-transformed product.

Instead of reviving local markets, the project managers chose to redefine the product and to create a new market. The new designs from famous fashion designers and the improved quality opened up the market potential. The project redefined the mojari from simple traditional footwear for the local market to a contemporary up-market fashionable accessory for the upper-end urban market.

The India International Trade Fair in New Delhi in 1998 was the first showcase for the revised product. One of the RUDA managers said, "when we took the products, initially the customers were sceptical because they were used to the old problems with the mojaris, for example, they would get blisters from the unidirectional shape. We then taught the artisans to explain the new features to the customers — the new leather, the open-backed shoes, the left-right differentiation. The stall was a hit and the artisans had to return to Rajasthan to bring more pairs." Another project coordinator recalls that he sold Rs. 5,000 worth of shoes in barely two hours: "the mojaris were selling like hot cakes".

RUDA subsequently sponsored the artisans for many more exhibitions and *melas* (fairs) across the country. RUDA also arranged a trip to the International Shoe Fair in Dusseldorf, one of the two biggest annual events in footwear. The artisans were responsible for making their own sales at these events, but all their expenses were covered by the project. At the beginning, they also received wage payment for each shoe from project funds. At these exhibitions, the artisans made links with Delhi traders, and even with exporters. With their own linkages to outside markets, the artisans started getting bigger orders. As one project manager said, "even we never thought we would be that successful." Almost overnight, orders poured in from across the country and abroad.

Before the project, almost all the mojari shoes were sold in local markets. As a result of the exhibitions, the artisans started to produce mainly for more distant markets. The focus had shifted — 80% of the increased volume of goods was sent to external markets with only 20% staying in Rajasthan.

Since the new design changes and patterns had caught the imagination of the urban market, demand soared and so did prices. The Udaipuria artisans recall that in the early 1990s each household made barely 15–20 pairs a week, but after OpM they started producing 100–150 pairs a week.

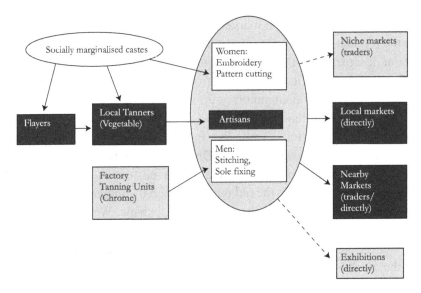

Figure 2: The mojari value chain: before and after.

Note: Before OpM (dark boxes), the Mojari Value Chain was largely restricted to local flayers, tanners, artisans, and markets. As a result of OpM (additions shown in grey boxes), factory tanned leather became more common, women started playing a larger role because of the emphasis on embroidery and embellishments, and new markets opened up through exhibitions and the creation of a niche market both domestically and abroad. However, even with the new markets, old markets and traders also benefited from the boom in the sector.

If they received a large order, some larger households could even go up to 500 pairs.

Before the project, the artisans made hardly any profit on the shoes because selling prices were close to the costs of raw material at between fifty and seventy rupees a pair. However, after the project, shoes started selling for between Rs. 100 and Rs. 350 a pair, depending on quality, leaving the artisans with around Rs. 10 or Rs. 15 a pair in profits. At exhibitions, the profit margin for artisans became much higher, reaching as high as Rs. 150 a pair because all their travel and lodging expenses were usually covered by the project. This combined increase in volume and price meant that total household profits rose to over Rs. 2,500 a week compared to Rs. 300 a week before the project. The following flowchart shows the profit made by each stakeholder in the value chain, before and after OpM (see Fig. 3).

Before Operation Mojari

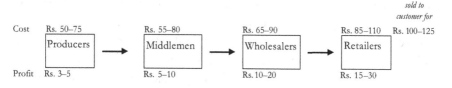

After Operation Mojari

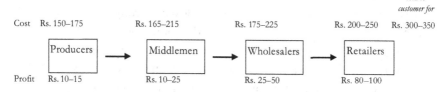

Figure 3: Value addition for mojaris.

Soon artisans started to change back to mojari making — some people who had abandoned the practice in previous decades came back to their traditional livelihoods. In Udaipuria, over three quarters of the households had left mojari making before OpM, but with the increased demand all of them were again fully involved in this trade. The demand for shoes had grown so dramatically that many households even started to hire labourers from other villages to increase their household production.

SHYAM LAL

Shyam Lal comes from a family of 11 that has been making mojaris for over a century. In the 1990s, only two of his brothers and his father were involved in this trade, making around 30 pairs a week.

With the surge in demand which OpM introduced, "everyone in the household got involved", he says, "even my *bhabhis* (sisters-in-law) started working on the embroidery and embellishments, ... even children worked part-time after school." The household started making over 100 pairs a week.

While women from artisan households had traditionally also helped to make mojaris, particularly in leather cutting and embroidery, their role became more important with the introduction of new designs, which required more intricate pattern cutting and more embellishment and embroidery. Usually, the households divided the various processes in mojari making by gender, with the more delicate stages allocated to the women — thus, due to OpM, women started playing a key role in the main household earnings.

Lifestyles changed in the village. There are now well-constructed brick houses where there used to be mud huts. Slowly, through their improved incomes, artisans bought televisions and mobile phones. "We started receiving faxes for our orders," recalls one artisan, "whereas before we had never even heard of a fax, and we didn't even know our a-b-c." Most children in the village are now enrolled in the neighbouring private schools instead of the cheaper government schools. "Our children study in English medium schools," says a proud artisan, "some are even going to college."

However, not all the five districts under OpM enjoyed such spectacular gains. Artisans from Jaipur district had the double advantage of being close to the OpM project headquarters as well as to the Jaipur and Delhi traders. While Nagaur district was also home to many artisan households, the exhibitions provided most of their sales, as the markets are too far away. This district never made the same market linkages nor did it benefit to the same extent from the market boom.

TRADER'S WOE: EXHIBITIONS

One shop owner at the local Jaipur market complained that the many opportunities for artisans to go to exhibitions were hurting their sales. First, it hurt volumes as some goods went directly to the customer. Second, it also affected prices — while retailers needed to mark-up the goods to include their own commission, the artisans whose transport and lodging expenses for the exhibitions were covered by the government could sell the shoes directly for a slightly lower price. Customers then expected retailers to match this price.

TRADER'S DELIGHT: INCREASED SALES

Although OpM connected the artisans directly to external markets, this did not mean the end of the local middleman. Even with the emphasis on distant markets, because of the increase in the numbers of artisans and the shoes produced per artisan during this time, the one fifth of the shoes which were sold locally also constituted good business. Thus, the traders found that they still had a good livelihood.

Many artisans also chose to concentrate on making the shoes, leaving the travelling to the traders. Thus, it was often the village traders who bought the goods in bulk from different artisans and took them to external markets. In the village of Udaipuria, some artisans themselves turned traders and bought shoes for resale from their neighbours. During the peak demand, enough shoes were made in the village to support twenty village traders. "I would take these shoes to retailers in Delhi and even as far as Assam," recounts one such village trader-cum-artisan.

Thus, higher sales and higher profits benefited all members of the value chain, including both the artisans and the traders.

OpM also had to transform the artisans into entrepreneurs. Before OpM, the artisans had no concept of the difference between profits and wages. They simply aimed to recover their costs and make a bit extra. Thus, in addition to training in pattern cutting and designs, OpM also taught the artisans about pricing, marketing and sourcing raw materials.

The artisans learned how to sell their products to new types of customer. Through the exhibitions and fairs, the artisans had to be able to market their products directly to the customer. They were encouraged to move beyond their traditional markets, and to think beyond their traditional products. The project staff hoped that, when the project ended, they would be able to continue to create market linkages without assistance.

In 2001, towards the end of the project, in order to continue the benefits, the central government set up the Society for the Marketing of Artisans and Rural Things (SMART), in collaboration with the FDDI of New Delhi. SMART was set up as a non-profit society, and its main objective was to bring work to the artisans by building market linkages; it was to act as a clearing house for orders, to farm out the work to artisans and to pay them wages per shoe. Its collaboration with FDDI was to ensure that designs were regularly updated to maintain market interest.

Operation Mojari finished as planned, in 2003. With the end of the project, the staff left the villages. SMART was supposed to take over the role of supplying the artisans with technical and design inputs and acting as a link to external markets.

Although SMART's main objective was to improve the livelihoods of the mojari artisans, it did not manage to secure the trust of the artisan community. It was never an association of artisans, but rather an association for artisans, and this was perhaps the cause of some of its problems. Many artisan groups like those at Ramgunj and Udaipuria refused to work with SMART because they did not believe they were getting adequate returns compared to the risks they ran.

The artisans at Ramgunj remember that the managers were unforgiving about what SMART perceived as "quality flaws", which the artisans argued were the inevitable results of handcrafted goods. Rejections during quality checks meant that the artisans often made no profits on orders. "If we were commissioned to make 10 pairs, and they rejected two, then all our profit got eaten up in those two shoes," explains one artisan, "not only did we not receive wages for those two pairs, we were not even compensated for the raw materials we had used in them." These artisans find it more profitable to sell directly in the market.

Artisans at Udaipuria share the same complaint on rejections. They add that the logistics of selling the shoes to SMART also work against them. The travelling and lodging costs for multiple trips to show the product, then deliver it, and then get their payment take away all their profits.

In addition, in order to meet larger orders quickly, SMART mechanised some of its operations and set up a factory with various machines, such as a sole-cutting machine. SMART employs 20 artisans at this factory to operate the machines and also to do some of the stitching. Only the work that cannot be done in the factory is outsourced to collaborating households, who are given wages for their work. This process of in-house manufacturing further limits the benefits to artisans in the villages. Thus, even in its more successful days, SMART only ever had, at most, 400 artisan households as members. By 2008 the number had fallen much lower than this.

SMART defends the quality checks as an important part of building its brand for repeat orders. SMART are actively looking for more artisans with whom to collaborate, but only those who can do high quality work. As part of this effort, they have in recent years conducted some training programmes in neighbouring villages.

SMART has not only lost many of its links with artisans, but it has recently also faced a downturn in sales. On its inception, SMART trademarked the name "Mojari", and for many years focused on the export market. They were producing around 60,000–70,000 shoes a year in 2000 and 2001. But by 2005 mojaris had gone out of fashion in many of SMART's biggest markets, such as Italy and France. With a downturn in export orders SMART had to make the transition to the domestic market. In 2008, around 80% of its orders are domestic; this has brought down its returns because of the lower profit margins in the home market.

Faced with a decline in markets and returns, SMART is taking innovative steps to increase their orders, such as starting a website (www.mojari.com) to retail their goods. They set up their third retail outlet in India in early 2008, where they sell high-end mojaris priced at around Rs. 600–750 a pair. They have also diversified into other products, like bags and pencil cases. However, the main problem remains that SMART is improving the livelihoods of a very small group of artisans.

Most of the 3,500 households which benefited from OpM never graduated to working for SMART. Furthermore, although the government tried to continue some aspects of the project, they mainly reach only the artisans who take the initiative to connect with the government. RUDA organised two missions to the field, which included training and design inputs. The government also continued to sponsor below-poverty-line artisans to visit various exhibitions across the country. However, the piecemeal manner of conducting these activities has diluted their impact.

The artisans were thus, by and large left on their own after OpM. At the end of the project, the mojari market was still booming. The Jaipur artisans recall that they could barely keep up with the demand. However, this golden period did not last long. By around 2005, the artisans found that their incomes, which had gone up dramatically, were sliding down again.

The artisans blame this market decline on undercutting of prices, with subsequent compromises on quality. During the peak demand, many artisans hired apprentices to help them meet the demand. Many artisans blame these apprentices, saying that the apprentices soon returned to their own villages to start their own businesses. Their incomplete skills led to lower quality, which started the price decline.

The Delhi traders, who also stocked other cheaper machine-made shoes, put a lot of pressure on the artisans to provide mojaris at lower prices. They took advantage of the competition amongst artisans. "If I were selling at Rs. 100, then someone else would offer it for Rs. 95", explains one artisan, "then I would also cut the price to stay competitive." But with reduced profits, artisans started cutting corners on quality. In turn, the reduced quality led to even lower prices. This led to a downward spiral.

The increasing price of leather at this time was also an important factor in the reduction of quality. Synthetic materials were commonly used instead of leather for both soles and uppers.

Traditionally, since the flaying and tanning were both carried out in the villages, the tanned leather had always been supplied direct to the mojari artisans. Rajasthan is an arid desert state with little agriculture, but it does have a large livestock population, which meant reasonable prices for leather. However, around the time of OpM, flayers in the villages found that they could get much higher prices for raw leather from industrial tanneries in other states, such as those at Agra and Kanpur. Thus, raw leather from Rajasthan was sent to other states for processing, and then the processed leather was bought by the Rajasthani artisans.

As tanning was relocated from the local villages to factories in other states the mojari artisans had to pay higher prices for finished leather, which forced them to cut quality and shift to synthetic materials. This did mean that the flayers in the villages now had an independent market which was not tied to the fate of mojaris, but it led to even further downward pressure on the prices of the shoes.

A MODERN CUSTOMER

A customer in the local market in Jaipur is buying a mojari for Rs. 90. It's a pretty white shoe, with lots of glitter on top; it is clearly made from synthetic materials. She knows that the shoe is

(Continued)

(Continued)

not durable, and she will not be able to wear it "more than 10–12 times". "But that's OK" she says. She has a new dress, the shoes match it, they're pretty and they're affordable. The shop-owner notes that he has completely stopped stocking leather products and high-end products.

A further problem was that with the end of OpM, there were no more innovations in the designs and patterns. The markets, however, were tired of the same designs. "What new items do you have?", is the customer's constant question, says one Jaipur shoe trader. The constant innovation and new designs made the shoes into fashion items, but by 2005 the markets were saturated with the same patterns, and the designs were seen to be out-dated. As often happens with fashion items, once the upper-end market tires of a product, it moves down the market chain.

BANWARI DEVI

Bhanwari Devi's husband died in 1999. She heads a household of six people, including her husband's younger brother and his wife, her mother-in-law and her two daughters.

With the death of her husband, who used to be a mojari artisan, she was forced to take over the role of breadwinner in a traditional society where women still cover their faces in public. When she could not earn enough money as a day labourer, she enrolled in OpM. Through the project, she received both physical inputs and training.

Recalling those years, she says that she could easily make an income of Rs. 15,000 a month, or even as much as Rs. 20,000, because each pair of mojaris sold for around Rs. 250. She improved her household's lifestyle, and even repaid some old debts.

However, with a decline in market prices, she is now forced to sell her shoes for only Rs. 80 a pair. She feels helpless against the

(Continued)

(Continued)

middleman, she says, because he refuses to give a higher price. With a monthly income of between Rs. 1,000–1,500, Bhanwari Devi is fighting to make ends meet. She was forced to send two of her children to live with relatives, and can barely afford the cost of food and school fees for her two daughters who live with her.

Thus, although the artisans maintained their market linkages with Delhi, they started to target the low-price low-quality market. Their incomes decreased drastically, both because of declining prices and declining demand. Migration from mojari making to other livelihoods started again.

The Udaipuria artisans estimate that once again barely a fifth of the households in the village rely on mojari making for their livelihood. They are producing only around twenty pairs a week per household, and although they sell them for around Rs. 70–90 a pair, the costs of inputs have increased so much that they are barely making a profit. With the costs of living also having increased a lot, one artisan half-jokingly says, "the price covers the cost of the coffee I drink while I make the shoe".

The artisans in the other districts did not suffer in the same way as those in and near Jaipur, primarily because they never benefited as much. Even though Jodhpur is a big tourist city, the artisans were too far from the Delhi traders to form as many linkages as the Jaipur artisans did. They did fare better than the even more remote Nagaur artisans. Artisans in Jodhpur have long been famous for their delicate embroidery

Table 1: Before, during and after project mojari sales and prices.

	Before OpM	During OpM	After OpM
Price per pair	Rs. 50	Rs. 350	Rs. 80
Sales per household	20 per week	100 per week	20 per week
Profit per household	Rs. 300 per week	Rs. 2500 per week	Rs. 500 per week

skills, which no other artisans have been able to replicate. Since their goods were so distinctive, and so different from a plastic sandal, they faced less pressure than their Jaipur peers to downgrade quality. They instead concentrated on the high-quality low-volume market, selling mainly to the export houses based in Jodhpur. They also sell direct to the tourist market.

Even while the mojari market declined, the flayers continued to benefit from the project's technical guidance and their links to the factories, because there was still a large demand for other leather goods in domestic and export markets. Thus, although they are still socially marginalised in many ways, the flayers have better livelihoods and lifestyles. Many of their children are also now enrolled in schools.

RUDA is looking for new ways to strengthen the market links. They have set up "Direct from Artisan" retail shops across the country, where the artisans will be given free floor space on a rotational basis to sell their goods. They are also looking at e-marketing platforms. The RUDA Chairman, Rohit Brandon, says that they are exploring ways of "professionalising marketing by shifting it to marketing agencies".

There is also a growing consensus in the Rajasthan government and some of the former managers of the project that the artisans must be organised into producer societies. The Secretary of Industries in the Rajasthan Government, Mr. Puroshottam Agarwal, emphasises that while OpM was "a good example of how artisans can be linked to markets", the next step must be to "organise, empower and enable the artisans."

These societies would enable the cooperating artisans to make credit linkages and to create brand identities. Like SMART, these "Producer Companies" would have the capacity to meet large export or domestic orders. They would eventually be able to be completely self-sustaining, and even to hire the services of designers to create new patterns for the shoes. These companies would have built-in quality control measures, which could include local monitoring of the products by master craftsmen in the village.

When this idea of forming a producer company was introduced to the artisans in Udaipuria in February 2008 they were very enthusiastic. Within two days of distributing forms for registration to create a company for the village, 100 forms had been filled in and returned. The artisans understand that now they must be the ones to take responsibility. While they will have some initial hand-holding from an NGO, they know that in the long-term they have to take the initiative to ensure that their producer company makes profits and sustains. They hope that through the company they can access loans to buy raw materials to meet big orders. There is a renewed sense of optimism. One artisan has just refused an order of 40,000 pairs because he does not have the capacity to meet the order. These are the kind of orders a producer company could work together to fill.

The government is now actively working towards creating a three-tier structure for the leather sub-sector. At the bottom tier are the producer companies. The next level consists of NGOs that would handhold these producer companies until they are sustainable, and at the top is an apex agency that overlooks the entire leather sub-sector (see Fig. 4). The government will only play a facilitation role and will fund the initial stages of setting up the project, such as paying the costs of the NGOs. Eventually the producer companies would become self-sustainable.

It is not clear, however, how many producer companies and how many artisans the market can support without over-supply and lower prices. There are still some 30,000–40,000 households with the traditional skills of making mojaris, although only a few of them still work in this sector. Mr. Mathur, the former Manager of OpM, believes that the artisan leather sector should be able to support as many as 12,000 households. They would need to diversify into other leather products, such as handbags and folders, as the same workmanship can easily be applied there also. The previous glut in the market was in part caused by the lack of new designs. In the future the artisans will need to constantly innovate to maintain demand. One former manager has suggested that the market could be segmented by quality; artisans can concentrate on meeting either the high-quality fashion products or the low-quality synthetic mass products.

Figure 4: Three-tier structure for the leather sub-sector.

Since the high price of leather was one of the factors in the downward spiral of quality and prices of mojaris, the state government is also working to strengthen raw material production. They are exploring ways of building decentralised processing units in Rajasthan to bring leather processing back to the state. It is hoped that this will bring leather prices down and will make processed leather more physically accessible to the many artisans who rely on it.

CONCLUSION

All the stakeholders in Rajasthan look back at OpM as a success. It successfully took a product whose market was slowly dying and transformed it into a fashionable high-end product with a niche market.

In terms of the value chain, OpM essentially tried to empower the artisans to become entrepreneurs. Where most of them had never been out of their local markets before, they now knew of the possibilities in Delhi, the country and even the world. It gave them new designs that would appeal to this wider market, and helped to transform the shoe to meet urban expectations.

The success of OpM in building markets and livelihoods for these artisans was because of its holistic approach to the problem. Although there have been subsequent interventions since 2003 that aim to bring new designs and skills to the artisans, these have not been as successful as OpM because they were not comprehensively designed.

However, OpM did not build in enough mechanisms to ensure that artisans had continuing access to new designs and markets. Although it was a holistic intervention, OpM did not enable individual artisans to build their bargaining power with distant markets. SMART was set up to fulfil this function, but it was an after-thought which was not included in the original design of OpM. This was reflected in its failure to represent most of the artisans and to carry forward the mission of the original project.

It is to be hoped that the new producer companies will genuinely empower the artisans to play a stronger role in the value chain in the long term. Producer companies should be better qualified to get large orders from Delhi and abroad and to interact directly with export houses. These producer companies should be able truly to empower the artisans to control their own company and thus to build a sustainable value chain.

Chapter **7**

What Do the Case Studies Tell Us? Lessons for the Future

The case studies in this book were selected from a large number of possible candidates because they satisfied several quite demanding criteria. They had to include small farmers, or other non-farm participants, who might have been expected to be excluded from a "modern" value chain. The value chains could be initially cross-subsidised from other activities in the initiating firm or financed from external sources, but in the long-term they had to be sustainable and profitable for all parties; "corporate social responsibility" initiatives, which might be dropped when management's attention was drawn to some other more visible or attractive area, were not admitted. The value chains had to be on a fairly large-scale, or to have the potential to be scaled up to include thousands of producers; they could not be based on a minor specialised niche market.

The value chains had to be based on existing products, rather than being totally new items. They had to have involved a minimum of change to the livelihoods or activities of the producers, and as few new skills as possible. The intention was to identify approaches which could fairly easily be introduced, rather than those which required radical transformation. The value chains could be initiated by large scale private sector companies, by producers' associations, by financial institutions, NGOs or government agencies, but they had in the long-term to be financially and managerially sustainable without the assistance of any external agency or financial assistance.

Readers will have to decide for themselves whether all the case studies which were selected do actually conform to all these standards. It is important to admit, however, that the term "inclusive" has been fairly liberally defined. By no means are all the producers poor or marginalised, although each value chain does include a fair proportion of very small producers, and little is known in any of the cases of those who may have been excluded from the new value chain, or even damaged by it.

It is by definition not possible to see people who are excluded and are therefore not present, whether they are producers themselves, or labourers, or household members, or other people who may have been left out or deprived of a livelihood by the arrival of a new value chain. The "middlemen" (and women) from whose so-called "clutches" the producers have been released are generally not rich, and many of them may be poorer than the producers themselves. It may be that some of them have been marginalised and impoverished by the new value chain. Some of these people, such as the labourers and the *"kacha aadthis"* in market yards who have been by-passed by the Kohinoor company's organic value chain for basmati rice in Uttarkhand, may have been performing redundant tasks, but these tasks did constitute their livelihoods; "modernisation" is rarely a totally "win-win" solution. The producers in these value chains have all benefited, very significantly, but we should not be deluded by this into believing that there have been no damaging but unobserved side-effects.

Table 1 summarises some of the key features of the value chains which are described in this book.

Eight of the 14 value chains were initiated by institutions which themselves planned to play a major part in the value chain, and to profit from it. It is obviously not possible to draw any definitive conclusions from this sample, which covers a wide range of different types of products and producers. It is however clear that it is possible for private sector companies, without external subsidy, to develop and maintain value chains which include small producers and are profitable for all parties. Progress does not have to exclude the poor, and their inclusion does not have to depend on government support or on local or foreign donors.

The above figures also suggest that the value chains which were initiated and promoted by private for-profit businesses grew much faster than those which were promoted by non-government organisations or government and donor sponsored agencies, such as PRADAN, RUDA or EDA Rural Systems. Even when the relatively large number of growers who participate in the Agrocel organic cotton value chain are excluded, the average number of producers who were added per year by the for-profit promoters was almost 600, while the development agencies only managed to expand by just over 400 producers per year.

This difference is quite significant, but the overall numbers are in all cases tiny in relation to the scale of the problems of agriculture in India. Modern retailing and integrated value chains have only come to India in the last 10 years or less, and on a very small scale, but small-scale farmers and artisans in India have been in deep distress for many years. A quarter of a million indebted Indian farmers have committed suicide since

Table 1: Some salient features of the value chains.

Value chain	State location	Year started	No. of producers included	Initiator
Namdhari Fresh	Karnataka	2000	4,000	For-profit agri-business
ITC Choupal/ GMED	Punjab	2004	1,600	For-profit agri-business + foreign donor
INFAM/ Wayanad	Kerala	2000	2,000	Church and local NGO
Spencers	Gujarat	2001	2,000	Corporate retailer
BASIX/PepsiCo potatoes	Jharkhand	2005	1,440	Financial Institution/ NGO
Kohinoor basmati rice	Uttarakhand	2003	860	Corporate agri-business
Agrocel cotton	Gujarat +	2000	25,000	Corporate agri-business
BioRe cotton	Madhya Pradesh	2002	8,000	Corporate agri-business + Swiss importer
Falcon fisheries	Orissa	2003	1,200	For-profit exporter
Honey EDA	Bihar	2002	1,500	Govt. and Ford Foundation sponsored
Rural Systems Araku Coffee	Andhra Pradesh	2001	8,000	NGO + donor assistance
PRADAN broiler chickens	Madhya Pradesh	1988	3,700	NGO
"Mangaldeep" agarbatti	Karnataka +	2004	5,000	Corporate consumer goods firm
Operation Mojari	Rajasthan	1997	3,500	State and donor assisted agency

1997. Some commentators have argued that this number is no more than would be expected from so large a population over that period, but most agreed that this ghastly statistic is but one symptom of a deep malaise.

Our case studies are about the very small number of producers who have been fortunate or enterprising enough to participate in these inclusive value chains, and they have generally benefited a great deal. There is a need for large number of similar value chains, each reaching far greater number of producers. The Amul co-operative dairy system is probably the only example of an effective integrated value chain which has reached the scale which is required. It was started long before the term "value chain" came into vogue, but it reaches around two and a half million people (www.amul.com), mainly women, who operate very small-scale individual dairy units. It depended heavily on subsidy in its early days, but is now very profitable for all concerned. It has not made its producers rich, but it does provide them with a reliable supplementary source of income; there is a need for many more value chains like it.

Most effective interventions in India take place in the South of the country, such as the microfinance movement. Our value chains were not in any way chosen on the basis of their location, but they are fairly widely spread throughout the country, including even the state of Bihar which is one of the poorest and most disadvantaged places in India and where so few initiatives seem to take place or to succeed. This also shows that sustainable and inclusive value chains can be developed anywhere in India; they do not appear to depend on good government, or adequate infrastructure, or higher than average levels of public services such as education and health care. This is heartening, since these assets are in such short supply in much of India.

The promoters of the value chains have used a variety of methods to create and sustain the links between the markets and the producers. Table 2 lists a small number of these methods, and shows which are used in each of the fourteen value chains.

It is or has until recently been almost axiomatic in India, and indeed elsewhere also, that poor people must be in groups of some kind in order to better their situation. These groups may be formal co-operatives under the 1904 co-operative act or its state-level derivatives, such as the societies which the honey and the broiler chicken producers have formed, or, as in the Araku Valley coffee case, they may be mutually aided co-operative

Table 2: Methods and markets used in the value chains.

Value chain	Producer groups or cooperatives	Value chain development subsidised	Fair trade	Producers contracted	Organic	Export/ domestic market
Namdhari fresh	No	No	No	Yes	No	Export +
ITC Choupal/GMED	No	Yes, USA govt.	No	No	No	Domestic
INFAM, Wayanad	No	Yes	No	No	Yes	No
Spencers	No	No	No	No	No	Domestic
BASIX/PepsiCo potatoes	Yes	No	No	Yes	No	Domestic
Kohinoor basmati rice	Yes	Indirect from govt.	Planned	No	Yes	Export
Agrocel cotton	No	Some from Swiss	Yes	No	Yes	Export
BioRe cotton	Yes	No	No	No	Yes	Export
Falcon fisheries	No	No	No	Yes	No	Export
Honey EDA rural systems	Yes	Yes	No	No	No	Domestic
Araku coffee	Yes	Yes	Yes	No	Yes	Export
PRADAN broiler chickens	Yes	Yes	No	No	No	Domestic
"Mangaldeep" agarbatti	No (but SHGs)	No	No	No	n/a	Domestic
Operation Mojari	No	Yes	No	NO	n/a	Export

societies, or MACS, formed under the more recent act which was initiated in Andhra Pradesh and which has been widely imitated elsewhere. Or, they may use the still more recent form of producer companies, as is proposed for the farmers in Kerala and the cotton farmers who work with Agrocel. They can also be unregistered self-help groups, such as those of which the "Mangaldeep" agarbatti producers are members.

There are many obvious reasons why these group enterprises are useful, both for small producers themselves and for any institution which wants to assist their members or to buy from or sell to them. Groups have always been attractive to NGOs and to governments. It is easier and less expensive to reach groups of people rather than individuals, and groups tend to need continuing assistance and nurturing. This ensures that those who are employed in NGOs or other assistance agencies will be able to keep their jobs, and it maintains the "beneficiary" relationship which can be used to secure continuing gratitude, or votes. Individual entrepreneurs are less biddable than compliant and thankful group members, however much these members may have been "empowered" by their membership. It is quite common for staff of assistance agencies to say "we shall form them into a cooperative", as if such an institution could be formed by anyone other than its members themselves.

It is significant, however, that groups of any kind are used in less than half of the case studies in this book. In the other eight cases, the farmers or other producers work as individuals, selling their products into the value chain with none of the alleged benefits of group membership. Group formation is a very slow and difficult task; the PRADAN broiler chicken producers work in a cooperative group structure, but this initiative was started in 1988. This is a successful programme, but it is by far the oldest intervention in the collection, and the assistance agency continues to play a vital role in the maintenance and expansion of the activity. The programme of BASIX and PepsiCo to promote potato cultivation in Jharkhand has not thus far succeeded, and one major reason for this is that the promoters seriously underestimated the time it would take to help the potato farmers to build a viable group enterprise. As so often happens, the agency found it easier in the short-term to manage the activities itself than to build the capacity of the group, but this level of involvement could not be sustained.

We can therefore conclude with some confidence that it is not always necessary to form small producers into groups, of any kind, in order to enable them to play their part in modern and sustainable value chains. Group approaches may be needed, but small producers, like any others, should first be approached as individuals. Group methods should be a last resort and not the automatic first choice.

A new value chain, like any other innovation, requires investment to set it up before the results can yield a return. Large businesses, such as ITC, PepsiCo or Kohinoor, may make this investment from their own resources, or they may look for external assistance to reduce their own expenditure. ITC has made use of assistance from the United States government, which part-financed the GMED programme, and the company has also indirectly tapped government resources by working with self-help groups which have been capitalised by subsidised credit and grants. The promoters of five of the other value chains have made no use of subsidy, but Agrocel and Namdhari are both members of long-established family-controlled business groups which have a record of philanthropy.

The work of EDA Rural Systems in Muzaffarpur was initiated with assistance from the Small Industries Development Bank of India, a government sponsored institution, which has received large amounts of funds from international donors, and the more intensive later stages of the work with honey producers was supported by the Ford Foundation. Both the organic cotton initiatives received Swiss assistance, albeit to a fairly modest extent, RUDA's assistance for mojari producers was partly funded by the United Nations Development Programme and from the United Kingdom, and Naandi's work with Araku Valley coffee growers has been supported from the Netherlands and elsewhere.

There is nothing wrong with foreign assistance in itself, and the institutions which have promoted these value chains have clearly looked for funding from whatever sources are most available. Given the scale and severity of the problems of small producers in India, and the buoyancy of government revenues as well as the wealth of many private companies and individuals, however, it is perhaps rather odd, or even regrettable, that more of the support for these value chains has not come from domestic sources.

The majority of the value chains, however, were not subsidised, from any source. This shows that inclusive value chains can be good business, and that their development can be treated as a commercial investment which can be financed like any other. Inclusive value chains are not dependent on groups, or on subsidy.

Five of the value chains are focused on organic products. We saw earlier that small farmers enjoy particular comparative advantages in organic agriculture, and the rapid growth in demand for organic products, worldwide, has significant positive implications for the future livelihoods of small-holders who might otherwise be expected to be excluded by more modern integrated value chains. The majority of the organic produce is destined for export markets, which is unsurprising since there is as yet only a very limited demand for such crops in India. This demand is growing, however, and the farmers who have already been introduced to the skills needed for this type of farming will be in a strong position to capture a share of the domestic market as it develops. The members of INFAM in Kerala are already beginning to benefit from this.

Organic produce commands very substantial premiums over the price of conventionally grown crops, and the tribal producers of organic coffee in Araku, as well as the cotton farmers who work with Agrocel and bioRe, and the basmati rice farmers in Uttarakhand, are benefiting substantially from these higher prices. There are some additional costs, such as the expenses involved in ensuring that all the produce can be traced back to the farm where it was grown, and, at least in the case of paddy, the reduced yields from other crops such as wheat which are grown on land which has been certified organic and cannot therefore be treated with chemical fertilisers, herbicides or pesticides.

In most cases, however, organic cultivation appears to be less expensive than conventional methods, and it can also generate higher yields. Even if the produce commands the same prices as a conventionally grown crop, with no organic premium, it may be more profitable. This is sometimes true in the short-term, but if the long-term health and fertility of the soil is taken into account, as it must be in particular for small-holders, organic methods are definitely more economic. Organic farming may be much more than a speciality for foreign niche markets. It may offer a solution for many of the problems of India's farmers, and these value chains show how this can be done.

The farmers who grow organic coffee in Araku Valley, and those who grow organic cotton for Agrocel, have also been able to qualify for "fair trade" status. The organic paddy cultivators are also applying for this, with the assistance of the Kohinoor Company. This status enables them to receive substantial sums of money to finance community assets such as schools or clinics, but is also provides a strong incentive for transparency and good governance throughout the value chains in which they participate. If the lead institutions fail to maintain this, or the farmers themselves lose interest in the management and equity of the institutions through which they are selling their crops, they will forfeit the benefits which fair trade status confers.

Fair trade status as yet means little in the Indian domestic market, but it is to be hoped that in due course it will become part of the mainstream as it already has in some markets in Europe, where fair trade bananas, coffee, tea, chocolate and wine have already gained a significant market share. Here again, these value chains are showing the way forward.

"Modern" integrated value chains depend on regular and predictable supplies, and this is one reason why the firms which set up such value chains generally avoid small farmers. The easiest approach is of course for the processing or marketing company itself to own and manage the farms which produce their supplies. Many sugar, paper and palm oil mills, as well as other agri-businesses, cultivate their feedstock on a plantation basis, where they can control every aspect in the interest of the profitability of the complete operation. They may also buy from independent small-holders, but their "captive" plantation is usually their main source of supply.

It is not generally feasible in India for one agri-business company to own and manage enough land to supply all its needs. Land ceiling regulations and the underdeveloped state of land markets make it almost impossible for any one institution to own the hundreds or even thousands of acres that may be necessary. Value chains that handle agricultural produce must necessarily include large numbers of small independent farmers.

There are also, as the case studies have shown, a number of good reasons why it may be better to deal with large number of small suppliers, in spite of the obvious practical difficulties. Falcon Fisheries, like many other large-scale shrimp exporters, tried to have its own captive sources of supply. This was permitted, but the Company eventually concluded that it was best not to own its own ponds and to have a mix of medium and small-scale suppliers.

One common way of maintaining some element of control over such producers is to bind them by contract to supply material at the times and prices and in the quantities which are needed for the value chain to operate at an optimum level. A contract of this sort may in any case felt to be necessary because the company to which the small producer will supply has provided seeds or other inputs on credit to the producers, often accompanied by extension and other capacity building services. If the smallholder sells the produce to another buyer, the company will earn no return on its services and may not even be able to recover the cost of the inputs it supplied.

Master weavers, and other "middlemen" in artisanal trades also operate in a similar way. They are often criticised for the effectively extortionate rates of interest which are charged on such transactions, but they do provide a reliable if not very remunerative market for the producers, and they also bear most of the risk if the goods are for any reason difficult to sell.

There are many advocates of "contract farming", as this form of relationship is generally called, and it is perhaps surprising that such contracts are only being used in three of our 14 examples. Falcon Fisheries contracts the shrimp pond operators to supply to the company, in order to protect its investment in interest free advance supplies of fingerlings and feed, Namdhari Fresh uses the same system to secure its supplies of fresh vegetables and BASIX attempted to bind the small-scale potato farmers to sell only to PepsiCo. These contracts are not easily enforceable, particularly in India where legal sanctions are virtually useless in cases of this sort. Falcon is said to deal leniently with its few defaulters, and BASIX was unable to recover its advances from those farmers who sold their crops on the open market when the price briefly exceeded the prices which had been agreed with PepsiCo.

The remaining procuring companies use a variety of other methods to ensure their supplies. Organic farmers have every reason to supply to the lead company, because the prices are significantly higher than on the open market. As yet, there is no open market for organic produce in India and it seems unlikely that there will be such a market in the foreseeable future, because of the practical difficulties of inspection and traceability. Even Spencer's, which belongs to a strongly profit-oriented group of companies, has chosen to use what they call "contact growing", as opposed to contracts, and they depend on the business sense of their suppliers to ensure reliable deliveries.

Generally speaking, the success and robustness of most of the value chains depend on the fact that it makes economic sense for the producers to supply to the company which has developed the chain. It is not necessary to make vain appeals to "loyalty", as is so common in so many co-operatives; farmers are in business, like the other players in the value chains, and most of them are quite poor. It is unreasonable to expect them to accept lower returns today in expectation of vague promises of prosperity tomorrow.

We saw earlier that six of our 14 value chains were initiated and are being driven by agencies which are not themselves principal players in the chains and whose survival does not depend on their economic success. INFAM is mainly a campaigning and promotional NGO, which is driven by the church and by its farmer members. BASIX is nominally a for-profit livelihoods promotion business, but it has a strong social orientation and although it has a financial stake in the potato value chain its main objective in the whole exercise was to improve the farmers' livelihoods, not to make money. EDA is a development consultancy and project management firm. PRADAN and Naandi are development NGOs and RUDA is a state-government sponsored enterprise promotion agency. The other eight promoting institutions are for-profit businesses which are active members of the value chains which they have promoted.

We have already seen that the value chains which were promoted by for-profit companies, as part of their normal business development process, have grown faster than those promoted by separate agencies, funded from sources other than the prospective profits they will earn from the value chain itself. There are a number of reasons why "commercial" promoters of this kind are more likely to build effective value chains, more rapidly and sustainably than "external" agencies.

Their incentive is clear. Some of the companies may have been clever enough to secure access to subsidised resources from external sources, such as Kohinoor's collaboration with the OBEP state agency in Uttarakhand, funded by the Tatas and the State Government, or ITC's work with the GMED project, which is funded by taxpayers in the United States. Most of their costs, however, are an investment in the future profits the company will earn from being an active participant in the value chain. The staff who work on these initiatives are strongly motivated to build a strong value chain, rapidly, in order to minimise the investment and maximise the return.

These staff are also likely to be familiar with the business area of the value chain. ITC is traditionally a tobacco business, and thus understands the procurement of raw material from farmers and the marketing of fast-moving consumer goods, such as agarbatti, perhaps as well as any company in India. BioRe's Swiss partners know the market for organic cotton, Agrocel understands small farmers' input needs, and Falcon Fisheries has itself been in the business of raising shrimps in coastal ponds. Agencies such as BASIX, EDA Rural Systems, RUDA or the Naandi Foundation have extensive experience of working with the rural poor, but not in fields which are directly related to the businesses with which the respective value are engaged. Experience can be acquired, but it takes time.

More important than domain knowledge, and less easy to acquire, are the attitudes of business. Value chains are first and foremost business structures; they can also, as our case studies show, be a powerful weapon against rural poverty and agrarian distress, but this is not their prime purpose. NGO staff understand poverty alleviation, and they are or should be strongly oriented to their "market", poor and disadvantaged people. They are not, however, oriented to the needs of customers who eat organic rice, or wear high-fashion slippers, and they tend not to think like profit-oriented business managers.

Businesses are often criticised for taking a short-term view, but the companies who have built the value chains described in this book are building for the long-term; their management anticipate that their investment in the value chains will continue to yield a return for many years. "Exit" or withdrawal are the last issues they consider. The development agencies, however, must from the outset plan for their own departure, which may be precipitated by the end of a project funding cycle rather than by the completion of their task. Their goal is to build the producers' independent capacity to manage the value chain as soon as possible, and to leave behind a system which operates smoothly without any external support.

This expectation begs the question of whether small-holder coffee farmers, or shoemakers, or beekeepers, really should try to manage the downstream functions of the value chains to which they belong, either directly or through cooperatives or other entities. It can be argued that farmers should be free to be specialists, to focus their attention on the task of farming, and to leave the ownership and management of other parts of the value chain to others who are experts in those tasks. Irrespective of this issue, however, any agency which plans to extricate itself from a given role in a value chain is likely to be less committed to it than a company whose business depends on the continued profitable operation of the whole chain.

There are of course many reasons why temporary external agencies are sometimes called upon to build value chains. It may be that no for-profit company would ever become involved, because the whole proposition is too risky. Or there may be a number of different and competing players in the potential value chain, such that no one of them is likely on its own to find it worthwhile to invest in building it. This was almost certainly true of the broiler value chain in Bihar which PRADAN has so successfully built. There are large numbers of rather small distributors and retailers in the poultry business, and it was necessary for an outside agency to intervene in order to secure a place for a small-scale village producers. The Dabur company is a major customer for honey, and it might have itself intervened in the value chain which EDA Rural Systems eventually built for the beekeepers, but one important result of the new value chain was that the price of honey rose by a large multiple. Dabur would probably not have initiated a change which resulted in such an increase in the cost of one of its raw materials.

This brings us to the main reason why many people in the development community at any rate believe that inclusive value chains have to be initiated and built by development agencies, and paid for from government or other non-commercial sources. Private for-profit businesses, it is believed, will inevitably "exploit" small producers. The examples in this book show that this is not necessarily the case.

"Exploit" does not in itself necessarily imply inequity or oppression. The word has taken on this sense, particularly in the context of unequal power relationships in value chains, because so many such chains are inequitable, and, it can be argued, are for that reason also not sustainable in the long term. "Exploit" means "make use of", or "derive benefit from", and benefit is exactly what all parties in an inclusive value chain should get from the other members. If they do not benefit, and the chain has to be protected and preserved by subsidies, grants, or charity, it ceases to be sustainable in an economic sense, however noble may be the motives of those who support it.

The 14 case studies in this book involve many different commodities, in different places, and they were promoted by different types of institution, for different motives. The BASIX-PepsiCo potato chain, the INFAM initiatives in Wayanad and RUDA's work with mojari producers were only partially successful, and the other 11 cases seem generally to have succeeded well, although many challenges remain, as they always will.

There are however some general lessons which can be drawn from the cases. Some relate to what was done in the value chains, and some to what was not done, but all may be useful as guidelines for other institutions which may in the future wish to promote similarly inclusive and profitable value chains.

- It is not always necessary to put small producers into groups in order to enable them to participate profitably in a new value chain. Such groups can serve a valuable purpose in some circumstances, but they are not a standard necessity.

- Inclusive value chains, which are profitable for all participants, including the smallest and most vulnerable producers, do not have to be subsidised, even at the initial development stage. If the potential for a new and inclusive value chain is identified, and there is no obvious potential promoter who might undertake the task without subsidy, it may be necessary to provide some subsidy. But it is by no means always necessary.

- Organic methods are particularly suited to small-scale producers, and they can significantly increase the prices which the producers receive. Such methods also reduce the need for external inputs, and credit. In many cases organic farming can also improve yields, and reduce costs, irrespective of prices. Organic farming can be a solution for marginalised farmers even when there is no opportunity to charge premium prices for the crops.

- The most profitable and secure markets are those where the products are sold on the basis of their high-quality, not their low-price. This contrasts strongly with the usual government approach to promoting small producers' products, such as handloom cloth, which is based almost entirely on discounts and low prices, rather than on the other

"Ps" in the marketing mix, the product, the place where it can be purchased and the way it is promoted.
• Developing improved products and new markets may require the
removal of bureaucratic restrictions, such as taxes on the movement
of goods, or official market monopolies or out-dated trade or registration rules. Governments often find it easier to start to do new things
than to stop doing old ones, but any institution which promotes value
chains should be prepared to deal with this type of problem. The
process of liberalisation is by no means complete in India, particularly
at the State and District level.

A number of micro-finance institutions, such as BASIX was before it
widened its remit to cover livelihood promotion in general, are becoming
engaged in livelihood promotion and the development of value chains. It
may be necessary to provide finance to enable small producers to participate in modern value chains, but finance is not always necessary, and it is
rarely if ever the principal constraint. The promoters of the value chains
described in this book have provided a number of services to the small
producers.

They provide extension services to introduce new technical knowledge, such as organic methods of cultivation; they have improved product
designs, as in the case of the mojari slippers; they have secured changes
in regulations, such as reducing taxes and harassment against honey producers; they have devised ways of avoiding dysfunctional official procedures,
such as the market systems in Uttarkhand; they have promoted new producer-owned intermediaries for coffee and broiler producers; they have
identified and introduced new private for-profit "middlemen" to facilitate
the collection and processing of raw honey; they have initiated new on-
farm product grading systems; they have also provided working capital,
as for shrimp producers and organic cotton growers. Above all, they have
linked producers to new markets.

The vital aspect of this list, which is incomplete even for these case
studies, is that each situation has required a unique set of inputs, and that
no single input is a sufficient basis for the value chain. The promoters have
not assumed that any particular intervention is the "magic bullet", and they
have not allowed the package of services to be influenced by what they
themselves can provide, rather than by the needs of the situation. It may be

significant that the least successful intervention is probably that of BASIX in Jharkhand. BASIX aspires to be a full-service livelihoods promotion institution, but its origins lie in financial services, and for the majority of its customers and some of its staff BASIX is still a financial service institution and no more. This may in part have led the company's staff to underestimate the difficulty of building the capacity of the potato farmers' association.

Livelihood promotion, and the development of inclusive value chains, require above all an open mind with no preconceptions as to what inputs are needed. "If it works, don't fix it", is a useful rule; we should not assume that every aspect of every value chain participant's operations need to be improved, and we should above all be careful not to provide the inputs we know how to provide, rather than what the situation requires. The existing situation has to be objectively appraised, quantitatively and qualitatively, in order to identify what changes are needed, if any.

Most people are sceptical about "corporate social responsibility", and some readers may treat the claims in some of the preceding case studies with scepticism. They may be justified in doing so, but one important lesson from all the cases is that the traditional approaches to development for marginalised and disadvantaged people should also be viewed sceptically. Groups, subsidies, credit, and the whole edifice of rural development programmes, and the institutions which deliver them, have in general failed to achieve their objectives. Our case studies show that large for-profit businesses can build value chains which enable very poor farmers and artisans to improve their livelihoods.

Glossary

Agarbatti	Incense sticks.
Agrocel	A farm-services company, owned by Excel (q.v.) and the State of Gujarat.
Ahmedabad	The capital of Gujarat (q.v.).
Amul	The brand name for milk products from cooperatives in the State of Gujarat.
Araku Valley	A hill resort and coffee growing area in the State of Andhra Pradesh.
Aviva	A British multinational insurance company.
Basix	An Indian microfinance and livelihoods promotion group.
Basmati	A high quality variety of rice, which commands a premium price.
Batti	The stick to which a paste with incense is added to make an incense stick.
Bhendi	A variety of vegetable (q.v.). See Okra.
Bidadi Hobli	A sub-district of Ramanagar (q.v.) district.
Bihar	The second largest Indian State, known for its poverty.
bioRe	A Swiss organic cotton processing and marketing company.
Block	An administrative area, between a district and a village.
Brinjal	Aubergines or egg-plant.

Cargill	One of the world's largest commodity trading companies.
Chennai	(also Madras) The capital city of Tamil Nadu.
Choupal	A traditional village meeting place.
Crore	10 million.
Dehradun	The capital city of Uttarkhand State of India (q.v.).
Dehraduni	Produced in Dehradun (q.v.).
Deogarh	A district of Jharkhand (q.v.).
Desi	Traditional, village-based.
EDA Rural Systems	An Indian development research and project management company.
Escorts	A large diversified Indian agro-services company.
Excel Industries	A large Indian farm services company.
Foodland	An Indian supermarket retailing business.
Gaya	A district of Bihar State (q.v.).
Godrej	A large Indian diversified group of companies.
Godown	A warehouse or store.
Gram Panchayat	Local village council.
Gram Sabha	Local village assembly.
Gujarat	An Indian State in the North West of the country.
Haat	A traditional village market.
Haryana	A state in India, near to Delhi.
ICICI Lombard	An insurance company.
ICT	Information Communication Technology.
Indica bees	Traditional non-hybrid hardy Indian bees.
Infosys	A large Indian international software company.
ITC	The Indian Tobacco Company, a large Indian farm product and food company.
Jamun	A flowering tree whose pollen is the source of a particular flavour of honey.
Jatropha	A tree whose fruit is a source of vegetable oil, often used for energy generation.
Jharkhand	An Indian state, largely populated by 'tribals' (q.v.).
Jilla Panchayad, also Zilla Panchayat	The lowest level of the Indian rural administration.

KVIC	Khadi and Village Industries Commision, a handicraft promotion agency.
Kacha Aadthi	Informal traders who operate in official wholesale market yards.
Karanj	The Indian name for Jatropha (q.v.).
Karnataka	An Indian state, whose capital is Bangalore.
Kasba	Traditional Urdu word for village market.
Kerala	A State in South India.
Khadi	Hand-spun and hand-woven cloth.
Kirana	A small local grocery shop, a "mom and pop store".
Kolkata	Also Calcutta, the capital city of West Bengal (q.v.).
Kushwaha	An Indian caste, traditionally bee-keepers.
Kutch	A dry and barren coastal district of Gujarat State.
Lakh	100,000.
Ludhiana	A large industrial city in Punjab (q.v.).
MP	Madhya Pradesh, a State in central India.
Mandi	A wholesale market for farm produce.
Mandvi	A district of Kutch in Western Gujarat.
Mellisfera bees	Hybrid highly productive bees of Italian origin.
Mojari	Traditional handmade leather slippers.
Moong bean	A pulse which can be grown in semi-arid conditions.
Muzaffarpur	A town in Bihar (q.v.).
Naandi	A large development foundation based in Hyderabad.
Naxals, Naxalites	Rural revolutionary groups, often of marginalised tribals (q.v.).
Okra	Ladies' finger, a green vegetable.
Ooty	Otherwise known as Ootacamund, a hill town in Tamil Nadu (q.v.).
Orissa	An Indian State on the Bay of Bengal, the poorest state in India.
Paddy	Rice before it is threshed.
Punjab	A State, the Indian portion of the Punjab which was split in 1947.
Puri	A coastal town in Orissa (q.v.).
Quintal	100 kilograms.
QMart	An India-based distributor of handicrafts and textile items.

Ragi	A variety of millet.
Rajma	A pulse grown in semi-arid conditions.
Ramanagar	A district of Karnataka (q.v.) State.
Ranchi	The capital city of Jharkhand (q.v.) and its surrounding district.
Rasam	A traditional Indian spicy soup.
Reliance	An Indian conglomerate business with major interests in supermarkets.
Royal Sundaram	An Anglo-India insurance company.
RUDA	An artisans' livelihood support organisation of the State of Rajasthan.
Samiti, Samity	Committee, or governing body.
SAARC	The South Asian Association for Regional Cooperation.
SGSY	An Indian government programme to encourage local group businesses.
SHG	Self-help Group, a group of around 20 people who save and take loans together.
Shandy	A traditional village market.
Shri Vivekananda	A Hindu philosopher, of the late nineteenth century.
Spencers	India's oldest organised retailer, now engaged in supermarkets.
Subhiksha	An Indian supermarket retailing business.
Suguna	A large Indian poultry production and marketing company.
Sunhera Kal	A training programme for unemployed urban youth.
Tamil Nadu	An Indian State in the extreme South of the country.
Tasar	Raw silk produced by uncultivated silk worms in some Indian forests.
Thapar	A diversified group of Indian companies.
Timul	A large milk and milk products marketing cooperative in Bihar.
Traidcraft	A British fair trade marketing company.
Tribals	The indigenous people of India, now largely marginalised in hill areas.

Udaipur	A city in Rajasthan State, with a long tradition of leather working.
Udham Singh Nagar	A district in Uttarkhand (q.v.) State.
UP	Uttar Pradesh, India's largest State, with some 170 million people.
Uttarkhand	A State in North India, largely in the Himalayas.
Vadodara	Otherwise known as Baroda, a city in Gujarat State.
Vericott	A British organic textile importing and garment company.
Vikas Nagar	Literally, "development town", a town in Uttarkhand (q.v.) State.
Wayanad	A District of Kerala (q.v.).
WB	West Bengal, an Indian state on the West coast.
WTO	The World Trade Organisation.